PRINTED WRITINGS

BY

GEORGE W. RUSSELL

(AE)

A BIBLIOGRAPHY

Opinions of this book

The late Dr F. S. Bourke (Chairman in 1959 of the Bibliographical Society of Ireland) wrote:

"I must confess to some disappointment when I read through your *Bibliography* of AE. But let me hasten to re-assure you; I was disappointed because I was unable to add anything to it . . . I congratulate you on a very fine piece of work."

The late Dr R. I. Best wrote:

"Your work is most painstaking and accurate. It will do much to revive an interest in AE, of that I am convinced."

Dr Edward McLysaght (Chairman of the Irish Manuscripts' Commission) writes:

"I cannot think of anything to add to your excellent *Bibliography*."

WHO WAS AE?

George William Russell (1867–1935) the Irish mystic poet, painter, journalist and philosopher best known by his pseudonym "AE". He was an expert exponent (in the *Irish Homestead*) of rural Irish economic co-operation, and in later life achieved world-wide fame with his wise commentaries on public affairs and aesthetics in the weekly *Irish Statesman*. The poems and landscape paintings mirror AE's gentle personality. In them he expressed his appreciation of the radiantly beautiful Irish landscape, and his strong (but undogmatic) belief in the intrinsic value of individual human endeavor. His comprehensive knowledge of rural Ireland had illustrated to him the need for collective social endeavor as a means to developing a stable national economy. Throughout his life he won the friendship of many distinguished men and women. Seeming wholly unselfish, he watched and listened to his friends, and illuminated their lives with his truthful and calm appreciation of their aims and achievements.

A NOTE ON THE COMPILER

Alan Denson is English by education and domicile. His lineage is mixed; English and Scottish. Mr Denson has edited *Letters from AE (G. W. Russell)*. His new book *John Hughes, a Great Irish Sculptor* is ready for the press. He has also edited *Poems by Charles Weekes (with a Memoir)*, and is now engaged in writing two other books concerned with Irish writers and artists. In 1952 the late Dr Oliver St John Gogarty wrote of him: "I do not know anyone who is better equipped to write about AE".

PRINTED WRITINGS
BY
GEORGE W. RUSSELL
(AE)

A BIBLIOGRAPHY

WITH SOME NOTES ON HIS
PICTURES AND PORTRAITS

COMPILED BY
ALAN DENSON

Foreword by
Padraic Colum

Reminiscences of AE by M. J. Bonn

A Note on AE and Painting by Thomas Bodkin

NORTHWESTERN UNIVERSITY PRESS
Evanston, Illinois
1961

Open access edition funded by the National Endowment for the Humanities/Andrew W. Mellon Foundation Humanities Open Book Program.

George W. Russell. Printed Writings by George W. Russell (AE) A Bibliography.
Evanston, Ill.: Northwestern University Press, 1961.

ISBN 978-0-8101-3945-9 (paper)
ISBN 978-0-8101-3946-6 (ebook)

Original edition LCCN 61-16862

TO

DR M. J. BONN

THOMAS BODKIN PADRAIC COLUM

HERBERT PALMER CYNTHIA STEPHENS

CONTENTS

ILLUSTRATIONS

FOREWORD

by Padraic Colum

In a garden in Harcourt Terrace, Dublin, two acts of a three-act play were performed on January 2, 1902. I have a notion (but I am not sure) that news of this interesting way of celebrating a boy's birthday reached an amateur of the theater, Frank Fay, with results that were momentous in the history of Irish dramatic literature.

There had been the final production of the association that named itself "The Irish Literary Theatre" the year before. That production had in the main failed, and with it had failed the prospects of the theater that W. B. Yeats, Edward Martyn, and George Moore had envisaged. The main production was *Dermot and Grania*, written as a collaboration between W. B. Yeats and George Moore. However, the promoters of the Irish Literary Theatre had attached a play in Irish—perhaps the first attempt to put a play in Irish on the stage—to the production that had a London company for its cast. This one-act play was written by the President of the expanding Gaelic League, Dr Douglas Hyde, with him as the chief personage in the cast. This short play, written by an amateur dramatist and supported by an amateur cast was a success, as the long play by distinguished writers supported by a distinguished cast was a failure. And now a man working with an amateur company got wind of a "prospect".

And now to Frank Fay. He was teacher of elocution in Dublin, and, I make bold to say, the best teacher of that art Dublin ever had. He gave recitals in verse and appeared as an actor when he got the opportunity. With his brother William G. Fay he formed a small company to play comedies and farces. The pair had made contact with the "Irish Ireland" groups: one had produced a patriotic play and the other had acted in it. And now an Irish play was cropping up. Frank Fay read the two acts that appeared in the *All-Ireland Review*. The lines appealed to him as an elocutionist. The cast that had been assembled for the production of an English farce—some of them had been recruited from the patriotic societies and had appeared in the patriotic plays that the Fays had helped to produce—were given scripts of *Deirdre* by AE, and rehearsals were started on a play that was to initiate a national theater.

What a strange combination was then effected! A group from a theosophical society coalesced with a militant nationalist organization, the coalition being activated by two men whose interest was the theater, one a good comedy actor and the other a man whose enthusiasm was for the speaking of verse. It was through this conjunction that as a youngster not yet twenty who had become a follower of the Fays that I first met AE. He had come amongst us to read the third act of *Deirdre*, finished at last.

He was a big man, bearded, with twinkling eyes behind glasses, and a pipe that was constantly being taken from his pocket to his mouth and from his mouth to his pocket. He mixed easily with the group, talking to us personally and collectively. His contribution to the rehearsals was his chanting of the part of the Druid Cathvah. His chanting must have appealed especially to Frank Fay: to all of us it was extraordinary.

Deirdre, he told us, had been written in reaction from the production of *Dermot and Grania*. There was a cult of the Irish heroes initiated by Standish O'Grady and carried on by Maud Gonne to be brought to a culmination by Padraic Pearse. The Yeats-Moore play was divested of heroism. When Finn came on the scene, Standish O'Grady who had presented an heroic Finn, put his hands before his eyes, AE told us. It was to restore the heroic element that he had written *Deirdre*.

The rehearsals went on for months; I saw a good deal of AE during them, walking back with him. As he went along the streets toward Rathmines he flowed on in discourse on Irish mythology which through discussions in the Hermetic Society was emerging as an esoteric doctrine. Then Yeats came amongst us with *Kathleen-ni-Houlihan* which then went into rehearsal, and our group, some of whom had training and some who were merely amateur, got ready for what was to be a national theater with a three-act heroic play and a one-act patriotic play in a peasant setting.

And now it was shown that the Dublin audience was with AE and Standish O'Grady in homage to what was heroic in the sagas. In the second act of *Deirdre* when Naisi, speaking of the companions he had left behind, says to Deirdre, "And there was one, a small, dark man whom many thought to be a god in exile. His name is Cuchullain," a thrill could be felt going through the audience. It was the first time that the name of the foremost of the epic characters had been spoken on an Irish stage. When the author in response to the call for him appeared—he still, I remember, wore the robe of the Druid he had enacted—his speech, finely delivered, renewed the heroic appeal. Deirdre and the son of Usna had perished because of a king's broken word. "Better," AE told the audience, "to perish through an excess of noble trust than to keep life through ignoble precautions." I am relying on my memory for the words, but "Better to perish through an excess of noble trust" has kept a place in my mind.

But of that historic production what remains in my mind more firmly than anything else is AE's appearance and utterance as the Druid, Cathvah. Tall, bearded, commanding, he chanted the verse that had the very rhythm of sorcery:

Let the Faed Fia fall;
Mananaun Mac Lir.
Take back the days
Amid days unremembered.
Over the warring mind
Let thy Faed Fia fall,
Mananaun Mac Lir!

Let thy waves rise,
Mananaun Mac Lir.
Let the earth fail
Beneath their feet,
Let thy waves flow over them,
Mananaun:
Lord of ocean!

AE's *Deirdre* has been eclipsed by Synge's and Yeats'. When I look back on it now I see it as a pageant rather than a play. I don't suppose it could ever be done again with anything like the enthusiasm of its first appearance.

March 1961

PADRAIC COLUM

"À LA RECHERCHE DU TEMPS PERDU"

by M. J. Bonn

My main justification for writing the following notes may be compressed into a single word: survival. I am the last of the men and women who gathered around Sir Horace Plunkett[1] at the turn of the century; with one exception, Sir Patrick Hannon, F.R.G.S., F.S.S., F.R.E.S., F.R.Econ.S., F.R.S.A.[2] He was much more of an insider than I, but dropped out in 1909. I ran into him in Cape Town in 1907, where he had gone to help the Government to develop a co-operative movement. With that charming effrontery of his he made its members give me a dinner having convinced them that I was a very important person—which at that time I certainly was not.

On a lovely August day in 1896 I found myself on the mail boat going from Holyhead to what was then called Kingstown. A very friendly priest began to talk to me having probably realised that I was a strange bird in those latitudes. I come of a family who had many international ramifications, but none of them knew anything about Ireland. I went there on what might be considered a wild goose chase. I had been studying economic history, and had spent many dreary hours in the British Museum trying to visualize earlier stages of economic civilization. I didn't get on very well. Then I had a flash of inspiration. From what I had heard and read the Ireland of those days seemed one of the few countries in western Europe where the long arm of the past still kept a strong grip on the affairs of the present. I wanted to see things with my own eyes, especially as I had discovered very early that most books on Ireland were written by partisans. So I went to the Honorable George Peel[3], who was then secretary of the Gold Standard Defense Organization. Inflationist bi-metalism was very rampant in those days and I had been taught the dangers of inflation by the inflow of great quantities of silver on the Spanish

[1] Sir Horace Curzon Plunkett (1854–1932).

[2] Sir Patrick Joseph Hannon (born 1874).

[3] The Hon. Arthur George Villiers Peel (1868–1956).

economy of the sixteenth and seventeenth centuries. I told him that I wanted an introduction to an impartial Irishman who could tell me where to go and what to see. "There is no such being alive," he said to me, " and if there were I couldn't find him." But a few days later he sent me a line saying "I have found him." His name was Horace Plunkett. I saw Horace Plunkett and he very kindly provided me with introductions to his associates who would, he was sure, show me everything I wanted to see, and tell me everything I ought to hear. He would, he said, see me later in Ireland and help me as much as he could. Thus began a rather strange friendship (for Plunkett was twenty years older than I) in which my wife joined later on. It lasted for thirty-six years, and was not even broken during the first World War. At that time we were both in the United States, on opposite sides. My wife and I were at lunch with the German Ambassador when somebody mentioned that Sir Horace Plunkett had arrived, and was staying at the British Embassy. "May I use the telephone to speak to him?" said my wife, to the great amusement of the Ambassador. She rang up the British Embassy, told an almost fainting secretary who she was, and asked to speak to Horace. He immediately came to the telephone and they arranged a meeting in New York. It had to take place at our hotel for he was staying with a belligerent American, Laurence Godkin[4], the editor of *The Nation*, who was so anti-German that Horace didn't dare to take me into his house.

Plunkett had given me letters of introduction to his main collaborators: at that time T. P. Gill[5], R. A. Anderson[6], and Father T. A. Finlay[7] the Jesuit. All of them received me very kindly and gave me letters of introduction to all sorts of people on whom I called during my first peregrination of Ireland. T. P. Gill had been a brilliant newspaperman—I think he had been on *The Speaker* with Sir Wemyss Reid[8]. He liked to disport a kind of slight Parisian verve. R. A. Anderson, on the other hand, was of the Anglo-Scots-Irish type with a lot of common sense and both feet on the ground. Father Tom Finlay was a brilliant member of the Society of Jesus with whom I could discuss Irish problems on an abstract logical plane; whilst I learnt facts

[4] Laurence Godkin (1860–1929).

[5] Thomas Patrick Gill (1858–1931).

[6] Robert Andrew Anderson (1861–1942).

[7] Father Thomas Aloysius Finlay (1848–1940).

[8] Sir (Thomas) Wemyss Reid (1842–1905), edited *The Speaker* (London) from 1890–9.

from Anderson and got an insight into the sparkling Irish mind through T. P. Gill. Ireland came up to my expectations.

It was very attractive. At the Dublin horse-show and at the race-meetings, you saw more beautiful women and handsome men than anywhere else. In "dear dirty Dublin" with its magnificent Georgian mansions, and in many little poke-holes, you could have brilliant conversation.

I remember a dinner-party at the Chief Secretary's residence when George Wyndham[9] and Professor Mahaffy[10] tried to outshine each other in a fire-works display of argument and counter-argument. They were debating rather than engaging in conversation; for the object of debate is to make minced-meat of your opponent's arguments. But good conversation is a splash and a counter-splash of ideas which may have little contact with each other, and need not be based on provable facts. It is talking for talking's sake, depending on the ability of the participants to outdo each other.

There was a small club-room somewhere in (I think) Grafton Street, where a literary côterie met, under the guidance of T. W. Rolleston[11]. He very kindly invited me sometimes. The air vibrated with scintillating epigrams which seemed to blow the dust from the wooden chairs and tables, and settled down again once a session was over.

Somewhat later I had the good luck to be present at a meeting of the leaders of the Celtic revival. They too could talk with endless enthusiasm, but their romanticism seemed to me a little artificial. Whilst vaunting the glorious Celtic literature of the past they had to do so in the language of the Sassenach, which some of them could polish to shining perfection. If they had any "Irish," it was that of babbling babes. Only one of them, Douglas Hyde[12] (later President of the Republic), was a Celtic scholar of international standing. I kept in touch with him, until his life ended.

What I was really after was to find out how an—to use a modern term—under-developed country could be advanced by its own effort and a certain amount of external help. That brought me deep into Irish

[9] George Wyndham (1863–1913).

[10] Sir John Pentland Mahaffy (1839–1919).

[11] Thomas William Hazell Rolleston (1857–1920): he translated into English Dr Bonn's book *Modern Ireland and her Agrarian Problems* (1906).

[12] Dr Douglas Hyde (1860–1949).

history. I was finally confronted with the problem of why Great Britain, whose colonial efforts had been successful nearly everywhere, had failed in Ireland. I had to delve deep down into Irish history with not too much help from my predecessors, few of whom had been impartial. The outcome of it was a very bulky book *Die Englische Kolonisation in Irland* (Stuttgart and Berlin, 1906: Cotta. 2 vols), on which I spent nearly ten years of my life. But all this only developed by and by. For three years I passed my summer holidays in Ireland. Through my ever-increasing intimacy with Plunkett I met nearly everybody who was somebody in Ireland: from the Lord Lieutenant and the Chief Secretaries, such as George Wyndham and Gerald Balfour[13]; to nationalist politicians such as John Redmond[14] and Tim Healy[15], and near-revolutionaries such as Michael Davitt[16] and Joe Devlin[17]. I remember a delightful evening I spent with Tim Healy: we started on agrarian problems but soon got to quoting poetry to each other.

As far as Plunkett's work was concerned I was naturally an outsider, and remained an outsider. I could not help him on the practical side of his movement, but I sensed its inner meaning and could help him to formulate it. The great agrarian reforms which had been carried out by several British governments, culminating in the Land Act of 1903, made the Irish tenant an independent peasant owner. But it broke up the unity of the estate. The decent Irish landowners—not all landlords lived in Castle Rackrent—had done more than collect rents. They had helped the tenant to make improvements and better their ways of farming. Even in the worst cases the estate had been a unit. It was now broken into parcels. The fundamental achievement of the co-operative movement which Plunkett had started in 1891 was to create a new unit by voluntary association of self-help.

I was able to help Plunkett to elaborate his ideas in his book *Ireland in the New Century* (London, February 1904: John Murray). After having had my fill of the Irish atmosphere in 1896, 1897 and 1898 I went to work on the material I had collected. I did not return to Ireland before 1903. During the summer months I hired a cottage next

[13] Gerald Balfour (1853–1945).
[14] John Redmond (1856–1918).
[15] Timothy Michael Healy (1855–1931).
[16] Michael Davitt (1846–1906).
[17] Joe Devlin (1871–1934).

to that of Horace at Foxrock. In the autumn we rented a house in Malahide. In that house *Ireland in the New Century* was finished. I generally went to town with Horace, to spend the day in the National Library, and came back in the late afternoon. In the evening we always had company, mainly with a purpose. Horace was very overworked at that time. I generally managed to keep him in bed on Sunday, when we read the proof sheets of *Ireland in the New Century*. I admired it as a literary achievement, but I was quite sure that its publication would be a political mistake. Brilliance in a writer may be an asset; it is a devastating liability in a man who wants things to be done by plain people for plain people. I'm afraid I was right. During that time I got deeper and deeper into Irish affairs, for by now I knew a lot more about the past than most of the people who discussed the present with me.

It was at that time that I first came across AE. He interested me from the beginning. He was quite as unassuming and gentle as Horace. He had, like him, a very strong sense of reality. But notwithstanding his practical realism, he was a dreamer. He was, to my mind, neither a great poet nor a great painter. His poetry looked upon as a work of art was far inferior to that of Yeats, but it was sincere and spontaneous. He wrote poetry as a bird sings, because he had to do it, not because he wanted to create a work of art. A Beethoven symphony is far more musical than the song of a nightingale but there is something in that song which even the greatest composer has been unable to achieve. AE's landscapes cannot stand comparison with any of the great landscape painters, but there is an ethereal beauty in them which even Turner never reached. He lived in two worlds. In everyday life he was a practical man, but behind it he lived in a land of elves and of the little people whose language he understood and spoke. He did not create them by an act of will or stimulated imagination; they were *there* to greet him and he opened his house and heart to them. He and Horace were near-saints, absolutely selfless. I think I was able to understand AE even though I could never hope to share the rhythm of his inner life.

I left Ireland in the spring of 1904 with the half-finished manuscript of my work. I never lived there again, though I frequently went over as Horace's guest. I married in 1905 and was deeply grateful that my wife and Horace understood each other and became as close friends as he and I were.

I remember on a visit in 1908 being at the meeting of the British Association, in Dublin. I had written a rather dull statistical paper from which it was quite clear that it was not so much the magic of property which had improved Irish economy, as cheap English credit and old age pensions. It roused the indignation of the Undersecretary in the Department of Agriculture, Thomas W. Russell[18], who attacked me and an American economist [19] who had made some unwelcome observations. My American friend collapsed and meekly apologized. He should have known, he said, that talking in Ireland about Irish questions was like walking with a lit candle into a room filled with gas. I was less humble; I said I knew that I was walking with a lit candle in a room filled with gas and of course there was an explosion: but I knew too that it was Irish gas which made a lot of noise and wouldn't hurt anybody. Everybody laughed but official Ireland was not very pleased, as I recognized when I was presented to His Excellency the Lord Lieutenant[20].

My last visit to Ireland before the war was in 1912. Horace asked me to go to Belfast to watch the taking of the Covenant (September 28). It was a most impressive sight. I had a feeling that I was viewing a march-past by Cromwell's Ironsides.

My last visit to Ireland took place just thirty years ago. The National University had asked me to give them a course of lectures. I was dined and wined by the Government. But somehow the old charm had gone. Horace remained in England and many of my old friends were dead. I visited in her Dublin apartment the Dowager Lady Fingall[21], whose radiant beauty as mistress of Killeen Castle had so often enthused me, and whose brilliant mind had been a great help to Horace. It was sad to see her crippled by arthritis in a Dublin flat. I went to Glasnevin to lay a few flowers on the grave of an Irishwoman with whom I had been deeply in love—unfortunately a quite one-sided affair. She had played a part, a great part, in the national movement and the knowledge of my visit to her grave seemed to have spread all over Dublin. It resulted in an invitation to see Mr de Valéra. My impression was that the greatest living Irishman seemed to be quite unlike any other Irishmen I ever had met.

[18] Thomas Wallace Russell (1841–1920).
[19] John Graham Brooks (1846–1938). Meeting in Dublin, September 9, 1908.
[20] Lord Aberdeen (1847–1934).
[21] The Dowager Lady Fingall (1867?–1944).

I am not very sure that I shall ever reach *The Land of Heart's Desire*:

A land where even the old are fair
And even the wise are merry of tongue.

But if I do I shall find Horace near my wife, and I hope not far behind them, AE.

October 4, 1960. M. J. BONN

PREFACE

THIS *Bibliography* is the second in which AE's books have been listed. The pioneer was the unsigned "Bibliography of AE" printed in the *Dublin Magazine* (Dublin) vol 5 No 1 pp 44–52 (January 1930), with its supplement in vol 10 No 4 pp 74–76 (October 1935). That was compiled by Michael Joseph MacManus (1888–September 21, 1951), literary editor of the *Irish Press* (Dublin) from 1934 until his death. But P. S. O'Hegarty (1879–1955) attributed that bibliography to "Seumas O'Sullivan", in vol 22 No 3 p 60 (July 1947). MacManus' list omitted AE's book *The Avatars*.

The information in this book should prove accurate, and the compiler's intention has been to dispel the errors and confusion of fact, biographical and bibliographical, with which AE's reputation has been burdened. (AE was inconsistent in writing his pseudonym. Sometimes he wrote the diphthong, sometimes inserted stops.)

Some problems have proved insoluble. Zealous binders have sometimes guillotined tall pamphlets. Bound-in with other pamphlets, those by AE often seem to contradict the accurate measurements given in this book. Such binding cuts booksellers' prices, too.

Parts 1, 2, 4, 5, and 6 are listed chronologically: *Parts* 3, 7, 8, and 12a and b are listed in alphabetical order. Linear limits across the page are indicated by a vertical bar [|]. Type styles on the title-pages are varied; for this book all type-styles are printed uniformly. Black print on white paper should be assumed: exceptions are noticed. Capitals have been retained only for the first word in each title, and for some proper nouns. The name and texture of the paper are not given, nor *signatures*. The title-page of the first edition should be read for subsequent reprints: formal variations are described in detail. Measurement to the nearest millimetre: vertical first. The size of the cover, or outer wrappers, is given, not the inner textual pages.

W. B. Yeats and AE planned, *circa* 1904, to produce a magazine with the title *The Bell-Branch*. The magazine was never issued.

Advised by their reader Mr Colin Summerford, Messrs Methuen & Co., the London publishers, tried to accumulate prose or verse by members of the Irish Academy of Letters (*circa* 1934). That anthology was never compiled.

Charles Alexandre Weekes (1867–1946), Russell's steadfast friend from about 1889, reviewed several AE books, but this compiler has not yet located those reviews.

Parts 12a and 12b list key references. The compiler is not unmindful of Ecclesiastes' admonition (chapter 12 verse 12).

ACKNOWLEDGEMENTS

The Directors and staff of Messrs Macmillan & Co Ltd (London) answered every question addressed to them by this compiler, promptly and with good grace.

The Directors and staff in several libraries have assisted the compiler by their courteous service: National Library of Ireland; Trinity College, Dublin; the Reference Library of the Theosophical Society in Great Britain; the British Museum Library (and their excellent Newspaper Library); the Secretary (Miss M. Digby, O.B.E.) and librarian of the Plunkett Foundation for Co-operative Studies (London); the Houghton and Widener Libraries in Harvard University; the splendidly equipped and hospitable public reference libraries in Birmingham and Manchester (England); Yale University Library; University of Kansas Library, Lawrence, Kansas; University of Texas; and the Curators in the Lilly Library, the University of Indiana, at Bloomington. The kindness shown by the Lilly Library staff has been one of the most encouraging features of the later stages of this work: every question promptly answered, photocopies quickly supplied. Everything done to make their valuable collections serve even this obscure and remote compiler.

Professor William A. Jackson, at Harvard University; Dr William O'Sullivan (Trinity College, Dublin); Professor Denis Gwynn; Mr Dan H. Laurence; Mr George Goossens; Mr Alfred MacLochlainn, M.A., and Mr Thomas O'Neill, M.A. (National Library of Ireland), have given their expert services cheerfully.

Mr George Paterson, O.B.E., M.A., M.R.I.A., Curator of the County Museum, Armagh, has given his help constantly over many years. His interest and encouragement, like that the compiler has gratefully received from Dr Edward MacLysaght, the late Dr R. I. Best, the late Dr F. S. Bourke, and the late Joseph Hone, has been entirely constructive.

Professor Herbert Howarth, characteristically resourceful and kind, searched voluntarily some American serial publications which are not available in the United Kingdom: *Pearson's Magazine*, *The Reader*, *The Freeman*, *Reedy's Mirror*. Professor Howarth's generous personal friendship has been particularly helpful because he knows how great a strain, mental and physical, is work of this type. Several other distinguished men have proved their friendship by similar timely interest and encouragement. Among them, and pre-eminent, is that exemplary scholar Professor Richard Ellmann, whose interest in this work has been so great a boon. His enthusiasm and discreetly given constructive advice, resembled the unerring pertinacity and wisdom which have informed all the comments on this work made by the late Professor Thomas Bodkin.

Professor Bodkin most generously permitted his invaluable "Notes on AE and Painting" to be reprinted in this book. With extraordinary modesty Dr Bodkin suggested that this compiler might care to revise those notes, or to make some factual alterations. The notes were written in 1937, and are reprinted here exactly as Dr Bodkin wrote them, because this compiler was unwilling to tamper with them in any way.

The "Reminiscences" by Dr Bonn and the *Foreword* by Mr Padraic Colum were specially written at the compiler's request.

Many other people have answered the compiler's questions. Without their help the book would not have been complete, for printed sources have not been very useful; although the compiler has referred to *Allgemeines Lexikon der Bilden den Künstler* by U. Thieme & F. Becker (1907–1940), and *Künstler Lexikon* by Hans Vollmer (1955: *in progress*) (both published in Leipzig by Verlag E. A. Seeman); W. G. Strickland's *A Dictionary of Irish Artists* (2 vols Dublin: 1913. Maunsell); *Catalogue of the Engraved Irish Portraits (mainly in the Joly Collection) and of Original Drawings*, compiled by Rosalind M. Elmes (Dublin: [1937], 1938. Stationery Office); *Art Index*, (1930–) and *Who's Who in Art* (London: 1934 and 1958 editions).

The compiler is profoundly grateful to his publisher, especially to the Director of the Northwestern University Press, Mr Robert P. Armstrong, for his considerate kindness; and to all his excellent staff, amongst whom Mr Frank Shiras, Miss Karen Jensen, and (in London) Mr Frank Pike have proved efficient guides. Nobody could be better served by any publisher, and nobody could be more grateful for the splendid skill exemplified by the incomparable printers of this book.

Mr Séan Keating, P.R.H.A., the late Donald Gilbert, F.R.B.S., R.B.S.A., Mr John Irvine, and Mr P. H. Muir have answered questions generously.

Dr S. P. Choong and Mr A. Kamal helped the compiler check part of the proofs, earning his gratitude by their vigilance.

The compiler's keenest sense of obligation is acknowledged in the dedication. Those friends' unfailing interest, their concern to see this work concluded, and their heartening confidence in the compiler's ability, eased the burden by setting such drudgery in perspective. This book and *Letters from AE* are preliminary tools. This compiler's summary list of textual variants in AE's published poems will be expanded when he is given access to the extant manuscript collections. From collation of all MS with the printed texts a comprehensive edited collection of AE's poems should be made.

The compiler ventures to express his hope that the *Letters* and *Bibliography* may revive interest in AE's life and achievements, and encourage a gifted writer to compose a worthy biography of Russell—prompted as he has been solely by sympathetic admiration.

Additions (translations, for instance) or corrections to this book should be addressed to the compiler, care of his publisher. He would welcome from librarians and private collectors detailed lists of their holdings.

London, July 23, 1961. ALAN DENSON

CHRONOLOGICAL TABLE

Year		*Event*
1867	April 10	George William Russell born to Thomas Elias Russell (book-keeper) of William Street, Lurgan, County Armagh by his wife Marianne Russell (*formerly* Armstrong). Mrs Russell's name wrongly registered on the birth certificate as "Mary Anne Russell."
1871	February	G. W. Russell enrolled as a day pupil at the Model School, Lurgan.
1878		T. E. Russell invited to join his friend Robert Gardner's business, chartered accountants, Dame Street, Dublin. The family left Lurgan to reside at 33 Emorville Avenue, Dublin. G. W. Russell generally passed part of his school holidays with an aunt resident in Armagh.
1880	[Early]	G. W. Russell enrolled at the Art School, Kildare Street, Dublin, as a day pupil.
1882	[Early]	G. W. Russell enrolled at Dr C. W. Benson's Rathmines School: (*School Roll* No. 1272).
1883	October	Attended evening session art classes at the [Metropolitan] School of Art, Kildare Street, Dublin. Continued attendance until July 1885. Probably met John Hughes, W. B. Yeats, and Charles Johnston. Perhaps met Oliver Sheppard.
1884	October 13	Mary Elizabeth Russell, G.W.R.'s sister, died aged 18, in Dublin.
	December	G. W. Russell left Rathmines School. Studied privately?
1885		The family moved to 67 Grosvenor Square, Dublin.
188–57		G. W. Russell attended evening sessions at the School affiliated to the Royal Hibernian Academy.

1887	December 11	W. B. Yeats introduced G.W.R. to Katharine Tynan.
1888	[Early]	Attended meetings of the Dublin lodge of the Theosophical Society. Perhaps joined the T.S. late 1888, or 1889?
1890	August 1	Appointed a clerk with Messrs Pim Bros., drapers, Dublin. Salary £40 *per annum.* Resigned November 1897 (£60 p.a.).
	December 9	G.W.R. was admitted to probationer membership of the Esoteric Section of the Theosophical Society, "having signed the pledge." The small certificate of enrolment was signed by H. P. Blavatsky: Russell's counterfoil numbered 939.
1891	April	Mr and Mrs Frederick J. Dick, tenants of 3 Upper Ely Place, Dublin, established a small residential community of Theosophists: with D. N. Dunlop, H. M. Magee, Edmund J. King, and G. W. Russell. Magee left in 1894 the room he had shared with Russell being taken over by A. W. Dwyer. Dunlop left, probably in December 1892, to marry Eleanor Fitzpatrick. This small community moved to 13 Eustace Street, in December 1896 or January 1897.
	May 8	H. P. Blavatsky died in London.
1891	October 6	Charles Stewart Parnell died aged 45.
1892	May–June	T. E. Russell and family moved from Rathmines to 5 Seapoint Terrace, Monkstown.
1895		G. W. Russell joined the Irish Literary Society, Dublin. From 1901–4 he was a member of their Publications Committee.
	February?	Miss Violet North (from Bow, London) and James M. Pryse moved to Dublin, and perhaps took up residence in 3 Upper Ely Place.
1896	March 21	Death of William Quan Judge in New York, aged 45. James M. Pryse left Dublin, returning to New York.

1897	October 9	Marianne Russell (61) died, 5 Seapoint Terrace.
	November 3	G. W. Russell resigned his employment with Messrs Pim Bros.
	November 11	G.W.R. had been mentioned to Horace Plunkett by P. J. [*later* Sir Patrick] Hannon. Plunkett had met Russell at Pim's store and interviewed him on Nov 11, and appointed him a Banks' Organiser (under the co-operative credit system devised by F. W. Raiffeisen [1818–88]) in the "Congested Districts" of western Ireland (Donegal, Mayo, Galway, parts of Sligo and Kerry) in the Irish Agricultural Organization Society.
1898	March	Russell seceded from the T.S., disappointed by the new head of the organization, Mrs Katherine Tingley.
	April 7	G.W.R. resided, 6 Castlewood Avenue.
	June 9	G. W. Russell was married to Miss Violet North (daughter of the late Archibald North), in the Dublin Registrary. Both resident at 10 Grove Terrace, Rathmines. Marriage witnessed by John Hughes and A. W. Dwyer.
	[Mid-]	T. E. Russell moved from Seapoint Terrace to "Hillsborough" Blackrock.
	November 2	Russells moved residence to 28 Upper Mount Pleasant Avenue, Rathmines.
	[Late-]	G. W. Russell appointed joint assistant secretary of the I.A.O.S., with P. J. Hannon.
1899	February?	G.W. and Violet Russell's first son, Brian, was born. The official search revealed neither birth nor death registration. The child died in early infancy.
1900		Their first surviving child, Brian Hartley Russell, was probably born. The official search did not reveal the registration.
	April 23	Russells moved to 25 Coulson Avenue, Rathgar.

1900	October 31	Thomas Elias Russell died aged 78 at "Hillsborough," Blackrock.
1902		The Irish National Theatre Society formed: *President*, W. B. Yeats, *Vice-Presidents*, Douglas Hyde, Maud Gonne, G. W. Russell.
1902	April 2, 3, 4	*Deirdre* by Russell and *Kathleen ni Houlihan* by W. B. Yeats first performed by W. G. Fay's Irish National Dramatic Company at St Teresa's Hall, Clarendon Street, Dublin.
	November 17	G.W. and Violet Russell's younger son born, Diarmuid Conor Russell.
1903	July 14	Plunkett, T. P. Gill, Professor J. R. Campbell, and Russell appointed by I.A.O.S. Committee to devise means for adjusting relations between the I.A.O.S. and the Dept. of Agriculture and Technical Instruction (Ireland).
1903		Introduced to Sir Frederick Macmillan by S. L. Gwynn. Offers Macmillan & Co. *The Divine Vision*, and all his later poems.
1904	July?	Russell resigned Vice-Presidency of the Irish National Theatre Society.
	October 20	Colonel H. S. Olcott (1832–1907), President of the T.S. (Adyar), issued a charter establishing a "Second Dublin Lodge": members, Mr and Mrs G. W. Russell, Mr and Mrs Powis Hoult, W. G. Fay, J. S. Starkey, Mrs Greene, Mrs Charles Kelly, John Quigley: secretary, H. F. Norman. Met weekly in 34 Wicklow Street until March 25, 1909. The group seceded from the T.S. (Adyar) in 1909 when Mrs Annie Besant succeeded to the Presidency. As an independent group the Dublin "Hermetic Society" persisted until Russell left Dublin in 1933: he had been its President. P. G. Bowen succeeded him.
1905	August	Russell was appointed Editor of the *Irish Homestead* (Dublin), in succession to H. F. Norman. Russell continued for several years

1905	August	to supervise the organisation of Co-operative Banks. (Norman was Banks' Organiser).
1906	[Early]	Russells moved to 17 Rathgar Avenue, Rathgar, Dublin.
1907	March 16	John O'Leary died.
1908	November 11	The Plunkett House, 84 Merrion Square, Dublin, opened as I.A.O.S. headquarters.
1909	March 24	J. M. Synge died, aged 38.
1911	March	George Moore retired to London after ten years' residence in Dublin.
1912	April 11	Third Home Rule Bill for Ireland introduced in the House of Commons. This inflamed resentment in Ulster, which issued in the formation of the Ulster Volunteers' Force.
		James Connolly began forming the Irish Labour Party.
1913	May	All rights in AE's poetry transferred from John Lane (The Bodley Head) Ltd, and T. B. Mosher, to Messrs Macmillan & Co Ltd.
	June	Russell at Breaghy, Ballymore, County Donegal arranging the sequence of his *Collected Poems*.
	July	Returned corrected proofs of *Collected Poems* to Macmillan & Co. Ltd. [Published September 23.]
	August 26	Dublin Tramways' workers' strike began, and was continued throughout Horse-Show week: organised by the Irish Transport and General Workers' Union, led by James Larkin.
	30	A meeting of union members was interrupted by the police. They arrested Larkin and Connolly, and killed two other people.
	September 12	Connolly and Larkin released from prison.
		William Martin Murphy successfully arranged a federation of 400 employers, to counter the strike by locking-out their 24,000 employees—depriving them of all honest means to earn subsistence. An Industrial Peace Committee was formed by people unattached to the unions;

1913		among them AE. The committee was later re-formed as the Civic League.
	October 5	Public rally in the Phoenix Park, Dublin. Larkin proposed the formation of an Irish Citizens' Army to be led by Captain Jack R. White.
	27	Larkin's trial for sedition: sentenced to seven months' imprisonment.
1913	November 1	In the Royal Albert Hall, London, a mass meeting to sponsor support for the Dublin strikers. Addressed by Bernard Shaw, F. W. (*later* Lord) Pethick-Lawrence, Ben Tillett, James Connolly, Mrs Montefiore, Miss Sylvia Pankhurst, Mrs Despard, Miss Delia Larkin (James' sister), AE, and two other speakers: Chairman, George Lansbury. Russell and Shaw were attacked by the press, S. L. Gwynn, M.P. dissociating himself from those attacks (*Freeman's Journal* November 5).
	14	Larkin released from prison. He moved to England to address trade unions.
	25	The Irish Volunteer Force launched at a rally in the Rotunda, Dublin.
1914	[Early]	The T. & G. W. Union strike collapsed in Dublin. But the Irish Volunteer Force did not collapse.
	April 24	Guns and ammunition for the Ulster Volunteers landed at Larne.
	June 23	Bill to amend the proposals for Irish Home Rule by stipulating the exclusion of Ulster (commercially the most prosperous part). Its introduction in the House of Lords was instigated by Sir Edward Carson and Andrew Bonar Law.
	July 26	Guns and ammunition for the Irish Volunteers landed at Howth.
	August 4	British declaration of war against Germany.

1916	April 20	[Thursday] AE left Dublin to spend the Easter week-end as a guest of Edward MacLysaght at Raheen, Tuamgraney, County Clare. Nationalist revolt in Dublin over week-end.
	26	Left Tuamgraney, probably arrived in Dublin April 27.
	May 8–12	Leaders of the revolt were executed.
1917		Defence of the Realm Act enforced in Ireland. 450 people arrested without right of trial.
	July 25	Inaugural session of the Irish Home Rule Convention, in the Regent House, Trinity College, Dublin. 95 members representing the varied secular and religious interests of the Irish community: representatives of *Sinn Fein* abstained from attendance. 15 of the delegates were British Government nominees, among them AE. Plunkett unanimously elected Chairman. Meetings adjourned until August 8.
	September 25	Russell co-opted to membership of the Grand Committee (re-formed) to settle procedural method.
	October 11	Russell one of the Committee of Nine, which sat in private, attempting to find a basis for general agreement.
1918		Under D.O.R.A. 1651 people in Ireland imprisoned without trial.
	February 1	Russell resigned from the Convention, believing its constitution precluded honest discussion and settlement of the Anglo-Irish dispute.
	November 11	The European war ended.
	25	Parliamentary General Election. 73 Sinn Fein candidates, 26 Unionists, and 6 Parliamentarians elected to Irish constituencies.
1919	January 20	Michael Collins summoned a meeting of the Irish M.P.s.
	21	Session at the Mansion House, Dublin, at which the proceedings were conducted in

1919		Irish. A "Declaration" drawn up, arguing the present existence of an Irish Republic.
	March	All Irish political prisoners were released.
	April 1	Mr Eamonn de Valera was elected President of Ireland by the executive members of the Irish Republican Brotherhood and its supporters, as Dáil Éireann.
	2	Mr de Valera nominated a cabinet of seven (including Collins and Griffith). This executive sought to undermine the local governmental boards by assuming directive authority; and the judiciary by adjudicating in disputes.
		A curfew imposed by the British administration.
	September 10	Dáil Éireann suppressed: led by Collins as a guerrilla force.
		The Royal Irish Constabulary was stiffened in resistance by two supplementary units from England: non-commissioned ex-soldiers, uniformly dressed in black-and-tan; and ex-officers styled Auxiliary Cadets.
		Under D.O.R.A. 15,818 Irish people imprisoned without trial during 1919.
1920	February 25	The fourth Home Rule Bill was introduced to the House of Commons by Lloyd George's Coalition Government. It prescribed Antrim, Armagh, Down, Fermanagh, Londonderry, and Tyrone to be excluded from an Irish republic.
	December 23	The Bill received the Royal Assent.
		Cork, Kerry, Limerick and Tipperary subject to martial law.
1921	January	Clare, Wexford, Waterford, and Kilkenny subjected to martial law.
	May 19	General elections in southern Ireland: Sinn Fein majority.
	24	General elections in Ulster: Unionist majority returned.
	June 24	Mr Lloyd George invited Mr de Valera to

1921	consultations in London with Sir James Craig (the Ulster leader). After protracted negotiations a treaty was drafted.
July 11	The British and Irish armies negotiated a truce.
[Later]	The Draft Treaty was revised by Dáil Éireann. That assembly then charged five plenipotentiaries (Robert Barton, Arthur Griffith, Michael Collins, G. Gavan Duffy, and Eamonn Duggan) with responsibility to negotiate its settlement with the British Government in London.
December 6	After some hesitation the Treaty was signed by all parties.
16	Treaty ratified by the British Parliament.
1922 January 7	Dáil ratified the Treaty by 64 to 57 votes. Because the Treaty did not yield full Republican status to Ireland Mr de Valera disapproved it, and resigned the Presidency. In his stead Griffith was elected: he nominated a pro-Treaty cabinet.
Jan–March	Anti-Treaty members of the Irish Volunteers repudiated their allegiance to the Dáil and to Mr de Valera. Led by Rory [Roderick] O'Connor this group commonly called "the irregulars": they proclaimed a military dictatorship.
March 15	Mr de Valera formed a new Republican party under his Presidency.
June 16	General election in Ireland (proportional representation). 58 pro-Treaty members elected, 35 other members incidentally pro-Treaty, and 35 members anti-Treaty. The anti-Treaty faction incited their followers to begin a civil war.
August 12	Griffith died. Collins President.
22	Collins killed in an ambush. Mr William T. Cosgrave succeeded as President.
December 29	Russell's "Open Letter to Irish Republicans" was printed in the *Irish Times*.

1923	January 8	Claude Falls Wright (one of Russell's early theosophical friends) drowned in Lake Nicaragua, near Bluefields: aged 56.
	April	The anti-Treaty supporters abandoned the conflict: excepting only Mr de Valera and his personal followers. They maintained an opposition of sorts "underground." Mr de Valera refused nomination to the Dáil until 1927.
1923	September 15	First issue of the [new] *Irish Statesman* (Dublin) edited by Russell, with J. W. Good and S. L. Mitchell as assistants. The *Irish Homestead* was merged with it: issued weekly. [September 8, 1922 Horace Plunkett had written to J. S. Cullinan (1860–1937), an American Corporation official, proposing the revival of the *Irish Statesman* "to advocate a persistent endeavour by the State to improve the conditions of every section of the Irish people . . ." Edward L. Doheny (1856–1935) invited likely supporters to dine at the Bankers' Club, New York, on October 16, 1922. Subsequently an organising Committee was formed: Doheny, Richard Campbell (1872–1935) Morgan J. O'Brien (1852–1937), James Byrne (1857–1942), John Quinn (1870–1924), Lawrence Godkin (1860–1929), George MacDonald, John A. Poynton (18–?–1934) and Cullinan, with James A. Healy as assistant secretary to Campbell. They secured 100 persons to underwrite an Agreement in equal amounts to total £30,000. The committee was to act in an advisory capacity to the Controlling Committee (Plunkett, Chairman; James G. Douglas, Lionel Smith-Gordon, Dr George O'Brien, and Lennox Robinson: with AE as editor, and Percy J. Gillespie as General Manager) in Dublin. AE had refused the editorial chair, but when pressed by Plunkett

1923 took it on condition that he would be free of any coercion, and that the *Irish Homestead* features would be retained. Plunkett arrived in New York on January 1, 1923; telegraphed Doheny's opinion to Cullinan—fewer than 100 should underwrite. Doheny agreed to underwrite $75,000, half the required amount, by three annual instalments. The first instalments were to be paid not later than March 1, 1923; second in December 1923; third in December 1924. James Byrne paid up the amount he had underwritten, dissatisfied with the small number of contributors to the fund. The paper's first year trading loss was £3,366: second year, £2,844. Each of the American supporters received securities to the extent of his participation unless such securities were sold to finance wider distribution; in which case he would be refunded his proportionate amount of sales. In 1925 further support for the paper was tardily won: ultimately funds were advanced from America and from Plunkett (£1000) and publication continued. In early 1928 AE's lecture tour in U.S.A. earned funds for the paper. President Cosgrave had urged Plunkett to avoid presenting any party viewpoint in the *Irish Statesman.* Plunkett wrote to Campbell (February 25, 1925), "I knew that AE would be a great editor, but I do think he has excelled himself in the guidance he has given to the Government of the Free State and in the way he has protected them from the Republicans."]

1926 March 4 Susan L. Mitchell died in Dublin, aged 60. Russell's younger son, Diarmuid, succeeded her as his father's editorial assistant (£100 *per annum*) until April 1929. From May 1929 until the *Irish Statesman* ceased publication his junior editorial assistant was Miss Irene Haugh, B.A.

1926	September 14	Russell arrived in Paris for his sole continental holiday, spent with Mr and Mrs C. P. Curran. Mme Simone Téry and James and Cynthia Stephens were also Russell's hosts there.
1927	May 25	Frederick J. Dick died at Point Loma, Calif., aged 71.
	July 10	Kevin O'Higgins murdered, aged 35.
	15	Constance Markiewicz (*née* Gore-Booth) died, aged 59.
1928	January 14	AE sailed for America: arrived in New York, January 25 and began lecturing there, to raise funds to maintain production of the *Irish Statesman*. He returned to Ireland at the end of March.
	June 18	Russell arrived in New York; his trip began on June 7.
	20	Yale University conferred on Russell an honorary D.Litt.
	October 29–November 13	Séamus Clandillon and his wife charged Dónal O'Sullivan, AE, and the *Irish Statesman* Publishing Company with responsibility for a libel which they read into a review of *Londubh an Chairn* (O.U P.) which they edited (*Irish Statesman* Nov 19, 1927). Mr Clandillon was Director of the Dublin broadcasting station. Dr O'Sullivan was Clerk to the Irish Senate. The High Court jury failed to agree after seven and a half hours' deliberation. Judge H. Hanna (1871–1946) refused the plaintiffs' request for judgment. Their subsequent appeal was dismissed. The defendants' costs were £2,500. A public appeal was immediately launched to defray those costs.
1929	May	Russell's younger son emigrated to America. [His elder son, Brian Hartley Russell, had emigrated to India in 1923, returning to England about 1931.]
	July 2	Trinity College, Dublin, conferred their honorary D.Litt. on Russell.

1929	[Later]	*Irish Statesman*'s American guarantors withdrew their support: probably affected by their own financial embarrassment occasioned by the Wall Street stock crash.
1930	April 12	Last issue of the *Irish Statesman.*
	May 2	Death of James Winder Good, aged 53.
	[Summer]	Lyon Phillimore, Oliver St. J. Gogarty and J. M. Hone with some other friends of Russell appealed by private circular letter for money to present to him as a token of public exteem for his character and work in Ireland.
	September 3	The Governor-General of the Irish Free State, Mr James McNeill (1869–1938), at a meeting in the Plunkett House, presented to Russell a cheque for £800, proceeds from the appeal.
	23	Arrived in New York, on the *Cedric* to lecture throughout the United States, mainly on "rural reconstruction." The purpose chiefly to earn money to provide his wife with the best medical attention.
1931	Mid-May	Returned from U.S.A.: first to London. He visited George Moore for the last time. Thence to Dublin.
	[Summer]	Russell wrote one article for publication in the year following the final issue of the *Irish Statesman.* Humbert Wolfe importuned him to review one of his books for the *Observer* (London).
1932	February 3	AE's wife, Violet, died aged 64, at their house, 17 Rathgar Avenue, Dublin. After the funeral he went to England to be solitary for a week, in the Euston Hotel.
	March 26	Sir Horace Plunkett died, aged 77.
	April 3	W. B. Yeats proposed formation of the Irish Academy of Letters. He invited AE to draft *Rules*, and to perform the various secretarial functions at which he regarded himself as

1932		inept. The Rules were registered on September 12, 1932, in Dublin.
	April 18	Thomas Matthew Russell [insurance inspector] (AE's brother?) died at Raven Lodge, Summerhill, aged 63.
	May 22	Lady Gregory died, aged 80.
1933	January 21	George Moore died in London, aged 80. Colonel Maurice Moore invited AE to compose and speak a tribute at the funeral. AE wrote a tribute which R. I. Best spoke over Moore's ashes. [First printed in full in this compiler's edition of AE's *Letters*.]
	July [Early]	Russell sold his home, 17 Rathgar Avenue, and gave away most of his possessions. Frank O'Connor has recorded that Yeats told him this procedure "wrung Russell's heart."
	July 8	Russell went to have a holiday with his friends Arthur and Lucy Kingsley Porter. He arrived at the Donegal rendezvous to meet Mrs Porter alone. Her husband had been accidentally drowned that day.
	August 2	He arrived in London. At his request Charles Weekes had arranged accommodation for Russell at 41 Sussex Gardens. Weekes and his wife had asked Russell to live with them, but he preferred to be unattached.
	September 28	G. R. S. Mead died, aged 70.
1934	March 8	Stephen MacKenna died, aged 62.
	April	Russell left London to reside in Donegal for May, June, and July.
	July 31	Arrived in Dublin.
	August 9	Returned to London. His former lodgings occupied, Russell moved to 1 Brunswick Square (demolished by bombs in the 1939 war).
	November 5–6	A. R. Orage died, aged 61. Invited to America to be the guest of the Roosevelt administration's Adviser to National

1934		Emergency Council, Mrs Mary Harriman Rumsey.
	December 13	Russell sailed for America from Southampton, on the *Aurania*.
	18	Mrs Rumsey died, aged 53.
	27	Russell arrived in New York. The Hon. M. L. Wilson, the Hon. H. A. Wallace (Secretary for Agriculture), and Judge Richard Campbell were mainly responsible for arranging Russell's heavy schedule of lecturing all over the country, on "rural policies."
1935	February	Russell ailing, sought curtailment of his trip.
	March 1	Russell sailed for England on the *Aurania*.
	16	Arrived in London. Moved his residence to 14 Tavistock Place.
	May 30	Daniel N. Dunlop died, aged 67.
	June 14	Russell signed his last will, witnessed by Mrs Sophie Jacobs and Miss Kathleen Goodfellow. He bequeathed all his real and personal property to his younger son.
	21	To a small nursing home run by Miss Phoebe Myers at "Havenhurst", Canford Cliffs, Bournemouth. Charles Weekes took Russell there from London by train.
	July 10	A surgical operation on his abdomen, in the Stagsden Nursing Home, Bournemouth.
	16	Mr C. P. Curran arrived at the nursing home and visited Russell. He was conscious and freely discussed his affairs, receiving gratefully messages of affectionate concern from his Dublin friends, H. F. Norman, Joseph O'Neill, Osborn Bergin, T. G. Keller, and others.
1935	July	The Gregory Medal, for distinction as a writer, was awarded to Russell by his fellow members of the Irish Academy of Letters.
	17	Oliver Gogarty flew from Ireland to be with AE. W. B. Yeats telegraphed an affectionate message (solicited by C. P. Curran and Pamela

1935	July 17	Travers): his silence had clouded AE's cheerfulness a little. Soon after 11 p.m. AE died in his sleep, surrounded by his friends C. P. Curran, Weekes, and Gogarty. A. R. Orage's widow arrived soon afterwards.
	18	Simone Téry, his gay young French friend (also a friend of Mrs Russell) arrived in Bournemouth from France. She had felt grave forebodings about AE, and came uninvited. Mr Curran had the thankless task of greeting her.
	19	Russell's body was taken by rail to Holyhead via London: James Stephens, Helen Waddell and other friends escorted the coffin. Thence by sea to Dun Laoghaire, with aeroplane escort on arrival. The death, caused by carcinoma of the rectum, was certified by James Alexander Walker [1901–December 22, 1953. Sometime honorary surgeon and resident obstetrician, St Mary's Hospital, Paddington, etc].
	20	The modified Church of Ireland service was conducted by the Rev C. C. Duggan. Principal among the congregated mourners was AE's elder son, Brian Hartley Russell: others in attendance included President de Valera, Mr W. T. Cosgrave, W. B. Yeats, R. A. Anderson, "Seumas O'Sullivan," Joseph O'Neill, F. R. Higgins, Gogarty, and Stephens. Frank O'Connor (representing the Irish Academy of Letters) delivered the *oraison funèbre* over the grave. The body was interred in Mount Jerome cemetery.
	22	Diarmuid Russell arrived in London by aeroplane from America. While settling his father's business affairs he was guest of Mr and Mrs Charles Weekes.
	August 27	Probate of AE's Will was granted to the

1935		Westminster Bank Ltd. Effects, £2,298 1s.7d. : resworn, £2,449 1s. 7d.
	November	A four-page leaflet *Memorial to George W. Russell* (*A.E.*) was circulated by C. P. Curran and H. F. Norman, the Honorary Secretaries of the A.E. Memorial Fund. W. B. Yeats was President; Senator J. G. Douglas, Chairman; James Montgomery and "Seumas O'Sullivan" Hon. Treasurers.
1939	October 4	*Indenture* between the A.E. Memorial Committee Members, and the Governor and Company of the Bank of Ireland. The funds
1939		subscribed by the public, less out-of-pocket expenses, were £898 0s. 4d. Accrued interest from the investments to which that sum was applied should occasionally be awarded as a cash prize to native Irish writers under 35 years of age, for meritorious creative or scholarly work, published or in manuscript.

CHRONOLOGICAL TABLE OF AE's MAIN PUBLICATIONS

Year	*Title*
1894	*To the Fellows of the Theosophical Society* (letter dated March 26, 1894).
	Homeward Songs by the Way (published in June).
1897	*The Future of Ireland and the Awakening of the Fires.* (? March).
	Ideals in Ireland: Priest or Hero? (? May).
	The Earth Breath and Other Poems (September).
1898	*Co-operative Credit* (? December).
1901	*An Artist of Gaelic Ireland* (? October).
1903	*The Nuts of Knowledge* (? December).
	Deirdre: a Drama in Three Acts.
1904	*The Divine Vision and other Poems* (January 14).
	[edited] *New Songs* (March).
	Controversy in Ireland (September).
1905	*The Mask of Apollo* (January 6).
1906	*Some Irish Essays* (January 22).
	By Still Waters (December 14).
1909	*The Hero in Man* (May).
1910	*The Building up of a Rural Civilisation* (? January).
1911	*The Renewal of Youth* (? May).
1912	*Co-operation and Nationality* (February).
1913	*The Rural Community* (? Summer).
	Collected Poems (September 23).
	To the Masters of Dublin (October).
	The Tragedy of Labour in Dublin (November).
	The Dublin Strike (November).
1914	*Oxford University and the Co-operative Movement* (June).
1915	*Ireland, Agriculture and the War* (? February).
	Gods of War with other Poems (September).
	Imaginations and Reveries (December 3).
1916	*Talks with an Irish Farmer* (i–xii) (January–September).
	The National Being (? September).

1917 *Templecrone* (? January).
Salutation (? January).
Thoughts for a Convention (June).
1918 *Conscription for Ireland* (May).
The Candle of Vision (October 22).
1919 *Literary Imagination* (? January).
Michael (December).
1920 *A Plea for Justice* (December).
The Economics of Ireland (? May).
1921 *Thoughts for British Co-operators* (May).
The Inner and the Outer Ireland (July).
Ireland and the Empire at the Court of Conscience (? September).
1922 *Ireland, Past and Future* (? April).
The Interpreters (November 7).
1925 *Voices of the Stones* (June 5).
1928 *Midsummer Eve* (June).
1929 *Dark Weeping* (October 9).
1930 *Enchantment and other Poems* (December).
1931 *Vale and other Poems* (March 3).
1932 *Song and its Fountains* (February 16).
Verses for Friends (December).
1933 *The Avatars* (October 3).
1934 *The House of the Titans and other Poems* (October 19).
1935 *Selected Poems* (September 17).

PRINTED WRITINGS BY GEORGE WILLIAM RUSSELL (AE)

Note—*AE's earliest signed writings known to have been published.* See below item 187 (*The Theosophist*). See also *Part* 12, *Rathmines School Magazine*, to which Russell may have contributed, although this compiler could not identify any work there which he would care to attribute to Russell. The distinctive characteristics of AE's prose and verse are not evident in his school magazine.

PART I

BOOKS AND PAMPHLETS

I

TO THE FELLOWS OF THE THEOSOPHICAL SOCIETY

To the fellows of the Theosophical | Society. | March 26th, 1894.|

Pp 8: heading, as above, on p [1]: text, pp [1]–8: at end of text signed, *Geo. W. Russell, F.T.S.* | *3, Upper Ely Place, Dublin.* | : [at foot of p 8, rule, and below: *Printed on the Irish Theosophist Press, 3, Upper Ely Place, Dublin.*]

Issued unbound, without title-page or wrappers, late March 1894. 20.2 × 13.6 cm.

A letter circulated among members of the Dublin lodge of the Theosophical Society, and possibly to members of other lodges. The topic: messages written on paper which had been produced, by William Quan Judge (1851–96), as communications issuant from "Masters" in psychic phenomena. The authenticity of those written messages had been questioned by some other members of the Theosophical Society. Some had assumed they had been written by Judge, of his own volition, without guiding intervention from any "Guru." The vigorous, capable and (in controversy) extremely formidable Mrs Annie Besant (1847–1933) had charged Judge with simple fraud: he had produced these messages to support his own ambitions within the T.S., to be the undisputed leader of the Society. Judge joined issue with Mrs Besant. (See item *B2* below.) Russell deplored the publicity which attached to such a scandalous charge against Judge: the Society was concerned with ethical values certainly, but this scandal resembled political legerdemain. Russell evidently believed Judge to have been innocent, and in this dispute entirely blameless. His letter earnestly pleads Judge's cause. The Dublin lodge maintained loyal allegiance to Judge.

[*Note:* p 3: "... perhaps our sad souls, which look no more on the eternal beauty, can easier read the mystery told in tears and understand sorrow better than joy." This sentence was adapted and reprinted in the Preface which AE wrote to his *Collected Poems* (item 21). AE preserved a copy of this pamphlet, inscribed on the top of p [1], apparently by his wife: *Señorita Violetta Norte.*]

2

HOMEWARD SONGS BY THE WAY

Homeward [*ornament*] | *Songs by* [*ornament*] | *The Way. A.E.* | *Dublin. Whaley* [*ornament*] | *46 Dawson Chambers 46* | *mdcccxciv. Price 1/6* [*ornament*].

Pp [2] + xiv + [52]: blank: half-title (verso blank): title-page (verso blank): dedication (verso blank): Preface (verso blank): Contents, ix-x: introductory poem (verso blank): blank leaf: text pp 1–51: printer's device and imprint on verso of p 51.

Issued in sage-green wrappers, lettered in brown on front cover as on title. *All rights reserved* on verso of front cover. Covers overlap. Published June 1894. 15.8 × 11.4 cm. [British

Museum copy date-stamped: 23 Ju 94]. Reprinted by Whaley
2A [A] January 1895. Taken over and re-issued by John Lane, The
2B Bodley Head (London) [no formal contract] [B] 1896. Reptd
2C [C] ? October 1901. Further reptd by Lane, "Fourth Edition"
2D [D] 1908. [17.1 × 12.9 cm.] [1000 copies] reset, with pp [2, blank leaf] + [12] + 13–64 text. With an arboraceous design on the front stiff-board grayish cover, printed in brown. Lettered on spine: *Homeward Songs by the Way*. The first American edition was pirated, with added poems [subsequently reptd in item 5 at pp: 11, 13, 14, 23, 29, 50, 51, 52, 53, 70,
2E 80, 81, 87, 88, 89, and 94]. [E] Portland, Maine: March 1895. Thomas B. Mosher. [Typography and designs by Bruce Rogers (May 14, 1870–May 18, 1957)]. 925 copies on Van Gelder paper. [Bound in stiff cream boards, title encased by filigree design on front cover; lettering in brown: lettered in brown on spine, at top, title (ornament) AE: at foot, 1895. 15.4 × 12.4 cm. The cover flanged to overlap except foot of the pages. 2 blank leaves: half-title [1], verso with original pbtn. details: title-page lettered in black and red, verso copyright and numerical details: dedication [v]; verso blank: [vii] Preface, verso blank: [ix–xi] Contents, verso blank: [13] Introductory poem; verso blank: [15] half-title, verso blank: 17–[87] text, verso publisher's and printers names etc:
2F 2 blank leaves. As with item 2, all edges uncut. [F] The same, but 50 copies printed on "Japan Vellum". Second American
2G edition: [G] Portland, Maine: ? June 1904. Mosher. 450 copies
2H on Van Gelder paper. [H] The same text, but 25 copies on "Japan Vellum". In item 2 all except pp 32 and 46 were reptd in item 21. Also item 2: pp 2, 3, 4, 8, 12, 23, 31, 41, 43 and 48 were reptd in item 8. And pp 6, 13, 14, 15, 16, 18, 20, 25 and 28 were reptd in item 14. Part reptd in item 54. *Dedicated:* To C.W[eekes] truest friend.

B2

A letter written by Russell was printed by the Irish Theosophist Press, and circulated to Members of the Theosophical Society during February 1895. This compiler has not seen a copy. G. R. S. Mead (1863–1933) quoted from the letter in *The Vâhan* (London) vol 4 No 8 (March 1, 1895) p 4 col 2:

"It is with real sadness that I find myself compelled to protest against the spirit and matter of a paper, issued by Mr G. R. S. Mead on I know not what authority, in which we are called upon 'to pass judgment' on W. Q. Judge." [Mead was Secretary-General of the European Section of the T.S., and editor of *The Vâhan.* His circular *Letter to the European Section* had been issued with vol 4 No 7 (February 1, 1895) of *The Vâhan.*] Judge replied in *The Path* (New York) vol 9 No 2 pp 433–4 (March 1895) maintaining his *Letters that have Helped Me* (serialised in item 96) were authentic. Statements by the joint Vice-Presidents of the T.S. in *The Path* (N.Y.) vol 9 No 5 pp 163–7 (August 1894), Judge, A. Besant. See also *Lucifer* (London) vol 15 pp 500–14 (February 1895), and in vol 16 (No 91) pp 68–9 (March 15, 1895) a letter from Geo. W. Russell (dated February 16, 1895) contesting Mrs Besant's opinions expressed in vol 15 (February, 1895). In the *Westminster Gazette* (London) Nos 537–46 (Monday, October 29 to November 8, 1894) F. Edmund Garrett's "Isis Very Much Unveiled" had been printed: an attempt at debunking H. P. Blavatsky (1831–91) founder of the T.S. Despite the "humility" observed at close quarters by her niece's husband, Charles Johnston, in *World Theosophy* (Hollywood) vol 1 No 8 (August, 1931) pp 617–18, Madam's contentious nature had stimulated resentment—and won staunch friends. Among them, H. T. Edge, Mead, W. R. Old, F. G. Fitch, Sarah Corbett, and A. P. Sinnett protested in *Westminster Gazette* Nos 542, 547–9, 553–6, and 559 (November 24, 1894) against Garrett's assault. That campaign included allusions to Judge's disputed honesty. In *The Vâhan* vol 4 No 6 p 9 col 1 (January 1, 1895) a letter was printed, dated November 26, 1894 from 3 Upper Ely Place, Dublin, expressing confidence in Judge, despite the *Westminster Gazette*'s criticism. Signatories: Robert Coates, A. Dick, A. W. Dwyer, Ellen Duncan, James Nolan, Fred J. Dick, Dan. N. Dunlop, James Duncan, Patrick Jordan, Geo. W. Russell. In *The Vâhan* vol 4 No 7 (February 1, 1895) p 12: "Additional signatures to the Dublin Lodge Circular" included from the Bow (London) Lodge, Violet North; and, from Dublin Lodge, Edmund King, E. J. King, Edith M. White, Eleanor Dunlop, A. Oldham, K. B. Lawrence, and E. A. Seale. (In vol 4 No 8 a letter from F. J. Dick to Mead was printed entire.) In vol 4 No 7 the 24 signatories to "A protest. To Members of the Theosophical Society in Europe" included J. C. Keightley, A. L. Cleather, Fanny and Edith Coryn, Annie and F. J. Dick, D. N. Dunlop, E. T. Hargrove, Basil Crump, K. B. Lawrence, Geo. W. Russell, Patrick E. Jordan, R. E. Coates, and Jas. Duncan. [In item 96 vol 3 No 5 pp 77–9 (Feb 15, 1895) an essay "On the Spur of the Moment" (sgd Æ) defends Judge, but does not include the quoted sentence.]

3

THE FUTURE OF IRELAND AND THE AWAKENING OF THE FIRES

The Future of Ireland | *and the Awakening of* | *the Fires.* [Four ornamental figures resembling two small leaves balanced on the apex of a triangle.] *By Æ.* | *Published at 13 Eustace Street.* | *Threepence.*

Pp 12: [1] title-page, poem on [2]: text pp [3]–10: [11] *Note.* in center: [12] blank.

Issued in gray wrappers, lettered on front wrapper as on t/p. All edges cut. Printed and published by the Irish Theosophist Press: ? March 1897. Reptd from articles in the *Irish Theosophist* (Dublin) vol 5 pp 66–9 and 85–9 (January 15 and February 15, 1897). "The Future of Ireland" had been discussed by the Dublin lodge members of the Theosophical Society on June 17, 1896. 24.6 × 18.4 cm.

[The original typescript of items 3 and 4, once owned by the late Dr Richard F. Hayes, he bequeathed to the National Library of Ireland: Mss No 10,755.]

4

IDEALS IN IRELAND: PRIEST OR HERO?

Ideals in Ireland. [ornament] | *Priest or Hero?* [ornament] *By Æ.* | *In same series.* [underlined] | *The Future of Ireland* |

and the awakening of | the fires. [ornament] | *Published at 13 Eustace Street, Dublin.* | *Price threepence.*

Pp 8: title-page, verso blank: text pp [1]–8: blank leaf.

Issued in gray wrappers lettered in dark blue as on t/p, but with "In the same series, etc." omitted. All edges cut. Reptd from the *Irish Theosophist* vol 5 pp 127–31 and 148–52 (April 15 and May 15, 1897). Printed and published by the Irish Theosophist Press: ? May 1897. 25.9 × 20.4 cm.

[The original typescript now in N.L.I.: Mss 10,755.]

5

THE EARTH BREATH AND OTHER POEMS

The Earth Breath and | Other Poems by A.E. | [design] *Published by John Lane, Sign of the | Bodley Head, New York and London*

Pp 96: half-title; on verso *By the same author: Homeward Songs by the Way*: title-page; on verso, *Fifteen of these poems have already been published in the American | edition of Homeward Songs by the Way.*; also on verso of t/p, *Copyright 1897 by John Lane* at head of page: pp [5–7] Contents; dedication on verso: [9–10] introductory poem, verso blank: text pp 11–94: [95] *The Earth Breath and other Poems. Printed for John Lane | by Will Bradely, Springfield, Mass., in August mdcccxcvii.* [MacManus noted on his copy: *Price 3/6* on t/p: and on p [95] after imprint: Printer's design, lettered *The Wayside Press.*] Published September 1897 [Brit. Mus. copy stamped 15 Se 97.] Type composed by AE. Royalty agreement dated June 25, 1897: 10 per cent on retail price, to author. 1000 copies published in America, and 1000 in Britain. During 1904 in America 301 copies were remaindered without AE's consent. In 1903 he passed publication of his poems to Macmillan & Co., but withdrew items 2D and 5 from Lane only in 1913.

Issued in gray boards, lettered in green on front cover: *The Earth Breath | And Other Poems by | A.E.* [Arboraceous design, as on title-page, identical to item 2D] On spine:

The Earth Breath [The green has faded into brown on some copies]. 15.9 × 12.4 cm.

5A Second edition, re-set: type not composed by AE. [A] *The Earth Breath and | Other Poems by A.E. | London: John Lane, The Bodley Head | New York: John Lane Company. mcmvi* Published 1906 (? 1000 copies). pp 94: [blank leaf]: half-title; on verso "Uniform with this volume | *Homeward Songs by the Way*": Title-page; on verso, *Copyright in the U.S.A.* | *Second edition* | *Fifteen*, etc [as in item 5]: pp [5–7] Contents: [8] Dedication: [9–10] Introductory poem, verso blank: text 11–94: [95–96] publisher's announcements: blank leaf. Issued in gray boards lettered on front cover and spine, as item 5, with identical design on front cover (not on title-page). 17.1 × 13.1 cm.

Omitting pp 29 and 51, and 74–9 (from which poem lines 23–30 were alone reptd in item 21, at p 152); all others reptd in item 21. Pp 9, 11, 13, 14, 23, 27, 48, 49, 72 and 94 were reptd in item 8: pp 24, 28, 33, 47, 52, 57, 80, 83 and 88 were reptd in item 14. Part reptd in item 54. *Dedicated*: To W. B. Yeats. [Some copies of item 5 and 5A were issued (first issue?) with a variant binding, quarter canvas, with a paper label on boards.] [See Yeats' article: *Daily Express* (Dublin), Sept 3, 1898: reptd in item 198.]

6

CO-OPERATIVE CREDIT

I.A.O.S.—Leaflet No. 2.—(Rural Banks). | *Co-operative Credit.* | *(Fortieth Thousand).* [Ruled line.]

Pp 4. Issued without title-page, unbound. Text [1]–4. At foot of p 4: *Published by the Irish Agricultural Organisation Society, Ltd.,* | *Dublin.* | [Unsigned]. [Advert. for the *Irish Homestead*] | *Printed by Sealy, Bryers & Walker, Mid. Abbey St. Dublin.* [Below ruled line under advert.] [This pamphlet should not be confused with the I.A.O.S. Technical Instruction leaflet series.] In the I.A.O.S. lists of publications this was variously named, occasionally by its sub-title *Rural Banks*, and as *Agricultural Banks*. Reptd in the *I.A.O.S. Annual Report for*

6A *1898* (Appendix G) at pp 63–4. Translated into Irish by Dr
6B Douglas Hyde, and published by the I.A.O.S. as their leaflet No 2A, in 1899. [See P. S. O'Hegarty's *Bibliography of Douglas Hyde* (off-print from the *Dublin Magazine* January 1939) item 13.] 40,000 copies of AE's leaflet had been printed for circulation by August 1900. This compiler discovered a copy of AE's leaflet and Hyde's translation in the British Museum Library. Those copies have now been lodged at pressmark: 8282dd. 22.1 × 13.4 cm.

7

AN ARTIST OF GAELIC IRELAND

An Artist | of Gaelic | Ireland | By A.E. [Above the title a zinc-block of a ship off-shore; colored by hand.]

Pp 4: title-page [I]: text [II–III]; at foot of [III] *Reprinted from the Freeman's Journal*; verso blank.

7A Another issue [A] on thicker paper, bearing a wood-cut on title-page hand-colored, of the sea, with a horse's head. Pp 4
7B [as item 7]. Reprinted from the [B] *Freeman's Journal* (Dublin) October 23, 1901, p 5 col 3. [Review signed by AE of Jack B. Yeats' exhibition, held in the Hall at 9 Merrion Row, Dublin, from October 23 to November 2, 1901.] Reptd in
7C [C] *Catalogue of Sketches of Life in the West of Ireland* by Jack B. Yeats [n.d.]. The copy once in the British Museum Library was destroyed by bombing during the 1939 war. It was there conjecturally dated in the catalogue: 1905? A copy was sold in the John Quinn Library Sale, New York, 1924 (Anderson Galleries), item 11324 [inscribed: "John Quinn from AE."] Jack Yeats' numerous exhibitions to which his subjects gave that title, included: *circa* August 30, 1902, and October 13, 1906, in Dublin; and at the Walker Galleries, London, in July 1914 (*The Times*, July 11). One sentence from item 7
7D and 7A was reptd in the [D] *Catalogue* of 29 paintings by Jack B. Yeats, exhibited in the Little Art Rooms, London, May 31–June 21, 1919, on p 4. [A copy of that *Catalogue* is lodged in the National Art Library, Victoria and Albert Museum, London.] Item 7 reptd (without illustration) in items

28 and 28A. A copy of item 7 is preserved in the County Museum, Armagh. 20.6 × 13.3 cm.

["REMEMBRANCE" a broad sheet. See below, item 133.]

8

THE NUTS OF KNOWLEDGE LYRICAL POEMS OLD AND NEW

The Nuts of Knowledge, Lyrical | Poems Old and New by A.E.

Pp [33]: fly-leaf blank: blank leaf: leaf with device printed in red, two double circles enclosing a sword; verso blank: blank leaf: title-page printed in black [verso blank]: Table of Contents on unnumbered page and its verso: unnumbered page with acknowledgement, "The Manager of the Dun Emer Press has to thank | Mr John Lane for permission to reprint ten poems | from *Homeward Songs by the Way* and ten from | *The Earth Breath.*" [Printed in black] with dedication on verso, also in black. P [1] Introductory poem [in red], verso blank: text pp 3–32 [3–31 in black; 32 in red]. P [33] at top, a note on the allusions in the title [in black], and at foot of the page [33] in red capitals—Here ends The Nuts of | Knowledge, written | by A.E., Printed, upon | Paper made in Ireland, | and Published by Eliz- | abeth Corbet Yeats at | The Dun Emer Press, in | The House of Evelyn | Gleeson at Dundrum | in the County of Dub- | lin, Ireland, finished | on the Tenth day of | October, in the year | nineteen hundred & | three. [verso blank]: blank leaf: fly-leaf white blank. Published December 1, 1903. [200 copies, unnumbered.]

Bound in blue-gray boards with a linen back extending 2.4 cm into covers. Lettered on front cover in black: *The Nuts of Knowledge by A.E.* [B.M. copy dated: 2 De 1903].

21.4 × 14.9 cm.

Dedication: For Brian [his elder son] etc.

Pp 3, 6, 7, 10, 12, 13, 15, 20, 22, 24 and 30 first collected. The other poems were reptd from items 2 and 5. Reptd in item 21.

9

DEIRDRE, A DRAMA IN THREE ACTS

The Green Sheaf Supplement to No. 7. | *Deirdre* | *A Drama in Three Acts* | *by A.E.* | *All Dramatic Rights Held by the Irish National Theatre Society.*

Pp 12: text and illustrations: inserted between pp 6 and 7, "Then in my dream I came nigh him" (Act 1) illus. by Cecil French; and "Do you not see them? The bright birds which sang at our flight!" etc. (Act 2), by the editor of the *Green Sheaf* (London) Pamela Colman Smith. Published in 1903, in London, [pp 12 unnumbered] Elkin Mathews.

28.1 × 22.1 cm.

9A First printed serially in [A] the *All-Ireland Review* (Kilkenny: Dublin): "The Flight of Deirdre" (July 6, 13 and 20, 1901: at pp 190–1, 201, 207); "The Recall of the Sons of Usna" (October 26, November 2, 1901: pp 254–5, 264–5); and "The Fate of the Sons of Usna" (February 8 and 15, 1902: pp
9B 435–6, 450–1). Reptd in [B] the *Celtic Christmas* issue of the *Irish Homestead* (Dublin) vol 8 [separate pagination for that issue] dated December 6, 1902: at pp 4–11.

9C [C] [ornament] | *Deirdre* [ornament] | *A Drama in Three Acts, by A.E.* | *Being Number Four of the* | *Tower Press Booklets* [dotted line] *Second* | *Series* [ornament] | *Maunsel & Co., Ltd.,* | *96 Middle Abbey Street,* | *Dublin* [ornament] *1907* | Published ? December 1907 [Brit. Mus. copy stamped 20 Mh 08]. 500 copies. Pp 54: fly-leaf: half-title, verso blank: [3–4] title-page, verso blank: [5] dedication *To* | *Seumas O'Sullivan,* verso blank: [7] *Dramatis Personæ,* verso blank: text pp 9–53: at foot of p 53, [rule] imprint *Printed at the Tower Press, 4 Skipper's Alley, Dublin,* verso blank: fly-leaf.

Issued in olive-green wrappers, lettered on front cover as on title-page, omitting date, and with line-block of a tower added in center. Unopened edges; wrappers overlap. 16.1 × 12.8 cm. [The Tower device was designed by Nicholas Murray Robertson in 1907. The original drawing, in ink, was sold by Elkin

Mathews Ltd in 1959.] One copy of 9C was specially bound in cloth-covered boards, multi-colored, and presented to James and Margaret Cousins to commemorate their association with the first performance of it. Sold late 1959 by Elkin Mathews Ltd, from Lennox Robinson's collections: included a photograph of an early performance, an inscription by AE, etc. Reptd in item 28. [Yeats' rev. of prefce: *United Irishman*, April 12 and 26, 1902.]

9D *Deirdre | A Legend in three acts | by A.E. | Maunsel & Roberts, Ltd. | 50 Lower Baggot Street, Dublin | 1922* This was a "Schools Edition". Pp 60. 18.5 × 12.4 cm.

[*Deirdre*, Acts 1 and 2 were first performed (dress-rehearsal) in George Coffey's house, 5 Harcourt Terrace, Dublin: performance to celebrate Diarmid Coffey's 12th birthday anniversary, in garden there, January 2 and 3, 1902. Naisi played by AE, Fergus by George Coffey, Ainle by R. I. Best, Buinne by J. H. Cousins, Deirdre by Miss Violet Mervyn (i.e. Miss Elizabeth Young), Lavarcam by her sister Miss Ella Young. Costumes supervised by Maud Gonne. T. W. Rolleston and E. E. Fournier managed the curtains indoors, January 2. First public performances of the complete play: in the Hall of St Teresa's Total Abstinence Society, Clarendon Street, Dublin, on April 2, 3, and 4, 1902: cast, *Deirdre*, Maire T. Quinn, *Lavarcam*, Maire Nic Shiubhlaigh; *Fergus*, P. J. Kelly; *Buinne*, P. Colum; *Ilaun*, C. Caulfield; *Ardan*, F. Ryan; *Ainnle*, H. Sproule (i.e. J. H. Cousins); *Naisi*, J. Dudley Digges; *Messenger*, Brian Callender; *Concobar*, F. J. Fay; *Cathvah*, AE. Those performances by the Irish National Dramatic Company included in the same programme W. B. Yeats' *Cathleen ni Houlihan*. They performed it privately at Dún Emer, Dundrum, on August 22, 1903, with cast substitutes: *Ilann*, Seumas O'Sullivan, *Ainle*, George Roberts, *Messenger*, P. Mac Shiubhlaigh. The "Theatre of Ireland" group played *Deirdre* at the Abbey Theatre, December 13 and 14, 1907, with AE as *Cathvah*. (Review in *Sinn Fein*, December 21, 1907).] *Names*: spelling varied as on programs.

9E Mr Gerard Fay owns the bound typescript Prompt-copy of the first performance of *Deirdre*, formerly owned by the late

Frank J. Fay. The play is marked in pencil with stage directions. Pp x + 40 + vi. Bound in deep blue-black rough cloth, title lettered in gold on front cover only (capitals). The typescript in purple ink (ribbon copy) on white paper. [See also Part 12B, item CLXIII.] 28.7 × 20.8 cm.

10

THE DIVINE VISION AND OTHER POEMS

The Divine Vision | and Other Poems | By A.E. | London | Macmillan and Co., Limited | New York: The Macmillan Company | 1904 | All rights reserved

10A [Some copies are dated: 1903. In all other details they (A) are similar, excepting the verso of the title-page which is blank.] [Price 3/- net.] Pp [xiv] + [96]: fly-leaf: blank leaf: [I] blank; on verso *By the Same Writer*, etc: [iii] half-title; verso [iv] publisher's monogram in centre: [v] title page, with *Copyright in the United States of America* on verso [vi]: [vii] dedication; verso blank: ix, Introductory poem; verso blank: xi–xiii, *Contents* [error on p xiii, *read* 78 for 77]; verso blank: text pp 1–91: [92] blank: 93–[95] a "Note" on mythological references; imprint, R. & R. Clark, Limited, at foot of [95], verso blank: fly-leaf. Printed in December 1903. Published in London and New York: January 13, 1904.

Issued in blue cloth, with single gold line bordering the front cover, and at head and foot of spine: lettered in gold, title and author, on front cover; the same, and at foot, *Macmillan* on spine. All edges uncut. 19.5 × 13.4 cm. Pp 8, 9, 17, 30, 57, 67, and 82 reptd in item 14. Excepting pp 27, 33, 46, 52, 66, and 75 reptd in item 21. Part reptd in item 54. Copy inscribed: [to Susan Mitchell] *Sioban from A.E. 15.1.04* [London: 1000 copies.]

Dedicated: To S. M[itchell], T. K[eohler], S. V[arian], G. R[oberts], E. Y[oung], J. S[tarkey], comrades in the craft.

11

CONTROVERSY IN IRELAND

Controversy in Ireland | An Appeal | To | Irish Journalists. | By A.E. | O'Donoghue & Co | 15 Hume Street, Dublin. | Price Threepence.

Pp 12: [1] Title-page: [2]–12, Text. The text comprises: [2]–3, *Prefatory Note* including a letter from AE which had
11A been first printed in *The Leader* (Dublin) September 17, 1904,
11B p 52 (letter dated 12th September): pp 3–7, *Physical Force in Literature.* | [*Reprinted from DANA, September 1904.*]; signed A.E.: pp 7–12, "*A Sober Nationalist.*" | [*Reprinted from THE LEADER, Sept. 10, 1904.*] unsigned. *Dana* (Dublin)
11C vol 1 No 5 pp 129–33 (September 1904), sgd Æ. *The Leader* article was printed in vol 9 No 3 pp 37–9 (Thursday, September 10), unsgd. Imprint at foot of p 12: [rule] | *The Sackville Press, Findlater Place, Dublin.*

Issued unbound, all edges cut. 19.5 × 13.6 cm.

Published probably September 26, 1904.

Russell was attacked again in *The Leader*, September 24, pp 75–6 (sgd Imaal). An editorial notice of his pamphlet was captioned "The Eel in Controversy", October 1, 1904, p 84
11D col 2. In the same issue a letter from Russell was printed at pp 88–90, captioned with editorial commentary "A Minor Poet in Eruption", taking issue good-naturedly with Imaal. Imaal replied, October 8, p 101. Russell was again attacked,
11E editorially, October 15, p 113: same issue his last words in a letter, pp 121–2. [*The Leader* was edited by D. P. Moran.]

12

THE MASK OF APOLLO AND OTHER STORIES

The Mask of Apollo | and other Stories | By A.E. | Dublin: Whaley & Co. | London: Macmillan & Co., Ltd.

Pp [vi] + [54]: fly-leaf: blank page, and on verso, *By the same Writer.*, etc: title-page, verso blank: preface, sgd A.E., verso blank: *Contents.*, [1], verso blank: text, pp 3–53: [54] imprint, *Printed by | Sealy, Bryers and Walker, | Middle Abbey Street, | Dublin. | 3807.5.04* | : fly-leaf blank.

Issued in terra-cotta boards, colored orange [faded into reddish-brown], with white cloth back extending 1.3 cm into covers. *The | Mask | Of | Apollo | By | A.E.* lettered silver on front cover. Uncut only top edges. 500 copies.

19.1 × 12.8 cm.

Published in Dublin and London on January 6, 1905. [Messrs Hodges, Figgis & Co. had ordered "a few copies" from Whaley & Co., by letter dated November 4, 1904. Compared to the printer's mark, the late publication may be explained either by some dispute caused by joint publication of the book; or perhaps through the unsettled conduct of the Dublin firm conducted by George Roberts.] Ella Young reviewed the book in the *United Irishman* (Dublin) January 7, 1905, p 3 cols 1–2.

12A These stories had been first printed: [A] "The Mask of Apollo"
in the *Irish Theosophist* vol 1 No 7 pp 67–8 (April 15, 1893):
12B [B] "The Cave of Lilith" in vol 2 No 5 pp 62–4 (February 15,
12C 1894): [C] "The Story of a Star" in vol 2 No 11 pp 160–2
12D (August 15, 1894): [D] "A Dream of Angus Oge" in *The*
12D *Internationalist* (Dublin) vol 1 No 1 pp 10–13 (October 15,
12E 1897): [E] "The Meditation of Ananda" (*formerly*: Parvati)
in the *Irish Theosophist* vol 2 No 2 pp 151–3 (November 15,
12F 1893): [F] "The Midnight Blossom" in vol 2 No 10 pp 140–3
12G (July 15, 1894): [G] "The Childhood of Apollo" in vol 5
No 1 pp 24–27 (November 15, 1896). Additionally "A Dream
12H of Angus Oge" was reptd [H] in *The Green Sheaf* (London)
12J No 4 (dated 1903), pp 4–7, and in *The Gael* (New York) [J]
issue dated April 1904, pp 153–4. Other stories were reptd in the *Daily Express* (Dublin) listed in *Part 8*, below. Ms of all except [C] and [D] were sold in the John Quinn Library sale (New York, 1924), item 8378 on 29 pages quarto. Page proofs were sold (item 8379). Present location not known.

Dedication: (in the Preface) to the friends he had in youth.

[Sir William Rothenstein (1872–1945) transmitted a copy of item 12 to Rabindra Nath Tagore (1861–1941), inscribed "To Rabindra Nath Tagore from AE." That copy is now preserved in the Rabindra Bhavana at Santiniketan, Bengal. In the letter announcing the despatch to Rothenstein of that book, AE wrote (*circa* 1914?) "... The Indian tales will doubtless seem illiterate to Tagore but I hope not in the spirit wrong or alien ..."]

13

SOME IRISH ESSAYS

The Tower Press Booklets | *Number One* [ornament] | *Some Irish Essays by A.E.* | *Dublin: Maunsel & Co., Ltd.,* | *60 Dawson Street. mcmvi.*

Pp 40: half-title, verso blank: title-page, on verso *Printed at the Tower Press,* | *Thirty-eight Cornmarket, Dublin.*: p 5, Contents: p 6, note as to original publication in journals: 7, Preface, verso blank: text pp 9–39, verso blank:

Issued in fawn wrappers with tower design on front, and series and book-name and author: inside the end wrapper is publisher's announcement of the next volume in the series. Published January 22, 1906. 500 copies. [The first series of the Tower Press Booklets were edited by "Seumas O'Sullivan" and James Connolly (died *circa* 1920–30: not to be confused with the Irish labor leader).] All edges uncut; wrappers overlapping. 17.7 × 10.8 cm.

13A [A] "Nationality and Cosmopolitanism in Art" was first printed in the *Daily Express* (Dublin) November 12, December
13B 10, 1898; reptd in item 61. [B] "The Dramatic Treatment of Heroic Literature" first printed in the *United Irishman* (Dublin) May 3, 1902, p 3; reptd in *Samhain* (Dublin) October 1902,
13C pp 11–13. [C] "On an Irish Hill" first printed in the *Kilkenny Moderator* (Kilkenny), perhaps in the Christmas issue 1896; the poems in this essay were reptd in item 21 pp 158, and 218
13D (also reptd in item 98, CC 1897, p 10). [D] "The Poet of Shadows" first printed in *The Reader* (item 177); reptd in

item 28. [See also ref. at end of item 28D: in vol 9 p 3651 (§5)—p 3653 reprinted item 13 pp 35–9.]

14

BY STILL WATERS, LYRICAL POEMS OLD AND NEW

By Still Waters, Lyrical | Poems Old and New by A.E. | The Dun Emer Press | Dundrum | mcmvi

Pp [34]: gray end-paper: 4 unnumbered blank leaves: unnumbered leaf with 2 double red circles, surrounding a sword device, in red; verso blank: unnumbered leaf, publisher's note in red, acknowledging source of poems; verso blank: title-page; verso blank: unnumbered, *Table of Contents*, and on verso: [1] Introductory poem, printed in red; verso blank: text pp 3–[33], of which [33] is printed in red, with a note at foot of that page, *Here ends By Still Waters, | Lyrical Poems Old and New | by A.E., Printed upon pa- | per made in Ireland, and | published by Elizabeth C. | Yeats at the Dun Emer | Press, at Dundrum in | the County of Dublin, Ire- | land, finished on All Souls' | Eve, in the year 1906.*; verso blank: 7 blank leaves, and final gray end-paper. [Brit. Mus.: 15 De 1906.] Published December 14, 1906. [200 copies, unnumbered.] 21.4 × 14.9 cm.

Issued in slate-gray boards, with linen back extending 2.4 cm into covers. Lettered on front cover: *By Still Waters: Lyrical | Poems Old and New by A.E.* [Not labeled on spine.] Top edges uncut; other edges untrimmed. Pp 4, 11, 12, 18, 19, and 32 first collected. The other poems reptd from items 2, 5, and 10. Reptd in item 21.

15

IRELAND AND TARIFF REFORM

Ireland and tariff reform by "Libra". Dublin: ? April 1909. Published by the *Irish Times.*

[This compiler has not yet seen a copy. The *Irish Times,*

Trinity College (Dublin), The National Library of Ireland, the British Museum have been searched, but no copy of that pamphlet has been found; nor has it been located by any of the other courteous librarians in European or American libraries. One copy was sold in the John Quinn Library sale (New York, 1924), item 8334: there cataloged as "Octavo, issued in wrappers". That copy was inscribed by AE: "To John Quinn, some 'pure excursions' of a poet for use as a sleeping draught. Dose. 'One article before going to bed.' Geo. W. Russell." Laid-in was the galley-proof of AE's poem "The City" (item 21, p 30) which was first printed in the *Irish Review* (Dublin) vol 3 p 228 (July 1913).]

The pamphlet reprinted articles first printed in the *Irish Times* (Dublin): (i) untitled, February 6, 1909, p 7 col 7 and p 8 col 1: (ii) "Reconstruction of Trade Conditions," February 13, 1909, p 7 col 8 and p 8 col 1: (iii) "Do we need protection for our egg trade?", February 20, 1909, p 7 col 8 and p 8 col 1: (iv) "Speculative Economics", February 27, 1909, p 7 col 8 and p 8 col 1: (v) "The Theory of Retaliation", March 6, 1909, p 7 col 7 and p 8 col 1: (vi) "Comparison of prices under Free Trade and Protection", March 13, 1909, p 7 col 8, and p 8 col 1. In the final article "Libra" forecast his intention to write "a judgment on the proposals" of the Tariff Commission, "from the Irish point of view", when their *Report* was issued. This compiler has not yet discovered that summary judgment.

AE mentioned these articles in a letter to C. A. Weekes, March 3, 1909 (now in the County Museum, Armagh).

The *Irish Times* file copy of the pamphlet was probably destroyed in the fire which gutted their premises on September 16, 1951.

16

THE HERO IN MAN

[Published without title-page: front wrapper lettered] *The Orpheus Series. No. 1.* | *The* | *Hero in Man* | *By* | *A.E.* | *6d.* | *Published by* | *D. N. Dunlop, Ashdale, Warwick Drive, Hale,*

Cheshire, | *and* | *Clifford Bax, Ivy Bank, Hampstead, London, N.W.*

Pp 32: [1–2] half-title, verso decorated only with an asterisk in center: 3–8, *Prelude* (prose introduction by Clifford Bax): [9] asterisk only, center: 10–30, text: [31] asterisk only, center: [32] publisher's advertisement, and at foot printer's imprint [rule] | *Women's Printing Society, Ltd., 31, 33, 35, Brick Street, W*

Issued in light-gray wrappers. Edges all uncut. Wrappers overlapping. Published in May 1909. 1000 copies. 19.6 × 14.5 cm.

The late P. S. O'Hegarty, in item 100 vol 22 No 3 p 60 (July 1947) described other copies of item 16 in his possession.
16A [A] He bought an issue of it on June 28, 1909, "and it looks like the first issue." His description tallies with that for item 16 above, excepting only the printer's imprint on p [32] which read: *Women's Printing Society, Ltd., Brick Street, Piccadilly.*
16B Mr O'Hegarty also owned another copy [B] "identical in every particular with the copy in wrappers" [item 16A] "save that the price on the cover is 1s. instead of 6d.", and it was bound in light-blue linen boards, lettered in black on front cover. That copy had a presentation inscription from Clifford Bax to J. C. Snaith, dated August 1909. [Item 16A, dimensions: 18.9 × 14 cm.] 19.4 × 14.5 cm.

16C Second edition: [C] *The Orpheus Series No. 1* | *The* | *Hero in Man* | *by* | *A.E.* | *1s.* | *The Orpheus Press, 1910.* Pp [36]: half-title, asterisk only on verso, center: [3–4] title-page, verso asterisk center: [5] publisher's note *First edition (1,000 copies), May, 1909.* | *Second Edition (1,000 copies), September, 1910.* [6] asterisk, center: 7–12, *Prelude,* by Clifford Bax: [13] asterisk, center: 14–34, text: [35] asterisk, center: [36] publisher's advertisement, with printer's imprint at foot of page *Women's Printing Society, Ltd., Brick Street, Piccadilly.* Lettered on front wrapper: *The Orpheus Series. No. 1* | *The* | *Hero in Man* | *by* | *A.E.* | *The Orpheus Press.* | *1910.* Issued in light-gray wrappers [now faded fawn-gray]: edges all uncut, wrappers overlapping Published in September 1910. 1000 copies. 19.6 × 14.5 cm.

The late M. J. MacManus described one copy of item 16 which
16D in fact [D] tallies exactly with item 16C in all particulars except: on t/p, he read price and publisher on same line, with date below; the date he read was 1909. Similarly his note on front cover varied in same particulars. His copy dimensions read: 19.2 × 14.7 cm., [by him read in inches.] [O'Hegarty's copies may have been acquired by the University of Kansas Library, Lawrence, Kansas.] [O'Hegarty's 16C, imprint as 16]. Clifford Bax's *Prelude* was dated: April 1909. AE's essays were first printed: (i) in *The Internationalist* (Dublin) vol 1 No 2 pp 24–6 (November 15, 1897): (ii) and (iii) in the *Irish Theosophist* vol 5 No 6 pp 112–14 (March 15, 1897) and vol 5 No 10 pp 181–5 (July 15, 1897). AE's essays reptd in item 28.

16E Reptd [E] in Bombay, India: ? 1945. International Book House.

17

THE BUILDING UP OF A RURAL CIVILISATION

The Building Up | of a | Rural Civilisation. | By | George W. Russell. | An address delivered at the Annual General Meeting of the | I.A.O.S., 10th December, 1909. | [double rule] | *Dublin: Sealy, Bryers & Walker | Middle Abbey Street* | [rule] | *1910.*

Pp 12: title-page, verso blank: text, [3]–11: [12] advertisement: Published in Dublin, ? January 1910.

Issued in gray printed paper wrappers: front wrapper lettered as t/p, with a triple-line black border, ornamented at corners, with *Price One Penny* at foot of page. 24.5 × 15.6 cm.

17A Reprinted in [A] the *I.A.O.S. Annual Report for the Year Ending June 30, 1909* (Dublin: 1910. Sealy, Bryers and Walker) at pp 38–46.

18

THE RENEWAL OF YOUTH

The Orpheus Series No. vii. | The | Renewal of Youth | by A.E. | The Orpheus Press | 3, Amen Corner, Paternoster Row, E.C.

Pp 24: [1] title-page, verso central asterisk: text pp 3–22: *Publisher's note* advertising "Orpheus" a magazine, and a list of the Orpheus Press booklets, 23–[24]: asterisk at end, and beneath, *Women's Printing Society* etc (as 16). Published ? May 1911. [1000 copies].

Issued in light-brown wrappers, overlapping. All edges uncut. Lettered in black, as title page, but address omitted, replaced by date, 1911. 19.6 × 14.8 cm

These essays had been first printed in the *Irish Theosophist*: (i) in vol 5 No 9 pp 168–70 (June 15, 1897): (ii) vol 3 No 11 pp 189–92 (August 15, 1895): (iii) vol 4 No 1 pp 15–18 (October 15, 1895). Reptd in item 28.

19

CO-OPERATION AND NATIONALITY

Co-operation and | Nationality | A Guide for rural reformers | from this to the next generation | By George W. Russell (Æ) | Maunsel and Company, Limited, | 96 Middle Abbey Street, Dublin | 1912

Pp [viii] + 104 + [iv]: half-title, verso imprint (Maunsel): title-page: verso, *All rights Reserved*: [v] dedication, verso blank: [vii] Contents, verso blank: text, pp [1]–[104]: 2 leaves with publisher's advertisements, and on versos, 4 pages. Published February 1912.

Issued in slate-gray wrappers, lettered (spine, title) in royal blue on front wrapper: Co-Operation | and Nationality | A Guide for Rural | Reformers from this | to the next Generation | Maunsel and Co., Ltd. | One Shilling Net [single line border]. Inside the front wrapper, and both sides of the back wrapper are decorated with the publisher's advertisements. Top edges cut; others uncut. 19.3 × 13.1 cm.

19A [A] First American edition: New York: 1913. Norman, Remington & Co. *Dedicated*: To Sir Horace Plunkett, Father T. Finlay, R. A. Anderson, (etc).

19B Reprinted [B] Chicago and New York: 1940. The Co-operative League of the U.S.A. Pp 5+70. [19A and 19B not seen by compiler.] Issued in paper covers: sold at 25 cents. [In the Library of Congress *Catalog* item 19B is described as 21.5 cm vertical.]

19C Chapters 1–6 in the book had been first printed in [C] the *Irish Review* (Dublin) vol 1 pp 32–6: 73–9: 117–23: 165–72: 219–29: 365–72 (monthly, issues March–October 1911). Additionally pp 82–97 (chapter 12) reprints "Ideals of the New Rural Society" from item 63.

19D Translated [D] into Finnish by Huvi Vuorinen, as *Osuustoiminta ja Kansan Hyvinvointi* (Porvoossa: 1912. Söderström Osa-keyhtiö. Paper wrappers: pp 92 [+4, publisher's advertisements]). [Item 19 was reviewed thoughtfully by J. M. Hone as "The Inconvenient Ardours of AE" in *The Saturday Review* (London) vol 113 pp 203–4 (February 17, 1912).]

20

THE RURAL COMMUNITY

The Rural Community | [rule] | *An Address to the* | *American Commission of* | *Agricultural Inquiry* | *by George W. Russell*, | *at* | *The Plunkett House, Dublin*, | *July 15th, 1913* [triple line border].

Pp 20: [1] title-page: [2] blank: text 3–20. Ornament below the text on p 20, and at foot of page [rule] and below, *Printed by The Rapid Printing Co., Ltd., 60 Mid. Abbey Street, Dublin.* [A notice of the Americans' visit to Dublin, with a photograph, was printed in item 98 vol 20 p 591 (July 19, 1913). Henry Agard Wallace was a delegate.]

Issued without wrappers, with title-page as cover. All edges cut. Published by the I.A.O.S., summer 1913. 18.4 × 12.3 cm.

20A [A] Substantially re-arranged, with some abridgement and captions added it was reptd in item 57, pp 357–74.

21

COLLECTED POEMS

Collected Poems | by | A.E. | Macmillan and Co., Limited | St. Martin's Street, London | 1913

Pp xvi + 275; fly-leaf: [i] half-title; verso, publisher's monogram and foreign addresses: [iii] title-page, (*Copyright* on verso): [v] dedication, verso blank: [vii] *Preface* (in which AE clarified the title of item 2: *Homeward, Songs by the Way*); verso blank: ix–xv *Contents*: [xvi] blank: 1, [Introductory poem]: text pp 2–271: [272] blank: *Note* [mythological references] pp 273–5; at foot of 275, *Printed by R. & R. Clark, Limited, Edinburgh.*; verso blank: fly-leaf.

Issued in dark-blue cloth, lettered in gold on front cover: *Collected Poems | A.E.* with a single-line gold border: backstrip lettered in gold as on front cover, with *Macmillan & Co.* at foot, and a single gold line at top and foot. Back cover, a single line impressed border, not gilded. Lower edges cut and trimmed; other edges uncut. Published in London, September 23, 1913. 19.5 × 13.6 cm.

Reprinted: November 1913: December 1914: April 1917 and
21A [A] with added poems (item 27, etc) July 1919: reptd October
21B 1920: and with more additions [B] (item 45: and pp 330–5 not elsewhere collected) March 1926: reptd October 1927: June 1928: a part of the June 1928 reprint was bound in red leather
21C and issued [C] in the *Cardinal Edition*, 1930. These various reprints were issued in format identical to item 21: item 21B having pp xviii + 373: it was again reptd in the ordinary edition, but the cloth cover a deeper blue, and without lettering on the front cover: instead 3 impressed lines surrounding front cover; and on spine gold lettered, title, author (publisher at foot), and 3 impressed lines horizontally grouped to divide it in 4 spaces and either side of the lettering; circle devices impressed beside the edges of the 3 centrally spaced lines;
21D that is item 21C, reptd April 1931. Finally reptd [D] with item 49 added, November 1935: pp xix [+ verso blank] + 430 +

[1 page advertising books by AE, verso blank.] Top edges uncut, others untrimmed. 19.9 × 13.4 cm.

21E [E] The first American edition was issued in New York: April 1915, by the Macmillan Company. Identical text to item 21. [See references in items 2, 5, 10, and 27 for poems excluded from this collection. Item 32 was also excluded, but was reptd elsewhere.]

The London issues were: September 1913, 1000 copies: November 1913, December 1914, April 1917, July 1919, all 1000 copies: October 1920, 1500 copies: March 1926, 1590 copies: October 1927, 1000 copies: the June 1928 reprint (part bound in 21C), 1000 copies: April 1931, 1500 copies: November 1935, 1060 copies.

Dedicated: To D. N. D[unlop] in memory of the Household [at 3 Upper Ely Place, Dublin]. [In item 21A and subsequent reprints the final quatrain on p 72 was altered. See AE's comment in item 50 pp 28–29.]

22

TO THE MASTERS OF DUBLIN

Reprinted from the "Irish Times", Tuesday, October 7th., 1913 | To the Masters of Dublin. | An Open Letter | [double rule] | *(by "A.E.") to the Editor of the "Irish Times".* The
22A original newspaper (p 6 col 4), [A]. Small broadside, printed on both sides. Unbound. 27 × 20.8 cm.

22B Reptd in *The Irish Worker* (Dublin) vol 3 No 22 p [1] cols 1–2, (Saturday, October 11, 1913). [In *The Irish Worker* No 25, p 3 col 1 (November 1, 1913) a letter was printed, from George Russell, "The Crime and the Punishment," concerned with James Larkin's imprisonment.] Reptd in items 24, 59, and 65.

22C Also quoted elsewhere, including: [C] *Constance Markiewicz* by Séan O'Faolain (London: 1934. Cape) at p 167.

22D Reptd with item 24 in [D] *One Thousand Years of Irish Prose:*

Part 1: The Literary Revival, edited by Vivian Mercier and David H. Greene (New York: 1952. Devin-Adair) at pp 227–33.

22E One copy of 22 is known, [E] printed on blue paper, instead of white paper; once owned by Mr William O'Brien of Dublin. [See also item 98 vol 20 pp 737–8 (Sep 6, 1913), and scarcely less valuable vol 20 pp 757–9 (Sep 13) and pp 777–9 (Sep 20, 1913).] AE was critical of the Union's leaders for their emotions drowning any intelligence they had. The I.A.O.S. Committee wrote to item 98 vol 20 pp 922–3 (Nov 8, 1913) publicly affirming the independence of AE, and of item 98, from the I.A.O.S., or the opinions of its officers. See also AE's dignified acceptance and comment: vol 20 p 942.

22F Again reprinted [F] in *Fifty Years of Liberty Hall*, edited by Cathal O'Shannon (Dublin: 1959. Published by the Irish Transport and General Workers' Union.) at pp 41–3 (also quoted in part on p 36).

23

THE TRAGEDY OF LABOUR IN DUBLIN

23 *Reprinted from The Times, Thursday, November 13, 1913* | *The Tragedy of Labour in Dublin.*

23A The original newspaper, [A]. Signed: George W. Russell (A.E.): p 10 col 3.

Single sheet, printed on one side only; verso blank.

Issued unbound. 29.8 × 24 cm.

23B Reptd [B] in the *Daily Herald* (London) November 14, 1913, etc. Reptd in items 24 and 59.

24

THE DUBLIN STRIKE

The Dublin Strike. | *A Plea for the Workers.* | *By "Æ" (George W. Russell.)* | *A speech delivered in the Royal Albert Hall, London, Nov. 1, 1913* | [rule]

Pp 8: text [1]–8: with rule at foot of p 8, followed by an advertisement for *The Christian Commonwealth*, and imprint: *Printed for and published by The Christian Commonwealth Company | Limited, at 133 Salisbury Square, Fleet Street, London, E.C. Price one penny.* On p [1] there is a footnote in small type: *No. 155, November 26, 1913.* But in *The Christian Commonwealth* (London: weekly) No. 1675 (vol 34) p 139 col 2, the pamphlet is announced to be "on sale this week", (Wed Nov 19, 1913). In the issue No 1674 p 120 (Wed Nov 12), ". . . . we shall publish "Æ's" speech at the Albert Hall as a penny pamphlet supplement to an early issue . . ." Perhaps the footnote date November 26 records a reprinting? In the November 19th issue of *The Christian Commonwealth* p 138, there was a note, "The proceeds of the sale of the pamphlet will be given to the Dublin Distress Fund." The text of the pamphlet is in three parts: first the speech, pp [1]–4: pp 4–7 reprints item 22: and item 23 is reptd at pp 7–8. [See also note of other reprinting, under item 22.] AE's own copy of this pamphlet, torn, and lacking pp 3–6, is corrected in ink by AE on p 2 (5 lines up in text): *Consul* cancelled, and *Council* inserted.

Issued without cover or title-page [heading title on p 1].

20.5 × 13.2 cm.

24A [Another edition]. [A] | *The Dublin Strike.* | [large photograph of AE, probably contemporary] | *By "Æ" (George W. Russell).* | [single rule] | *"Irish Worker" Press, Liberty Hall, Dublin, Ireland.* | [This description is taken from the copy of the pamphlet once owned by the late J. S. Starkey (Seumas O'Sullivan), now owned by the Lilly Library, University of Indiana, Bloomington. The photostat copy used by this compiler does not reveal whether the photograph had merely been pasted on to the pamphlet. Another copy seen by this compiler, of the same text issued by the same publisher, reads: | *The Dublin Strike.* | [rule] | *By "Æ." (George W. Russell).* | *I. A Plea for the Workers.* | *A Speech delivered in the Royal Albert Hall, London,* | *November 1, 1913, to an audience of 12,000 persons.* | [rule] [heading the front page and with text immediately below.] This compiler is certain that copy was exactly identical to item 24A when it was published. Since then the cover had drifted or been ripped off. Pp ii + 8 + ii. [i] front wrapper as t/p, [ii] blank: [1] headed as for the alternate copy described above, text extending to p 7: [8] blank: [iii] blank: [iv] end wrapper, publisher's advertisement for those books by AE *Which can be had from "Irish Worker" Library, 1 Liberty Hall, Dublin.* | [rule] [the book titles in two columns separated by a vertical rule] [rule below] | [a seven-line prose appraisal of Russell's personality] | [rule] | *Information upon the prices, etc., of Mr Russell's works can* | *be had at* | *"Irish Worker" Office, Liberty Hall, Dublin.* | *II. An open Letter to the Employers* extends from pp 4–6: followed by *III. An Appeal to Dublin Citizens* [i.e. *The Tragedy of Labour in Dublin*, pp 6–7.] On p 2 in item 24A (14 lines up, in text) *industry* mis-spelt.

Issued simultaneously with item 24 (November 1913), unbound, stapled in center: top edges unopened. 21.2 × 13.8 cm.

Russell's speech was quoted in the *Dublin Saturday Post* (Dublin) November 8, 1913: p 2 col 7.

[One copy of item 24A was sold among the AE items in the John Quinn Library sale: (AE, items 8312–81, sold Wed, February 13, 1924).]

24B

[In *The Christian Commonwealth* (London) vol 34 No 1678 (Dec 10, 1913) pp 190–3 "Confessions" of "The Faith I Live By" were printed with facsimile signatures from answers to that question. Annie Besant, L. Housman, G. Lansbury, Philip Snowden, Katharine Tynan, and H. G. Wells among the 84. AE's contribution, p 193: "I have never been able to state my own faiths clearly to myself. The mind is too feeble a net to catch leviathan. If there is anything in literature which recurs to me more often than other sayings it is the saying of Aratus, 'Full of Zeus are the cities. Full of Zeus are the harbours. Full of Zeus are all the ways of men. We also are his offspring.' And if you add to that this fragment of an old oracle, 'As for us who are his messengers, we are but a little part of him', you will have as nearly as it can be stated in brief the faith I live by."]

25

OXFORD UNIVERSITY AND THE CO-OPERATIVE MOVEMENT

[*One Penny.* | *Oxford University* | *and the* | *Co-operative* | *Movement,* | *by* | *George W. Russell* ("*Æ*"), | *Member of the* | *O.U.C.S. Honorary Council.* | [rule] | *Oxford University Co-operative Society, Ltd.* | *20 High Street,* | *Oxford.*

Pp 8: [1] title-page: [2]–7, text: [8] blank. Probably published May 1914. (Plunkett House Library copy was dated received: 30 Jun 1914. That copy is now in the Co-operative Reference Library, The Plunkett Foundation for Co-operative Studies, London.)

Issued unbound, stapled; all edges cut and trimmed.

18 × 12.3 cm.

[This pamphlet was AE's response to a request for an article, addressed to him by Eric G. Underwood (died June 10, 1952); perhaps encouraged by his Oxford friend Alan Anderson (1891–1914), R. A. Anderson's third son: characterised in *The Isis* (Oxford) February 14, 1914, and in the *Irish Homestead* vol 21 pp 898–9 (December 19, 1914). AE referred to the O.U.C.S. in his leader in item 98, vol 21 pp 381–2 (May 16, 1914).]

26

IRELAND, AGRICULTURE AND THE WAR

I.A.O.S. Pamphlet, No. 15. | *Ireland, Agriculture* | *and the war:* | *an open letter to Irish Farmers,* | *by the editor of the* "*Irish Homestead*". | *Reprinted by permission of the* "*Irish Homestead*". | *The Sackville Press, 11 & 12 Findlater's Place, Dublin*

Pp 16: issued unbound, perhaps in February 1915. Title heading p 1. 18.5 × 10.4 cm.

Reprinted from item 98 vol 22 pp 113–17 (February 20, 1915).

27

GODS OF WAR, WITH OTHER POEMS

Gods of War | With Other Poems | by A.E. | Printed for | Private Circulation | Dublin, 1915

Pp 40: [1] half-title, verso blank: [3] title-page, with acknowledgements note on verso: 5 *Contents*: [6] blank: 7–39, text: [40] imprint, *Printed at the Sackville Press, Dublin*

Issued in brown wrappers, overlapping. Lettered on front, in dark-blue: *Gods of War | A.E. | Dublin, 1915*. Top edges unopened; other edges cut and trimmed. Probably first circulated (?14) September 1915. 100 copies. 16.8 × 12.5 cm.

[Pp 7, 10, 16, 22, and 29 reptd from *The Times*, September 30, 1914 (and again, *Times' Poetry Supplement*, August 9, 1915): April 5, 1915: January 28, 1915: March 5, 1915: March 18, 1915. Pp 26, 29, and 32 not reptd. The others were reptd in item 21A, etc.] In a copy which AE gave to Miss Janet Cunningham he had canceled the first stanza on p 39; (in his own copy, acquired by the British Museum in 1951 he marked the same stanza "omit"), and p 20 (2nd stanza) altered to "*Our* eyes *are*" and in 5th line, to "*kinsmen*". [Evidently thoughtful for her, AE presented to Eva Gore-Booth a copy of this book, inscribed with her name "from AE—May 1916". Constance Markiewicz was imprisoned then. That copy is now owned by this compiler. William Rothenstein told AE Rev Stopford A. Brooke (1832–1916) had a copy. AE replied: ". . . I did not send him one. I only gave away about three dozen copies . . . but I am pleased one found its way to him, dear man . . ." [n.d.]]

28

IMAGINATIONS AND REVERIES

Imaginations | And Reveries | By A.E. | Maunsel & Company, Ltd. | Dublin and London | 1915

Pp xii + 256: [fly-leaf]: [i–ii] half-title, verso blank: [iii–iv] title-page, verso blank: [v–vi] dedication, verso blank: vii, *acknowledgment* note: [viii] blank: ix–x, *Preface*: xi–[xii] *Contents*, verso blank: text pp 1–255 (verso blank) printer's name etc at foot of 255: fly-leaf.

Issued in dark-blue cloth, lettered in gold on front cover (with single line gold border impressed) and on back-strip (single line gold at head and foot of back-strip): title, author, and *Maunsel* at foot of back-strip. Published December 3, 1915.
19.5 × 13.1 cm.

28A First American edition [A] identical contents: published in New York by the Macmillan Company, February 1916 (pp xii + 256).

28B An enlarged *second edition* [B] published by Maunsel and Roberts Limited, Dublin and London, in April 1921, (pp x + 316).
28C That edition was transferred to Macmillan & Co. Ltd., [C] in 1925: they re-issued it in London, with a new title-page, on November 7, 1925, (pp x + 316). Royalty Agmt, Sep 15, 1915. Author's royalty: 15 per cent on first 2000 copies, then 20. Mss to be delivered by Dec 15, 1915. Item 28C: dark-blue cloth cover, lettered in gold only on back-strip, with title, author, publisher, and single gold line at head and foot.
19.5 × 13.1 cm

28D [D] Reprinted: New York, 1932. The Macmillan Company, (pp viii + 316). In items 28B and 28C, D, the articles had been first printed: pp 1–11, see item 13: 12–21, see item 80: 22–7, see item 13: 28–33 in *United Irishman* (Dublin) May 24, 1902: 34–8, see item 13: 39–42 [review of W. B. Yeats' *Reveries over Childhood and Youth*] not yet traced: 43–53 in *Sinn Fein* (Dublin) March 23, 1912: 54–8 see item 83: 59–80, in *Shanachie* (Dublin) vol 1 No 2 pp 102–115 (Winter 1906: text of a lecture delivered at the Royal Hibernian Academy, February 1, 1906): 81–87, see item 7: 88–93, see *Portraits of AE*, item 2: 94–99 in *The Daily News* (London), April 15, 1912: 100–118, see item 63: 119–51, see item 33A: 152–60, see item 32: 161–7, in *The Times*, April 14, 1915: 168–73, see item 13: 174–82 in *Dana* (Dublin) vol 1 No 2 pp 45–9 (June 1904): 183–98 see item 18: 199–216, see item 16: 217–315, see item 12.

[*Note:* In *Irish Literature: Selections in Prose and Verse* edited by Justin M'cCarthy, M.P., and others (Chicago and Philadelphia: 1904. De Bower Elliott Co: *and* John D. Morris & Company) vol 7 pp 2737–40 there is another article on S. O'Grady, sgd "AE". Vol 9 pp 3651–3 reptd pp 39–42 above (on W. B. Yeats).] Quinn Sale, item 8353: inscribed beneath the printed dedication to Quinn, *from his friend the writer. 3 Dec 1915.* Another copy owned by Susan Mitchell's family: *For Susan on her birthday from "AE" on the birthday of his book. December 1915.* He gave her 28B: *To my dear friend Susan L. Mitchell from her colleague Æ 21 Apl 21.*

29

TALKS WITH AN IRISH FARMER

Irish Homestead Leaflets. | [rule] | *Talks With an Irish Farmer.* | *No. 1.* [2.] [iii.] [iv.] [v.] [vi.] [vii.] [viii.] [ix.]

Reprinted From The "Irish Homestead," Sept. 2, [*9*], [*16*], *1916.* [rule] | *Talks With An Irish Farmer.* | *No. x.* [xi.] [xii.]

Nos 1–ix, single leaves, folded: Nos x–xii, two leaves folded, and stapled on fold.

All issued unbound, without title-pages.

Published in Dublin as off-prints from the issues of the *Irish Homestead* [item 98] in which they were first printed:

[1] vol 23 pp 33–4 (January 15, 1916). Pp 4.
[2] vol 23 pp 49–50 (January 22, 1916). Pp 4.
[iii] vol 23 pp 65–6 (January 29, 1916). Pp 4.
[iv] vol 23 pp 81–2 (February 5, 1916). Pp 4.
[v] vol 23 pp 97–8 (February 12, 1916). Pp 4.
[vi] vol 23 pp 113–5 (February 19, 1916). Pp 4.
[vii] vol 23 pp 129–30 (February 26, 1916). Pp 4.
[viii] vol 23 pp 169–70 (March 11, 1916). Pp 4.
[ix] vol 23 pp 185–6 (March 18, 1916). Pp 4.
[x] vol 23 pp 549–51 (September 2, 1916). Pp 8. Text [1]–7: p [8] blank.

[xi] vol 23 pp 565–6 (September 9, 1916). Pp 8. Text [1]–6: pp [7–8] blank.

[xii] vol 23 pp 581–3 (September 16, 1916). Pp 8. Text [1]–7: p [8] blank.

Nos 1–ix, text pp 1–4. Title etc heads p [i] in 1–xii. Nos x, xi and xii have: [rule] | at foot of final page of the text with below imprint *Sackville Press, Printers, Dublin. Sizes*: [1] 22.4 × 14.3 cm. [2] 19.1 × 12.7 cm. [iii] [iv] [v] all 22.4 × 14.3 cm. [vi] [vii] [viii] [ix] all 25.6 × 15.8 cm. [x] 18.2 × 12.3 cm. [xi], [xii] 18.4 × 12.3 cm.

30

THE NATIONAL BEING

The | National Being | Some Thoughts on | An Irish Polity | By A.E. | Maunsel & Company, Ltd. | Dublin and London | 1916

Pp [x] + 176 + [ii]. Fly-leaf [i–ii]: blank leaf [iii–iv]: [v] half-title: [vi] *By the same author*, etc, in center of page: [vii–viii] title-page, verso blank: [ix–x] dedication *To the Right Hon. Sir Horace Plunkett*, etc, verso blank: 1–176, text, with imprint at foot of p 176, *Printed by R. & R. Clark, Limited Edinburgh.* Fly-leaf [i–ii] at end blank. [New York, Macmillan Co.] Published ? September 1916. 19.4 × 13.1 cm.

Issued in dark-blue cloth, lettered in gold, title and author, on front cover, and with *Maunsel* added at foot, similarly lettered on spine. Single line border in gold on front cover, single line gilt at head and foot of spine: single line blind-tooled as border on back cover. Top and fore-edges uncut.

30A Reptd [A] May 1918 by Maunsel, in Dublin. Pp [viii] + 176. Issued in light-green wrappers, lettered in brown on front wrapper, with book advertisements on the verso: [i–ii] blank: [iii] half-title: [iv] *By the same author*, etc: [v] title-page: [vi] *Popular edition | 1918*: [vii] dedication: [viii] blank: and text on pp [1]–176: adverts for books on both sides of the back wrapper. The wrappers overlapped the pages. Price retail (on front wrapper, at foot) *One Shilling and Sixpence net.* 18.5 cm vertical.

30B Reptd [B] December 1918. Similar text and format to item 30A.

30C Taken over by Messrs Macmillan & Co. Ltd., and re-issued with [C] a new title-page bearing that publisher's name and address: bound in dark-blue cloth, lettered and tooled in gilt on spine; title, author, publisher.
Published November 7, 1925. 19.4 × 13.1 cm.

30D Identical text to 30C, published in New York by the Macmillan Company, 1930. 19.5 cm vertical.

30E Reptd [E] *The* | *National Being* | *Some Thoughts On* | *An Irish Polity* | *By A.E.* | [publisher's lettered monogram intertwined S. and G.] | *S. Ganesan,* | *Publisher, Triplicane, Madras, S.E.* | *1923* [on verso of t/p: *First Indian Edition* | *All Rights reserved.* |] Pp [viii] + [136]. [i–ii] fly-leaf, verso blank: [iii–iv] half-title, verso blank: [v–vi] t/p, as above: [vii–viii] dedication, verso blank: [1]–134, text, with rule at foot of p 134 and below imprint *P. R. Rama Iyar and Co., Printers, Madras*: [135–6] blank fly-leaf. Published in 1923. 18.3 × 12.2 cm. Issued in pink wrappers, lettered in royal blue on front wrapper as on t/p, with *Price Re. 1/–* printed additionally below the publisher's monogram. Back outer wrapper decorated by publisher's advertisement for other books.

30F Part reptd [F] in *The Portable Irish Reader*, an anthology edited by Diarmuid C. Russell (New York: 1946, 1956. The Viking Press) as "Thoughts from *The National Being*", at pp 138–57. [Pp 138–44 reprinted pp 11–19 from item 30: and pp 144–57 reprinted pp 150–66 from item 30.]

The *Royalty Agreement* for item 30 signed by AE and Maunsel & Co., on January 25, 1916. The mss to be delivered by January 30, 1916, and to be published within 3 months. Author's royalty, 15 per cent on the retail price of the first 2000 copies sold; and 20 per cent on all copies sold above 2000: but 10 per cent on editions sold below the agreed retail price, 3/6. AE to receive 75 per cent of the proceeds on sale of American publication rights.

AE inscribed one copy of item 30A: "To my 'fellow-economist' Susan! A.E." [That copy was owned in 1954 by Susan L. Mitchell's heirs.]

In item 30 Russell reprinted paragraphs from his unsigned editorials, or "Notes of the Week" in item 98, the *Irish Homestead.* Item 98 vol 21 pp 729–30 (September 26, 1914) leader "The National Being" adapted into chapter 1 of item 30, at pp 1–2. Item 98 vol 21 pp 741–2 (October 3, 1914), "The Antecedents of Civilisation" reptd in item 30, adapted, pp 3–9. Item 98 vol 19 p 996 (December 7, 1912), reptd in item 30 pp 62–5.

The leading articles and "Notes of the Week" in item 98 supply proof of Russell's constant pre-occupation with the ideas expounded in item 30. Similar analogies are deployed to illustrate his argument: e.g. compare item 98 vol 17 pp 1033–6 (December 17, 1910) to item 30 pp 40–3, separate cells composing the human body, as individuals compose society.

In vol 22 pp 777–8 (November 27, 1915) is identical in mood, ideas and expressions to item 30 pp 150–9. Vol 22 pp 793–4 (December 4, 1915), the leader "National Brotherhood" resembles item 30 pp 159–66 equally in diction and thought.

31

TEMPLECRONE. A RECORD OF CO-OPERATIVE EFFORT

I.A.O.S. Leaflets, No. 22 (New Series.) | *Templecrone.* | *A Record of Co-operative Effort.* | *By "Æ."*

Pp 16. Text pp [1]–16.

At foot of p 16: | [rule] | *This leaflet is reprinted from "The Irish Homestead", and is* | *published by the Irish Agricultural Organisation Society at the* | *Plunkett House, Dublin. Leaflets dealing with agricultural co-* | *operation can be had on application to the Secretary at above* | *address* | [rule] | *I.A.W.S. Printing Dept.*

Issued without cover or title-page. Published perhaps early January 1917. 17.7 × 12.4 cm.

First printed in item 98 vol 23 pp 709–13 (November 11, 1916).

32

SALUTATION, A POEM ON THE IRISH REBELLION OF 1916

Salutation | [ornament] *A Poem on the* [ornament] | *Irish Rebellion of 1916* | *by A.E.* | *London:* | *Privately Printed, January 1917*

Pp 12: [1–2] blank leaf: [3—4] title-page, verso blank: [5–6] text: [7–8] *An Imperfect Bibliography* | *of "A.E."* | *(George W. Russell)* [9–10] *Of this poem twenty-five copies only* | *have been printed by Clement Shorter* | *with the kind permission of the author* | *Mr George W. Russell, for distribu-* | *tion among his friends.* (In ink: *No.* : initialled: *C.K.S.*); verso blank: [11–12] blank leaf.

Issued in thick paper wrappers, green. The front cover is lettered in black, identical to t/p, similarly bordered with a single black line. The wrappers lined with white paper. Fastened with silk cord. 24.1 × 19.2 cm.

The British Museum copy, No 17, date-stamped: 10 Mar 17. The copy once owned by Susan Mitchell was No 14: Russell had inscribed on p [1] *For Susan Æ.*

This edition printed the original short form of AE's poem. The short form was again reprinted by W. K. Magee ("John Eglinton") in *A Memoir of AE* (1937) pp 119–20. It had circulated privately in ms. The "complete" poem was first printed
32A in the *Irish Times* [A] Dec 19, 1917 p 6: but Shorter and Eglinton's text, 4th stanza, is there omitted (mentions Constance [Markiewicz]). The short version includes 5 stanzas, Nos 1, 3, 5, and 7 from the 7 of text 32A. 32A reptd in items 28B, C, and 158.

33

THOUGHTS FOR A CONVENTION

Proof Copy | *Private and Confidential.* | *Thoughts for* | *A Convention* | *Memorandum on the* | *State of Ireland by A.E.* | *Maunsel and Company Limited* | *Dublin and London 1917* | *Price one penny*

Pp [32] Text pp 3–29: pp 30–32, blank leaves.

The *Proof copy*, etc printed in the top left corner. Imprint on title differs from the published text (see items 33A, etc). The addendum to 33A etc, had not been written. A few copies of this pamphlet were privately circulated before publication: probably to the signatories of the letter dated May 30, 1917, printed pp 30–31 in item 33A etc.

Issued unbound, perhaps on May 29, 1917. 18.4 × 12.4 cm.

33A *Thoughts for* | *A Convention* | *Memorandum on the* | *State of Ireland by A.E.* | *Maunsel and Company Ltd.* | *Dublin and London* | *1917* | *Price One Penny*

Pp 32: [1] title-page: [2] *Printed by George Roberts, Dublin* | *Irish Paper*: text pp 3–28: 29 *Note: Addendum* on pp 30–31, two letters dated May 30, 1917: signed by James G. Douglas and others, and another letter from Horace Plunkett: [32] publisher's advertisement. [pp 30–31] reptd from *Irish Times* May 31, 1917.]

Issued without covers: all edges cut. Published early June 1917. 18.4 × 12.4 cm.

33B [B] Second edition, Dublin and London: 1917. Maunsel.
33C [C] Third edition, Dublin and London: 1918. Maunsel.
33D [D] The pamphlet reprinted articles which had been first printed
33E in the *Irish Times*, May 26, 28 and 29, 1917. Reptd [E] in *The New Age* (London) vol 21 pp 127–8, 149–50, 174–5 and 199–201 (June 7, 14, 21, and 28, 1917). Reptd in items 66 and 28B, 28C (in 28B, C, pp 3–28 of item 33A were reptd at pp 119–51, and the *Note*, p 29, at p 316: *Addendum* not reprinted).

34

CONSCRIPTION FOR IRELAND

Conscription for Ireland | [rule] | *A Warning to England.* | [rule]

Pp 4: text [1]–4. At foot of p 4: [rule] *Published by the Mansion House Conference, and printed by Cahill & Co., Ltd., Dublin.*

Issued without cover or title-page: title and sub-title preceding the text on p [1]. Published May 1918. 20.6 × 13.1 cm.

34A First printed [except the introductory explanation, §1] in [A] the *Manchester Guardian*, May 10, 1918, p 3 [a letter dated:
34B Dublin, May 8, 1918.] Reptd [B] in the *Freeman's Journal* (Dublin), May 11, 1918; and in item 59.

35

THE CANDLE OF VISION

The | *Candle of Vision* | *by A.E.* | [quotations from *Proverbs*, and from The Book of *Job*: 3 lines] | *Macmillan and Co., Limited* | *St. Martin's Street, London* | *1918*

Pp [x]+[176]+4: fly-leaf: blank leaf: [i–ii] half-title, with publisher's monogram and addresses on verso: [iii–iv] title-page, with *Copyright* and *First edition* date, and reprinting dates, on verso: [v–vi] dedication, verso blank: [vii–viii] *Preface*: [ix–x] *Contents*, verso blank: 1–175, text; with imprint at foot of p 175, *Printed by R. & R. Clark, Limited, Edinburgh.*: [176] blank: [1]–4, publishers advertisements: fly-leaf.

Issued in dark-blue cloth, a single line border impressed on front cover: lettered title and author, in gold, on front cover; gilt lettered title and author on back-strip, with publisher's name at foot, and a single gold line at head and foot (tending to fade into green, as on some copies of item 21 etc). Published October 22, 1918. 1500 copies. 19.7 × 13.3 cm.

35A,B Reprinted: [A] November 1918; 1000 copies: [B] January

35C,D 1919; 1000 copies: [C] March 1919; 1000 copies: [D] August
35E,F 1919; 1000 copies: [E] July 1920; 2000 copies: [F] December
35G 1927; 1500 copies: [G] March 1931; 1500 copies.

35H André Mermod planned French translation from some chapters in this book, for publication in the *Revue Européene* (Paris) [H]. This compiler has not yet checked that file. [See Russell's letter to Mermod: January 20, 1924.] M. Jacques H. Masui (of *Documents Spirituels*, Paris) advised the compiler he had translated item 35 into French:

35J *Le flambeau de la vision*, traduit du néerlandais par L. G. Gros. Pp 184. (In the series *Coll. Documents spirituel*, No 2). Paris, 1952. Cahiers du Sud [publrs]. (500 francs) 20 × 11.5 cm. [Pp 120–7 in *The Candle of Vision*: see note to item 187, below.] In the John Quinn Library Sale (New York, 1924) item 8364 comprised chapter one inscribed by AE "Saved from the fire", and additionally chapters 8–20 of the manuscript of this book, written on 96 quarto sheets. The poem on pp 174–5 had been first printed in item 27 p 30: reptd in items 21B, C and D.

35K [K] First American edition: New York, 1919. The Macmillan Company. *Dedicated*: To James Stephens, best of companions.

36

LITERARY IMAGINATION

[double rule at head and foot of page] | *Literary* | *Imagination* | *by* | *Æ* | *[Reprinted from "The Irish Homestead"]* | *The Talbot Press, Limited* | *89 Talbot Street, Dublin* | *T. Fisher Unwin, Limited* | *1 Adelphi Terrace, London*

Pp [4]. [1] title-page; [2] and [3] text, captioned at head of [2] *The Imagination of the Heart*, sgd at end [3] "Æ", with an emblem below incorporating two keys superimposed over a heart-shape, around which a fine double-line sprays out to resemble wings, linking the keys and the heart; [4] publisher's advertisement of the book reviewed by AE on this pamphlet, enclosed in a single rule, centered on the page.

Issued in January 1919, unbound. The pamphlet is a single sheet folded once to make four sides of which the front page [1] carried the title. 17.4 × 11.7 cm.

Reprinted from the *Irish Homestead* vol 25 pp 848 (cols 1 and 2) and 851 (col 1) (December 28, 1918); an unsigned editorial notice of *Dinny of the Doorstep* by K. F. Purdon, merely captioned without title "Review." Part only of that review was reptd on the pamphlet *Literary Imagination.*

[Miss Katherine F. Purdon wrote the "Gardening Notes" in the *Irish Homestead* from *circa* 1900 until her death which occurred in the summer of 1920. An obituary notice of her was printed in the *Irish Homestead* vol 27 pp 496–7 (July 3, 1920). AE had illustrated some of Miss Purdon's stories for publication in the *Celtic Christmas* issues of the *Irish Homestead,* 1907, 1908. In a letter to the late J. S. Starkey (now owned by this compiler) the late Susan L. Mitchell mentioned the large quantity of published prose manuscript bequeathed to her by Miss Purdon, whose close friend she had been. (In the letter, dated April 10, 1923, Miss Mitchell mentioned July *1921* as the date of Miss Purdon's death.)]

37

MICHAEL

Michael | by | A.E. | Dublin | Printed for the author | 1919

Pp [ii]+[12]: [i–ii] title-page, verso blank: pp 1–[12] text: blank leaf.

Issued without wrappers, sewn. Fore-edges unopened: other edges uncut. Issued in December 1919. 25 copies.

14.3 × 11.4 cm.

Reptd in the [First] *Irish Statesman* (Dublin) vol 1 p 622
37A,B (December 20, 1919) [A]: and [B] in [Littell's] *Living Age*
37C (Boston, Mass.) February 14, 1920; and [C] in *The Dial* (New York) March 1920, pp 326–34. Reptd in items 44, 45, 21B, C, and D; and in item 54. [One copy of this pamphlet was inscribed to W. K. Magee: *W. K. M. from Æ Christmas 1919.*]

38

A PLEA FOR JUSTICE

A Plea for Justice | being a demand for a | Public Enquiry into the | attacks on Co-operative | Societies in Ireland. | By | Geo. W. Russell, "Æ" | Published by the Irish Homestead | Limited, [ornament] *18 South Frederick Street, Dublin | Price* [dotted line] *Threepence*

Pp 24: title-page, verso blank: text pp [1]–24: end cover, blank inside: outside decorated with publisher's advertisement.

Issued in yellow wrappers, the front cover being the title-page. All edges cut. The t/p is bordered with a single black line. Published December 1920. 18.4 × 12.5 cm.

38A Reptd from item 98 vol 27 pp 899–908 (December 18, 1920).

38B Reptd [B] with additions: Dublin, 1921. The Irish Homestead Limited.

38C [See also: *Agricultural Co-operation in Ireland: A Plea for Justice by the I.A.O.S.* (Dublin: n.d. Sackville Press), pp 150]

39

THE ECONOMICS OF IRELAND, AND THE POLICY OF THE BRITISH GOVERNMENT

The Freeman Pamphlets | [rule] *The Economics of Ireland | and the Policy of the | British Government | by | George W. Russell | ("AE") | with an Introduction by | Francis Hackett |* [ornament] *New York | B. W. Huebsch, Inc. | mcmxx*

Pp 32: [1–2] title-page, and on verso a note, and *Copyright* etc: *Introduction*, pp 3–9, and text [11–24]: [25–32] book advertisements.

Issued in gray wrappers, lettered on front cover, identical to t/p, but with price, *25c* added in lower right corner. Back wrapper decorated with publisher's advertisements, inside and outer. All edges cut. Published 1920. 19 × 12.5 cm.

39A Reprinted: identical contents, but with date on t/p and front cover: *mcmxxi.* Size varied: 18.5 × 12.4 cm.

39B This pamphlet was reptd from Russell's article in [B] *The Freeman* (New York) vol 1 pp 153–7 (April 28, 1920): "Sir Auckland Geddes' Handiwork". [Sir A. C. Geddes (1879–1954), later Lord Geddes, lately appointed British Ambassador to Washington, had publicly praised the fourth *Home-Rule Bill* presented to the House of Commons. His speech was reported in most newspapers. AE attacked that Bill. Sir Eric Geddes (1875–1937) was Lord Geddes' brother.] Another AE article from *The Freeman*, item 69.

39C The article was off-printed and circulated, without Mr Hackett's *Introduction*, during 1920. [Not seen by this compiler.]

40

THOUGHTS FOR BRITISH CO-OPERATORS

[within single rule] *Thoughts for British | Co-operators | being a further demand | for a public enquiry into | the attacks on co-opera- | tive societies in Ireland | by | Geo. W. Russell, "Æ" | published by the Irish Homestead | Limited,* [double colon] *18 South Frederick Street, Dublin*

Introduction, dated 11th May 1921, by Sir Horace Plunkett, pp [1]–4: AE's text pp 5–12: list follows. Pp 12–36.

Issued in May 1921. All edges cut. Buff-manilla cover. The front wrapper is title-page: verso carries full-page textual advertisement of the Co-operative Reference Library. Recto of back wrapper, blank: verso, advertisement for the *Irish Homestead.* 18.5 × 12.4 cm.

40A First printed [A] in item 98 vol 28 pp 295–8 (April 30, 1921).

41

THE INNER AND THE OUTER IRELAND

The Inner | *and the* | *Outer* [ornament] | *Ireland* | *by A.E.* | *Reprinted by permission from* | "*Pearson's Magazine*", *U.S.A.* | *The Talbot Press* | *Limited* [ornament] *Dublin* | *1921* | *Price Twopence Net*

Pp 16: title-page, verso blank: text pp [3]–16.

Issued unbound, with front wrapper as t/p. First letter of *Inner* in title elaborately decorated. Three-line border, at edges twined in a Celtic design. Edges all cut. Published probably in July 1921. [P 8; the final word cancelled in some copies, and "reckless" rubber-stamped below.] 18.3 × 12.1 cm.

41A Reprinted from [A] *Pearson's Magazine* (New York) vol 46 No 11 pp 399-402 (May (1921). [See also item 113.]

No 11 pp 399–402 (May 1921). [See also item 113]. Issued unbound, with front cover as t/p. First letter of *Inner* in title elaborately decorated. Three-line border, at edges twined in a Celtic design. Edges all cut. Published probably in July 1921. [P 8; the final word cancelled in some copies, and "reckless" rubber-stamped below.] 18.3 × 12.1 cm. Reprinted from [A] *Pearson's Magazine* (New York) vol 46 No 11 pp 399–402 (May 1921). [See also item 113.]

41B Reptd in another edition: [B] *The Inner & the* | *Outer Ireland* | *by A.E.* | *T. Fisher Unwin Ltd* | *London: Adelphi Terrace* Pp 28: Fly-leaf [1–2]: blank leaf [3–4]: half-title [5–6] verso blank: [7–8] title-page, verso blank: [9] *First published in Pearson's Magazine, U.S.A.* | *Reprinted by the Talbot Press Dublin, 1921* | *This Edition published in London, August, 1921*: [10] blank: 11–27, text: [28] imprint, *Printed at* | *The Shakespeare Head* | *Stratford-upon-Avon*: [+2 blank leaves]. Issued in cream wrappers, overlapping and in front folded-in 5.2 cm, and end-wrapper folded-in 5.8 cm. Lettered in green on front cover, *The Inner & The Outer* | *Ireland* | *By A.E.* Single green line border on front. Only lower edge cut. [Brit. Mus. copy date-stamped 8 Aug 21.] 20.2 × 17.2 cm.

[AE inscribed one copy: Susan L. Mitchell from her friend AE. August 1921.]

41C French translation [C] by Maurice Bourgeois, *L'Irlande du dedans et du dehors*: Pp 24, issued unbound, stapled: p [1] as t/p and cover. Text pp 3–22. [A copy preserved by AE was inscribed by the translator at top of p [1]: "A Madame George W. Russell. Homage respecteux et reconnaissant . . ."]. This
41D was probably first printed [D] in *Démocratie* (Paris: vv 1–11, 1910–September 1921. New Series: vv 1–9, October 1921–October 1927?). Item 40C bearing imprint: *La Démocratie, 34 bd Raspail.* All edges trimmed.

41E Spanish translation [E] by E. Díez-Canedo, *Irlanda | por Dentro | y por | Fuera*. Madrid, n.d. [1922?]. Delegación de la República Irlandesa. Pp 15. The title etc on t/p is enclosed within a dotted line. Issued unbound: t/p as front cover is p [1]: p [2] blank: text at pp 3–15: [16] blank. Title enclosed by dotted rule.

42

IRELAND AND THE EMPIRE AT THE COURT OF CONSCIENCE

Ireland | and the Empire | at the Court of | Conscience | By A.E. | [publisher's monogram ornament] | *Dublin | The Talbot Press Limited | 85 Talbot Street | 1921* | [and printed below border] *Price Threepence net*

Pp 16. Title-page [1]: text pp 2–16.

Issued unbound, all edges trimmed. The t/p bordered with a single line. 20.8 × 13.7 cm.

42A First printed in [A] the *Manchester Guardian*, September 22, 1921. Reptd in *The Irish World and American Industrial*
42B *Liberator* (New York) [B] October 15, 1921; and in the *Irish*
42C *Press* (Philadelphia) [C] October 29, 1921, etc.

Captain Henry Harrison, O.B.E., M.C. (1868?–February 20, 1954), wrote *Mr George Russell and his Court of Conscience: an Intervener* (Dublin: 1921. Irish Dominion League). [That

League was founded June 1919, dissolved November 1921. President, Horace Plunkett; Secretary, H. Harrison; Hon Treasurer, R. A. Anderson. The founder was Henry Harrison, a Parnellite.]

43

IRELAND, PAST AND FUTURE

Ireland, Past and Future: by George Russell (A.E.) | Being a Paper read to the Sociological Society on 21st February, | 1922

Pp 20.

Issued unbound, all edges trimmed. 24.7 × 15 cm.

43A First printed in the *Sociological Review* (London) [A] vol 14 No 2 pp 93–110 (April 1922). Reptd, revised and adapted in item 68. [*Sociological Review* edited by Victor Verasius Branford and Alexander Farquharson.]

44

THE INTERPRETERS

The Interpreters | by | A.E. | [quotations from St Paul, Leroy, Lavelle: 4 lines.] | *Macmillan and Co., Limited | St. Martin's Street, London | 1922*

Pp viii + 180 + [iv]: fly-leaf: [i–ii] half-title, verso publisher's monogram and addresses]: [iii–iv] title-page, verso *Copyright | Printed in Great Britain*: [v–vi] dedication, verso blank: vii–viii, *Preface*: text pp 1–180, with *R. & R. Clark*'s imprint at foot: and publisher's advertisement of AE's books additional pp i–ii: [iii–iv] blank: fly-leaf.

Issued in dark-blue cloth, title and author lettered gilt on front cover and back-strip: publisher's name at foot of back-strip. A single-line border impressed on front cover. Light brown dust-wrapper with dark blue title, author, publisher's monogram on front: title, author, *6/- | net* and monogram on spine. Advertisement on back.
Published in London: November 7, 1922. 3000 copies. New

44A York: [A] The Macmillan Company. Published 1923. Identical contents. 20 × 13.1 cm.

In a letter to H. G. Wells, dated *Wednesday* [Summer 1909] AE briefly outlined the story which he wrote as item 44. *Dedicated*: To Stephen MacKenna for the delight I have in his noble translation of Plotinus.

45

VOICES OF THE STONES

Voices | Of The Stones | by A.E. | [quotation from *The Voyage of Bran*, 3 lines] | *Macmillan and Co., Limited | St. Martin's Street, London | 1925*

Pp [viii] + [62] + [2]: fly-leaf: [i–ii] half-title, monogram and publisher's addresses on verso: title-page [iii], on verso *Copyright | Printed in Great Britain*: v–vi, *Contents*: vii, Dedication: [viii] blank: text pp 1–61, with printer's imprint at foot, *R. & R. Clark*, etc: [62] blank: [1–2 numbered pages at end, advertising AE's books.]: fly-leaf.

Issued in dark-blue cloth, lettered gilt on back-strip with title, author, publisher, and a single line at head and foot: on front cover title and author, gilt; and an impressed single-line border.
Dedicated: To Padraic Colum.

Published simultaneously on June 5, 1925: London, Macmillan & Co., Ltd.: New York, The Macmillan Company. Reprinted
45A [A] in New York: 1931. The Macmillan Company.
[London: 2000 copies.] Reptd in items 21B, C, and D. Part reptd in item 54.

46

MIDSUMMER EVE

Midsummer Eve | By A.E. | [ornamental monogram] | *Crosby Gaige: New York* | 1928

Pp [32: unnumbered]: fly-leaf: [1–2] blank leaf: [3–4] half-title with *Geo. W. Russell "AE"*. Inscribed in ink by the author, below; verso blank: [5–6] title-page, and on verso, *Copyright 1928 by Crosby Gaige | Printed in U.S.A.*: [7–8] dedication, verso blank: [9–26] text: [27–28] blank leaf: [29–30] *Four Hundred and Fifty Copies printed at the | Printing House of William Edwin Rudge, Mount | Vernon, New York. Distributed in America by | Random House. Each copy signed by the author.* | ; verso blank: [31–32] blank leaf: fly-leaf.

Issued in pink board, lettered gilt on back-strip: *Midsummer Eve*. Dust-jacket, transparent paper. Issued in June 1928.

20.7 × 12.9 cm.

Dedicated: To Oliver St John Gogarty.

46A [A] Eight copies of this book printed on green paper, with identical text: signed by the author.

Reptd in item 49 at pp 18, 23, 3, 37, 7, 22, 4, 38, 10, and 50. Reptd in item 21D.

47

DARK WEEPING

Issued in gray fold-in wrappers. The front wrapper or title-page, devised by Paul Nash, reads: *Dark Weeping | "AE." | Designs by Paul Nash*. Pp [8: unnumbered]: [1–2] blank leaf: [3] design in seven colors, by Paul Nash: [4] blank: [5–6] text: [7–8] blank leaf. Front cover design printed in black upon the gray wrapper. On end wrapper, outside: *This is No. 19 of | The Ariel Poems | Published by Faber & Faber Limited | at 24 Russell Square, London, W.C.1 | Printed at The Curwen Press, Plaistow*. Tied with thread. Wrappers folded-in: front, 3.1 cm, end, 3 cm. [Paul Nash, 1889–1946.] Published in London: October 9, 1929. [3000 copies] 18.4 × 12.2 cm.

47A *Large paper edition*, 21.3 × 13.5 cm. Pp 14: [1–2] blank leaf: [3] *This large-paper edition, printed | on English hand-made paper, is | limited to four hundred copies | This is Number* [...] [sgd in ink: *Geo W Russell | "AE"*: [4] blank: [5–6] design in black and white lettered *Dark Weeping AE | Designs by Paul Nash*, verso blank: [7–8] title-page lettered: '*A.E.*' | *Dark Weeping* | *with Designs* | *by* | *Paul Nash* | *London*: | *Faber & Faber Ltd* | *1929*, with imprint on verso *Printed in England at the Curwen Press*: [9–10] design in colors by Paul Nash, verso blank: text, p [11] (verso blank) and [12] (verso blank): [13] *This is No. 19 of* | *The Ariel Poems* | *Published in London by Faber & Faber* | *Limited, at 24 Russell Square, W.C.1.*, verso [14] blank. Issued in gray thin boards, gilt lettered on front cover: '*A.E.*' | [three-star ornament] | *Dark Weeping*

Published in London: October 9, 1929. [Brit. Mus. copy No. 332]

47B [B] First printed in item 99, vol 11 pp 68–9 (September 29, 1928). Reptd in items 49, 21D. [Dr Oliver Gogarty remembered how deeply impressed AE had been by waking in tears one day. The poem originated in that incident.] [See *Paul Nash. The Portrait of an Artist* by Anthony Bertram (Faber, 1955), p. 150.]

48

ENCHANTMENT AND OTHER POEMS

Enchantment | *and Other Poems* | *by* | *AE* | *New York: The Fountain Press* | *London: Macmillan & Co., Ltd.* | *1930* [On title-page the author's pseudonym was printed in orange: the rest in black type.]

Pp [36]: fly-leaf: [1–2] half-title, verso blank: [3–4] title-page, on verso *Copyright 1930 by George Russell* | *Printed in the United States of America.* [5–6] dedication *To* | *Robert Frost*, verso blank: [7–8] *Contents*, verso blank: [9] *Enchantment*, followed by autograph ink signature *Geo W Russell* | *'AE'*, verso blank: pp 11–34, text: [35] blank: [36] *Of this book five hundred and forty-two copies,* | *of which five hundred are for sale, were printed* | *by James Hendrickson and Earl Widtman at Utica,* | *New York in June 1930. Distributed in America by* | *Random House and in Great Britain by Macmillan &* | *Company, Ltd.* | *This is number* [. . .] [Brit. Mus. copy marked in orange ink: *Out of Series*]: fly-leaf. [London: 250 copies.]

Issued in boards: orange design printed over a cream ground. In the center of the front cover a black square encloses lettering in black type: *Enchantment | And Other Poems | by | AE | The Fountain Press.* The spine covered with wide-mesh linen, extending 1.9 cm into front and back covers: linen dirty-cream color. A printed label stuck on the spine: *Enchantment.* Published December 1930. [Brit. Mus. copy date-stamped: 10 Dec 30] [English retail price, 31/6d.] 21.3 × 13.2 cm. Reptd in item 49 at pp: 9, 6, 14, 24, 12, 17, 30, 32, 51, 29, 45, 43, 44, 47, 52, 34, and 41. Reptd in item 21D. Partly reptd in item 54.

49

VALE AND OTHER POEMS

Vale | and other poems | by A.E. | Macmillan and Co., Limited | St. Martin's Street, London | 1931

Pp viii + 56: fly-leaf: [i–ii] half-title, on verso *By "A.E."* (and list of his books): [iii–iv] title-page, on verso *Copyright | Printed in Great Britain | by R. & R. Clark, Limited, Edinburgh*: [v–vi] dedication *To | Seumas O'Sullivan*, verso blank: vii–viii, *Contents*: 1, *Vale | and other poems*, verso blank: text pp 3–56, with printer's name etc at foot of p 56: fly-leaf.

Issued in dark-blue cloth, lettered gilt on front cover and spine: title, author; and publisher at foot, single line head and foot of spine. Front cover enclosed with blind-tooled single line. Dust-wrapper white, lettered dark blue, with title, author, publisher's monogram on front and spine; books by AE and others advertised on back of d/w. Inner flap priced *3/6d | net.* Published in London: March 3, 1931. 1500 copies. 19.7 × 13.1 cm.

49A [A] *Vale | & | other poems | By A.E.* | [ornament] | *New York | The Macmillan Company | 1931* |: on verso of t/p, *Copyright,*

1931 | *By George Russell* | [rule] | *All rights* [&c]. Pp viii + 50: 2 blank leaves: [i–ii] half-title, list of AE books on verso: [iii–iv] t/p: [v–vi] dedication *To Seumas O'Sullivan*, verso blank: [vii–viii] *Contents*: [1–2] title, verso blank: 3–50, text: [51–54] blank leaves: fly-leaf. Published perhaps before the London edition, perhaps late February 1931? Contents identical to item 49. Reptd in 21D. Partly reptd in item 54. Issued in beige nuanced to red, buckram. Black paper label stuck upper left of front cover, surrounded with gilt design, lettered title and author in gilt: black paper label stuck head of spine, title and author, gilt. Dust-wrapper black, lettered gilt on front and spine; inside front, flap, publisher's blurb and price, $*1.50* back of d/w blank. 20.2 × 14.2 cm.

49B [B] Reptd New York, June 1931.

49C [C] Reptd London edition: June 1931 [1000 copies].

49D [D] In item 49 "Blight" (p 6) was used in an illumination designed by Art O'Murnaghan, and made by Miss E. C. Yeats at the Cuala Industries, Dublin. That was displayed in Dublin at the Tailteann Art Exhibition, June 18 to July 10, 1932 (item 711). [In item 48 "Blight" was printed at p 13.] [AE supplied the designs for use by Miss L. Yeats in her tapestries made for Loughrea Cathedral, Galway, *circa* 1905: for St Patrick and St Lawrence O'Toole. Miss Yeats' other tapestry designs of men saints there were from original designs by Jack B. Yeats. (Letter, Miss L. Yeats to Miss S. H. Purser, January 5, 1926). Art O'Murnaghan died in 1957(?), aged about 70.]

50

SONG AND ITS FOUNTAINS

Song and its Fountains | *by* | *A.E.* | [quotation from *The Chaldean Oracles*, (5 lines)] | *Macmillan and Co., Limited* | *St. Martin's Street, London* | *1932*

Pp [2] + [vi] + 136. Fly-leaf: half-title with publisher's monogram and addresses on verso: [i–ii] t/p, verso *Copyright*, and printer's imprint, etc: [iii–iv] dedication *To | Violet | and | Diarmuid* [his wife and younger son]: [v–vi] preface, verso blank: 1–133, text: [134] blank: [printer's imprint at foot of 133]: [135] *By the same author*, etc: [136] blank: fly-leaf. All edges trimmed.

Issued in dark-blue cloth. Lettered gilt on front cover and spine, title, author: and on spine with publisher's name, and single gilt line tooled at head and foot. Single-line blind-tooled as a border on outer edge of front cover. Published: February 16, 1932. 2000 copies. 19.3 × 12.5 cm.

50A [A] The first chapter had been first printed, "Chapter from a book. Germinal." in item 100 vol 7 No 1 pp 4–10 (January 1932).

50B [B] American edition: New York, 1932. The Macmillan Company. Identical text.

50C [C] M. Jacques H. Masui has translated some chapters into French, since 1954. Their publication has not yet been traced by this compiler: probably in a periodical. [See also note to item 35.]

[Item 50 is a commentary on the genesis and meaning of some of AE's poems. First number, reference to item 50: number in parentheses, pagination in item 21D. 97 (348): 28–9 (72): 58–9 (358: lines 1–8, 259, 287–294): 30 (126): 84–5 (320): 88–9 (79): 13–14 (400): 63–4 (395: lines 30–54): 35–6 (151): 26 (155): 79 (394): 39–40 (114): 108–9 (item 53, p 29: lines 654–84): 6–7 (84): 48 (195): 74–5 (61): 70–71 (9): 115–6 (380): 46–7 (312): 132 (6): 29 (175): 130 (1): 122–4 (209): 55–6 (97): 79 (394): 63–4 (395: lines 30–54): 6–7 (84): 70–1 (54): 48 (195): 126–7 (305): 53–4 (130): 29 (175): 50 (128): 84–5 (3): 60–62 (212).]

C. M. Grieve ("Hugh MacDiarmid") reviewed this book as "AE and Poetry" in item 101, vol 3 pp 591–3 (October 5, 1933). A brief review by Humbert Wolfe in *The Observer* (London) February 28, 1932.

51

VERSES FOR FRIENDS

Verses for Friends | by | A.E. | Dublin: | Printed for the Writer | 1932

Pp [12]: front cover as title-page: text, 2–[12] with imprint at foot of p [12] *Printed by Cahill & Co., Ltd., Dublin.*

Issued unbound, stitched. 25 copies printed for private circulation. AE distributed them in December 1932. All except the proof copy were decorated by AE with crayon and ink drawings, on front (below title) and some had another sketch on the back page. Reptd in item 53: at pp 40, 39, 44, 41, 74, 69, 60, 48, 70, 72, 79, 87, and 88.

Proof copy now in N.L.I.: Hugh and Lota Law gave their copy to the County Museum, Armagh: Mr C. P. Curran owns a copy, as do Simone Téry (Mme Chabas), Mrs W. K. Magee, and Dr Heinz Höpf'l. The late Dr J. S. Starkey said he had several copies. 15.5 × 10.7 cm.

52

THE AVATARS

The Avatars | A Futurist Fantasy | by | A.E. | The Light is the real person in the picture. | Claud Monet | Macmillan and Co., Limited | St. Martin's Street, London | 1933

Pp [viii] + [190]: fly-leaf: [i–ii] half-title, publisher's monogram and addresses on verso: [iii–iv] title-page, verso *Copyright* and printer's imprint *R. & R. Clark*, etc. [v–vi] dedication *To | W. B. Yeats*, verso blank: vii–[viii] prefatory note, verso blank: text pp 1–188, with printer's imprint at foot of 188: [189–190] *By the Same Author*, etc, verso blank: blank leaf: fly-leaf.

Issued in dark-blue cloth, lettered gilt on t/p, title and author: and on spine, title, author, publisher, and a single line gilt at head and foot of spine. A single line impressed border on front cover, not gilded. All edges cut and trimmed. Published: October 3, 1933. London: 1500 copies. 19.2 × 12.6 cm.

52A [A] [New York: 1933. The Macmillan Company.]

[Part of p 55 was quoted in item 57. See below p 101, a further reference to Mr Séan O'Casey's quotation of the sentence.] See AE's letter to Macmillan & Co., April 11, 1933: and footnote.]

53

THE HOUSE OF THE TITANS AND OTHER POEMS

The | House of the Titans | and other poems | by | A.E. | Macmillan and Co., Limited | St. Martin's Street, London | 1934

Pp vi + [90]: fly-leaf: [i–ii] half-title, publisher's monogram and addresses on verso: [iii–iv] title-page, with *Copyright* and printer's imprint, etc, on verso. *R. & R. Clark*, etc: v–vi, *Contents*: text pp 1–[88]: [89—90] printer's imprint, etc, verso blank: fly-leaf.

Issued in dark-green cloth. Lettered in gold within double line close border, with Celtic twined lines grouped either side the lettering; on front cover, *The House of the Titans | A.E.* And on spine, gilt letters: short title, [square ornament], author, and at foot, publisher.
Published: October 19, 1934. 2000 copies. 19.2 × 12.4 cm.

53A [A] New York: 1934. The Macmillan Company. [Part first printed in item 51. And p 30 had been first printed in volume form in item 10 p 9 and item 21 p 37. Part reptd in item 54.] *Dedicated*: To Osborn Bergin.

54

SELECTED POEMS

Selected Poems | by | A.E. | [vignette reproducing Casimir Dunin Markiewicz's oil portrait of A.E.] | *Macmillan and Co., Limited | St. Martin's Street, London | 1935*

Pp [xiv] + 198: fly-leaf: [i–ii] half-title, publisher's monogram and addresses on verso: [tissue paper inserted to cover title-page]: [iii–iv] title-page, *Copyright* and *R. & R. Clark*, etc, imprint on verso: [v–vi] dedication, verso blank: [vii–viii] prefatory note, verso blank: ix–xiii, *Contents*, verso blank: text pp 1–[198] and *Index*, with printer's imprint at foot of 198: fly-leaf.

Issued in dark-blue cloth, with a tooled design on front cover: lettered gilt on spine, *Selected Poems* | [star] | *A.E.* | *Macmillan*, with triple line at head and foot of spine, gilt; and double lines gilt, thrice, with two gilt ring ornaments below each double line. Cream dust-wrapper lettered in brown: title, author (with [*George W. Russell*] below); vignette and legend; prefatory note; publisher's name, on front. Spine lettered, title, author, publisher. Back cover, *By the same author*, etc. Price printed inside front flap of d/w, *5/-* | *Net.* Published in London: September 17, 1935. [2000 copies.] 18.7 × 12.3 cm.

54A American edition: New York: September 1935. The Macmillan Company. Identical text to item 54: portrait omitted. Bound, light-blue cloth. Pp xiii + 197 + [1]. 19.5 cm vertical. Reptd
54B [B] London: February 15, 1951. Macmillan and Co. Ltd., "Golden Treasury Series", pp [xiv] + [198]: *Pan* figured in gold on front cover; in black, place of vignette on t/p. Bound, dark-blue cloth. 16 × 10.5 cm. [1130 copies.] Similar
54C reprint: New York: February 15, 1951. The St. Martin's Press. See letter AE to Mr Daniel Macmillan, April 17, 1935; and note. The poems in *item 54* were reptd from volumes; *pp 3–29 from item 2 at pp* 1, 2, 31, 12, 43, 3, 13, 14, 15, 16, 17, 20, 8, 30, 37, 9, 38, 48, 25, 23, 41, 36, 11, 18, 49, xi: *item 54 pp 33–53 from item 5 at pp* 11, 23, 20, 13, 72, 14, 18, 48, 88, 27, 71, 52, 83, 49, 47, 54, 93, 9: *pp 57–81 from item 10* p 1, and item 21 p 21, item 10, pp 40, 57, 16, 34, 8, 11, 20, 13, 68, 17, 3, 31, 6, 82, 81, 90: *pp 85–102 from item 14* pp 32, 4, and item 21 p 30, item 27 p 30, item 2 p 8, item 14 p 12, item 21 pp 233, 291, 195, item 10 p 71, item 21 pp 229 and 282: *pp 105–139 from item 45 at pp* 1, 7, 3, 10, 2, 18, 4, 27, 22, 5, item 21C p 330, item 45 pp 6, 14, item 21C p 334, item 45 pp 12, 34, 38, 46, 50: *pp 143–169 from item 49 at pp* 3, 4, 6, 7,

9, 14, 10, 17, 18, 29, 24, 30, 32, 22, 40, 25, 47, 43, 41: *pp 173–193 from item 53 at pp* 60, 41, 39, 47, 70, 64, 80, 41, 49, 30, 31, and 88. *Dedicated*: To Rose [Diarmuid Russell's wife]. The sections inscribed to: Weekes, W. B. Yeats, Hugh and Charlotte Law, Helen Waddell, Colum, O'Sullivan, Bergin. Originally one section was inscribed to F. R. Higgins.

55

SOME PASSAGES FROM THE LETTERS OF Æ TO W. B. YEATS

Some Passages from the Letters | *of Æ to W. B. Yeats.* | [two double circles, one within the other, encasing a sword emblem: printed in red] | *The Cuala Press* | *Dublin, Ireland.* | *mcmxxxvi*

Pp [viii] + [64]: blue fly-leaf: [i–ii] blank leaf: [iii–iv] blank leaf: [v–vi] title-page: [vii–viii] *NOTE* | *The punctuation and spelling in the original letters has* | *been kept with one exception, the name of the Polish* | *painter Markiewicz, which had undergone too great a* | *transformation to be recognisable.* [Printed in red], verso blank: text pp [1: numbered B]–[63] *Here ends "Some Passages From The* | *Letters of Æ to W. B. Yeats. Three* | *Hundred copies of this book have been* | *printed and published by Elizabeth* | *Corbet Yeats, (on paper made in Ire-* | *land) at The Cuala Press, 133 Lower* | *Baggot Street, Dublin, Ireland. Fin-* | *ished in the last week of June, nineteen* | *hundred and thirty six.* [Printed in red]: 4 blank leaves: blue fly-leaf/end-papers.

Issued in blue boards, linen spine extending 2.6 cm into covers. Lettered on front cover in black capitals: *Some Passages from the Letters* | *of Æ to W. B. Yeats.* Printed label stuck on spine: *Passages from the Letters of Æ to W. B. Yeats.* Published August 18, 1936.
[Brit. Mus. copy date-stamped: 21 Aug 36.] 21.8 × 14.9 cm.

The letters included, or extracts from letters, are dated as on the originals, or conjectured by W. B. Yeats: 1896 (4): February 2, 1897: April 3, 1897: 1897 (Winter): February 1, 1898: 1898: August 3, 1898: March 1899: 3 extracts from 1899 letters: April 1900: June 1900: July 1900: 1900 (2): January 28, 1902: April 1902: April 19, 1902: May 24, 1902: June 16, 1902: July 4, 1902: July 7, 1902: 1902: 1903 (8): 1904 (5): 1913: 9.2.21: 6.7.21: 1921: 16.1.22: 1922: 9.11.1928: 4.12.28: 22.2.1929: 19.4.30: 6.3.32: [May 1932]. Partly reptd in item 59, but all newly transcribed.

56

AE's LETTERS TO MÍNANLÁBÁIN

AE's Letters | to Mínanlábáin | With an Introduction | By | Lucy Kingsley Porter | New York | The Macmillan Company | 1937

Pp [viii] + 103: fly-leaf: [i–ii] half-title, with publisher's monogram and addresses on verso: [iii–iv] blank, and on verso a photograph of AE: [v–vi] title-page, on verso, *Copyright, 1937* etc, *First Printing* etc, and imprint at foot: *Printed in the United States of America | by the Stratford Press, Inc., New York*: [vii–viii] *Foreword* [dated November 1936] (verso blank): pp 1–19 *AE's Letters to Mínanlábáin* (an introduction to the text): pp 20–102, the letters (dating from December 3, 1930, to June 2, 1935): Facsimiles of his drawings, on pp 14, 21, 75, and 91: and of one complete illustrated letter, pp 71–74. The frontispiece photograph is noticed in list of *Portraits of AE*, No 37A.

Issued in light-blue cloth, lettered on spine: title, editor, and publisher at foot, in gold, single gold lines either side the title and publisher; a gold dot below publisher's name. White dust-wrapper, lettered in brown, with photograph on front; title etc, and editor's name beneath: double-line border, all printed in brown. Spine: title, editor, publisher. Back, publisher's advertisements for other books. On the front flap of the d/w: a blurb, and price marked, $2.00: on the back flap, quotations from the AE letters in the book. Published only in New York: February 1937. 21.5 × 16.4 cm.

57

THE LIVING TORCH

The Living Torch | *A.E.* | *Edited by* | *Monk Gibbon* | *With an Introductory Essay* | [vignette] | *Macmillan and Co., Limited* | *St. Martin's Street, London* | *1937*

Pp xii + [383]: fly-leaf: [i–ii] half-title, publisher's monogram and addresses on verso: [iii–iv] title-page [vignette, from *Portraits of AE* item 23], *Copyright* and *R. & R. Clark*'s imprint on verso: [v–vi] three-line quotation, with *Editor's Note* on verso: vii–xii, *Contents*: [1–2] *A.E.* in top left; verso blank: 3–81, Monk Gibbon's Introductory Essay, dated 1937: [82] blank: [83]–[382] text of AE's writings [see analysis, below]; printer's imprint at foot of p [382]: [383–4] publisher's advertisements: fly-leaf.

Issued in light-green cloth, lettered gilt: *The Living Torch* | [ornament] | *A.E.* | [ornamental torch symbol] | *Macmillan*, on spine. Cream dust-wrapper, lettered. Published in London: October 21, 1937. 2000 copies. 22.2 × 14.4 cm.

57A American edition: New York, 1938. The Macmillan Company. Identical text. Passages from AE's prose articles first printed in the *Irish Statesman* and elsewhere. No sources indicated. Pp 86–89 was reptd from the *Irish Statesman* vol 11 pp 516–7
57B (March 2, 1929: sgd Y.O.). It was reptd *A Gold Standard for Literature* pp 11 (abdgd as in item 57) in a ltd edition [illus bds 1 dollar]: ? New York, 1939. Periwinkle (pblr). Item 57 pp 252–6, a review of W. B. Yeats' *A Vision* was reptd abdgd from *Irish Statesman* vol 5 pp 714–6 (February 13, 1926: sgd A.E.). The publisher (London: January 15, 1926. T.
57C Werner Laurie) reprinted the review as a *Circular Letter* to booksellers. [This compiler has not yet seen a copy.] Mr Séan O'Casey quoted from Monk Gibbon's essay, pp 18, 60 [from *The Avatars*, item 52, p 55] etc in *Inishfallen, Fare Thee Well* (London: 1949. Macmillan) pp 208–31. [The ensuing source list indicates *Irish Statesman* unless otherwise stated. Volume and page numbers are followed by the date of the issue in which first publication may be seen. The numbers in

parentheses refer to item 57.] (86–89) item 57B: (90) 2 pp 397–8, sgd AE, Jun 7, 1924 abdgd: (91) 13 pp 436–7, Feb 1, 1930: (94) 6, pp 713–4, Sep 4, 1926 abdgd: (95–6) 7, pp 302–3, Dec 4, 1926 abdgd: (97A) 10, pp 255–6, Jun 2, 1928 sgd Y.O., abdgd: (101A) 4, pp 82 and 84, Mar 28, 1925 sgd AE, abdgd: (102) 1, p 182, Oct 20, 1923 abdgd: (103) 1, pp 84–5, Sep 29, 1923 sgd AE, abdgd: (104) 12, pp 311–312, Jun 22, 1929 sgd Y.O., abdgd: (107) 3, pp 399–400, Dec 6, 1924 sgd AE: (111) 1, pp 685–6, Feb 9, 1924 sgd Querist, abdgd: (114) 4, pp 15–16, Mar 14, 1925 sgd AE, abdgd: (118) 7, 14–16, Mar 12, 1927 sgd AE, abdgd [see *Bridge Into the Future* by Max Plowman (London: 1944. Dakers) p 244]: (121) 13, p 96, Oct 5, 1929 sgd Y.O., abdgd: (123) 1, pp 176 and 178, Oct 20, 1923 sgd Querist: (126) 11, pp 477–8, Feb 16, 1929 sgd AE, abdgd: (131) 8, pp 183–4, Apr 30, 1927 sgd Querist, abdgd: (133) 4, p 405, Jun 6, 1925 sgd Y.O., abdgd: (134) 2, pp 271–2, May 10, 1924 sgd Querist, abdgd: (143) 10, p 231, May 26, 1928 sgd AE, abdgd: (145) 6, pp 71–74, March 27, 1926 sgd AE, abdgd: (149) *Introduction* to item 89, abdgd: (151) *Foreword* to item 87: (154) 7, pp 355–6, Dec 18, 1926 sgd AE, abdgd: (158) 12, pp 230–1, May 25, 1929, sgd AE: (162) 12, pp 350–1, July 6, 1929 sgd Y.O., abdgd: (166) 4, pp 792–4, Aug 29, 1925, abdgd: (167) 9, p 443, Jan 14, 1928, abdgd: (168) 5, p 717, Feb 3, 1926, sgd Y.O., abdgd: (169) 3, pp 111–112, Oct 4, 1924, abdgd: (172) 12, p 266, Jun 8, 1929 sgd AE, abdgd: (174) 10, pp 227–9, May 26, 1928 sgd AE [reptd *New York Times' Saturday Review of Literature*, Jun 9, 1928: p 949]: (178) 11, pp 210–211, Nov 17, 1928 sgd Y.O., abdgd: (183) 10, pp 226–7, May 26, 1928 unsgd, abdgd: (184) 11, pp 429–430, Feb 2, 1929 unsgd, abdgd: (187) 7, pp 542–4, Feb 12, 1927 unsgd, abdgd: (191) 1, pp 134–5, Oct 13, 1923, unsgd, abdgd: (193) 1, pp 102–3, Oct 6, 1923 unsgd: (198) 3, pp 755–6, Feb 21, 1925 sgd AE, abdgd: (201) 8, p 286, May 28, 1927 sgd Y.O., abdgd: (205) 4, pp 500–501, Jun 27, 1925 sgd Y.O., abdgd: (226) 4, pp 389–390, Jun 6, 1925 unsgd, abdgd: (227) 1, p 432, Dec 15, 1923 sgd Querist, abdgd: (233) 1, pp 303–4, Nov 17, 1923 sgd Querist: (238) 1, pp 82 and 84, Sep 29, 1923 sgd Querist, abdgd: (240) 13, pp 191–2, Nov 9, 1929 sgd Y.O., abdgd: (242) 3, pp 334–5,

Nov 22, 1924 sgd AE: (247) 5, pp 517–9, Jan 1, 1926 unsgd, abdgd: (252) item 57C: (256) 1, pp 325–6, Nov 24, 1923 unsgd, abdgd: (259) 13, pp 11–12, Sep 7, 1929 sgd AE, abdgd: (262) 5, pp 176–7, Oct 17, 1925 sgd AE, abdgd: (264) 8, pp 597–8, Aug 27, 1927 sgd AE, abdgd: (267B) 10, p 212, May 19, 1928 sgd Y.O., abdgd: (267C) 11, pp 275–6, Dec 8, 1928 sgd Y.O., extract: (272) 2, pp 103–4, April 5, 1924 sgd Y.O., abdgd, etc. [other interesting unreprinted notices of exhibitions by Jack B. Yeats: 5, p 178, Oct 17, 1925: 7, pp 616–7, March 5, 1927: 13, p 95, Oct 5, 1929.]: (274) 9, pp 227–8, Nov 12, 1927 sgd Y.O., abdgd: (276) 11, pp 356–7, January 5, 1929 sgd Y.O., abdgd: (277) 5, pp 310 and 312, Nov 14, 1925 sgd AE, abdgd [other notices of Harry Clarke's work: 4, p 692, Aug 8, 1925 sgd Y.O. (Stained glass): 13, pp 320–321, Dec 21, 1929, sgd Y.O. (drawings)] (John Anster's trans of *Faust*, pubd London by Harrap): (280) 7, pp 520–1, Feb 5, 1927 sgd Y.O.: (286A) 8, pp 450–1, July 16, 1927 sgd Y.O., abdgd: (286B) 6, pp 133–4, Oct 16, 1926 sgd AE: (289) 5, p 314, Nov 14, 1925 sgd Y.O., abdgd: (290) 2, p 596, Jul 19, 1924 sgd Y.O.: (293) 10, p 436, Aug 4, 1928 sgd Y.O., abdgd: (295) 7, pp 184–6, Oct 30, 1926, abdgd: (297) 4, pp 47 and 50, Mar 21, 1925 sgd AE, abdgd: (300) 9, pp 350–1, Dec 17, 1927 sgd Y.O.: (302) 14, pp 31–32, Mar 15, 1930 sgd Y.O.: (305) 3, pp 787–9, Feb 28, 1925 sgd AE: (309) 9, pp 85–6, Nov 1, 1927 sgd Y.O., abdgd: (310) 9, pp 184–5, Oct 29, 1927 sgd Y.O., abdgd: (312) 11, pp 435–6, Feb 2, 1929 sgd Y.O., abdgd: (314) 4, pp 338 and 340, May 23, 1925 sgd AE, abdgd: (317) 7, pp 405–6, Jan 1, 1927 sgd Y.O., abdgd: (323) 13, pp 71–2, Sep 28, 1929 sgd Y.O., abdgd: (327A) 6, pp 297–8, May 22, 1926 sgd Y.O., abdgd: (328B) 11, pp 251–2, Dec 1, 1928 sgd AE, abdgd: (330A) 12, pp 89–90, Apr 6, 1929 sgd Y.O., abdgd: (330B) 7, pp 136 and 138, Oct 16, 1926 sgd Y.O., abdgd from review of Kipling's *Debits and Credits* (London: Macmillan): (332) 10, pp 272–4, Jun 9, 1928 sgd Y.O., abdgd from review of Shaw's *Intelligent Woman's Guide to Socialism* (London: Constable): (336) 6, pp 659–661, Aug 21, 1926 sgd Y.O., abdgd: (357–374 incl) reptd and re-arranged, with captions added, from this bibliography item 20: (374) 13, pp 65–66, Sep 28, 1929 unsgd, abdgd etc.

Entries in item 57 for which this compiler has not yet identified the first publication: Item 57, pp: 85, 96, 97B, 98, 99, 100, 101B, 116–8, 128–30, 137–40, 171–2, 179, 196–7, 200, 202–4, 207–25, 236, 245, 250–1, 267A, 268–71, 284–5, 291, 294, 319, 326, 327B, 328A, 329, 331, 332A, 333, 334, 339, 343–54, 376–82.

58

THE SUNSET OF FANTASY

The Sunset of Fantasy. The fragmentary first chapter of AE's memoirs has been printed only in item 100 vol 13 No 1 pp 6–11 (January 1938). A handwritten version is owned by the Lilly Library, Indiana University, another by Mr Diarmuid Conor Russell.

58A AE's last poem, "Upon an airy upland" was first printed in item 100 vol 10 No 4 p 8 (October 1935). Two of its three stanzas were reptd in item 57, p 76.

Again reptd entire by "Seumas O'Sullivan" in his anthology
58B [B] *Editor's Choice: Poems from the Dublin Magazine* (Dublin: 1944. Orwell Press), at p 7.

59

LETTERS FROM (AE)

Letters from AE. Selected | and edited by Alan Denson | With a foreword by Dr Mark Gibbon | Abelard-Schuman London New York Toronto. Pp [xliv] + [282]. Published October , 1961.

Includes reprints of items 22, 23, 32A, 34, and 55 (incomplete). At the editor's request his friend Mr T. G. F. Paterson, O.B.E., M.A., M.R.I.A. generously wrote some invaluable *Notes on Lurgan Armagh and District in the later Nineteenth Century* for inclusion as an appendix to the *Letters*. Mr Paterson's unrivalled expert local knowledge has thus been placed at the service of all future students of AE's life and early environment. The literary executor, AE's younger son, Mr Diarmuid Conor

Russell stipulated the commission of a *Foreword* from Dr Monk Gibbon; he performed his task gracefully, (10 pages). Illustrations include portraits of AE, reproduction of some pages from his letters, and portraits of his wife and several friends. Letters first printed include several to the late A. J. Balfour, Sir Horace Plunkett, W. B. Yeats, Charles Weekes, and others. The book is dedicated: *To Sir Thomas Beecham, Bart., C.H., and H.N., my true friend. Commemorating Ivy Maud Denson (née Williams) 1896–1958.*

59A The published *Letters* comprises approximately one-third only of the edited typescript selection from the mass of AE's letters seen and transcribed by the editor. He has presented to the National Library of Ireland, Dublin, one carbon copy of the complete typescript (item 59A). The editor's own carbon copy of the complete typescript was despatched by surface mail from London to the National Library (Dublin) early in 1960, to be bound. One parcel, containing pages 1–500, together with numerous unique photographs of AE's friends, paintings, portraits, etc, and the compiler's own annotated typescript of this *Bibliography*, was stolen in transit. This compiler would be grateful for the return of that parcel to him, c/o his publisher's office. Another only partly-edited typescript copy, together with early drafts of this *Bibliography* has been presented by the compiler to the County Museum, Armagh, as a small token of his gratitude to the Curator, his friend George Paterson.

59B Microfilm copies of the complete typescript are available only from the editor.

The letters from AE which were incorporated by "John Eglinton" in his unindexed book *A Memoir of . . . AE* were printed at the pages numbered in parentheses: Clifford Bax (1, 76, 83): E. A. Boyd (256): Van Wyck Brooks (14, 151, 160, 238, 255, 262–6): Frances Calvert (7): W. Denijs (195–6): St J. G. Ervine (4, 82, 92, 93, 127, 239, 247): Mrs Fiske-Warren (157–9): J. M. Gaus (206): T. P. Gill (48): C. M. Grieve (232, 234): Cecil Harmsworth [now Lord Rothermere] (125–6): J. S. Hecht (147): Grace E. Jameson (150, 172): Arthur Kingsley-Porter (249): Sir Henry Lawson (143–4):

N. Vachel Lindsay (231): W. K. Magee (23, 49, 50): Arnold Marsh (253–5): George Moore (110): A. Victor Murray (134): H. F. Norman (267): Séan O'Faolain (156, 164, 178, 233, 258): Joseph O'Neill (207–29, 268–9, 274–5, [281?, 282?]): Herbert E. Palmer (260–1): James M. Pryse (40): C. C. Rea [Mrs R. E. Coates] (18–21, 168, 184): Israel Regardie (13): Sir William Rothenstein (121–2, 140, 189–90): A. E. S. Smythe (33): T. Spicer-Simson (144): J. C. Squire (89–90): *The Times* (89): P. L. C. Travers (191, 230, 236–7, 270): H. A. Wallace (277, 280): C. A. Weekes (81, 94, 96, 117–8, 122, 129, 135, 170–1, 253, 278–9): W. B. Yeats (42, 45, 48, 89, 94).

Other AE letters have been printed in the books listed in *Part 5* items 98, 99A, 101: and in *Part 8* items: 130, 136, 137, 140, 147, 148, 150, 151, 152, 154, 155, 156, 157, 161, 162, 169A, 177, 185, 186, 187, 188, 188A, and 192. In *Part 9* items 197, [206?], 207, and 208. In *Part 12B*, items lxxx–lxxxiii, cxii, cxix, cxx, cxxi, cxxxv, cxlviii, clxiv, clxv, clxvi, clxvii, clxxix, cxcv, cxcvi, cxcix, cci, cciii, ccv, ccxiii, ccxiv, ccxix, ccxx, ccxxiv, ccxxvi, ccxxxix, cclii, cclxvi, cclxvii, ccxciv–v, cccix, cccxviii, cccxxiii, cccxxix, cccxxxvi, ccclx–i, ccclxvi, and ccclxxxiv.

Letters from AE which this compiler has not seen, include:

To E. L. Allhusen (1) [5 Hartington Gardens, Edinburgh: in November 1935. Seen by Magee.]

Ronald A. M. Armstrong (editor of *The Sufi Quarterly*, Geneva).

The Earl of Oxford and Asquith. [Not located among his papers which have been deposited in the Bodleian Library.]

Mrs McCraith Blakeney (3) [28 Sandford Road, Ranelagh, Dublin: November 1935. Seen by Magee. Mrs Blakeney had written a book (? unpublished) *Mirror of Memory* containing a chapter with AE as subject.]

Mr T. W. Cubbon (1). [Almere, Rossett, N. Wales: November 1935. Seen by Magee.]

Miss Willy Denijs (4). [25 Albert Neuhuysstraat, Utrecht, Holland. Seen by Magee, November 1935.]

Daniel Nicol Dunlop. [His family believe all AE's letters to both their parents were destroyed by them before 1935.]

Arthur William Dwyer. [Resident in Niagara Falls area in 1930.]

Miss Louella D. Everett (1). [107 Massachusetts Avenue, Boston, Mass. Seen by Magee, November 1935.]

Miss Ruth Fry. [Thorpeness, Suffolk. Ms. notes of a conversation with AE (date?): seen by Magee, November 1935.]

M. K. Gandhi. [None located by the Secretary to the Navajivan Trust.]

Maud Gonne MacBride. [All presumed destroyed by Madame MacBride during the Irish 'Troubles'.]

Paul Gregan. [None known to his son.]

Cecil Harmsworth, Lord Rothermere. (2). [Seen by Magee, 1935.]

Charles and Vera Johnston. [None known to their nephew.]

William Quan Judge. [None were found whilst the Theosophical Society papers were being sorted 1955–58.]

Hugh Alexander Law. (2). [Seen by Magee, November 1935. Present location not now known to his family.]

N. V. Lindsay. [None known to the late Mrs Elisabeth Lindsay.]

Arnold Marsh (2). [Seen by Magee, November 1935.]

Mrs Grace Mullen (4). [2 Upper Leeson Street, Dublin: November 1935. Seen by Magee.]

Professor Albert V. Murray (several). [Mislaid: seen by Magee, November 1935.]

Frank O'Connor (many). [Most were lost many years ago.]

Standish James O'Grady (several). [None known to his surviving son.]

Frederick Scott Oliver. [Perhaps owned by his widow?—at Edgerston, Scotland.]

James Morgan Pryse (several). [Dispersed singly by sale, after his death, by his brother the late John M. Pryse.]

George Roberts (several). [None owned by his widow.]

Frank Roberts (two early photographs of AE in youth.) [Mr Roberts was an early member of the Dublin lodge of the Theosophical Society. Seen by Magee, 1935. Then resident at 37 Third Avenue, Daison, Torquay, Devon].

Edwin Arlington Robinson. [Habitually destroyed his correspondence. Mrs Ruth Nivison has not found any AE letters.]

Mr J. C. Sherer (4). [Dundaff Muir, Camberley, Surrey: November 1935. Seen by Magee.]

Theodore Spicer-Simson. (Several?). [Seen by Magee, 1935.]

James Sullivan Starkey ("Seumas O'Sullivan"). [Sold 1958–9.]

Dr Walter Starkie (3?). [Mislaid.]

Rabindranath Tagore. (1). [Not located at Santiniketan.]

Mrs Pamela L. C. Travers. (Several) [Seen by Magee, 1935.]

Mr J. A. Waley-Cohen (Several.) [514 St Ermin's, Westminster, S.W.1, in November 1935. Seen by Magee, 1935?]

Mrs Florence M. Wilson (1). [101 Groomsport Road, Ballyholme, Bangor, N. Ireland. Seen by Magee, November 1935.]

[Additionally this compiler has not yet seen the letters known to have been written by AE to: Austin Clarke; those in Colby College; Professor Wm. Yandell Elliott (Harvard University); the late Alfred P. Griffiths (64 Northway, London, N.W.11, in 1935); Miss C. Keogh (53 Upper Mount Street, Dublin, 1935); Thomas Goodwin Keohler (*or* Keller); Mr N. O'Leary Curtis ("Ardmore", Westfield Road, Harold's Cross, Dublin: 4 letters to his father, the late W. O'Leary Curtis, in 1935); Vance Palmer (all destroyed); Bernard Shaw; the late Susan Varian.]

59C This *Bibliography*.

60

RULES OF THE IRISH NATIONAL THEATRE SOCIETY

Rules of the Irish | *National Theatre* | *Society* | [floral ornament] | *Registered Office,* | *34 Lr. Camden Street,* | *Dublin.*

Pp 12: [1–2] title-page, verso blank: [3]–[12] text. At foot of p [12] [rule] and printer's imprint: *Sealy, Bryers and Walker, Printers, Dublin.* End wrapper [13–14] blank.

Issued in brown paper wrappers, stapled. Front wrapper lettered in black, as t/p. 17.8 × 12.4 cm.

These *Rules* do not carry an author's name: they were drafted by AE, and registered in Dublin [Register No 1077] under specified sections of the *Friendly Societies Act, 1896*, by D. O'C. Miley, *Assistant Registrar for Ireland*, on December 30, 1903. The *Rules* were assented to on p 11, by W. G. Fay, Patrick J. Kelly, Frederick Ryan, Helen S. Laird, Maire Walker, James Starkey, F. J. Fay and George Roberts as Secretary. Copies of these *Rules* are stocked in the Houghton Library, Harvard University (Theater Collection). A copy is stocked in the Colby College Library.

AIMS OF THE IRISH NATIONAL THEATRE SOCIETY

60A *Aims of the Irish National Theatre Society* [1903] A printed *Statement of the Aims* of the I.N.T.S. was sold among the
60B late George Roberts' papers, in 1957. A "similar" [B] printed *Statement* was included in that sale, described as "2 leaves quarto". Now part of the Theater Collection, Harvard University.

60C

RULES OF THE IRISH ACADEMY OF LETTERS

Rules | of the | Irish Academy of Letters | [On page 1, as on front wrapper.] Pp 8 : [1]Rules i–iii: 2, rules iv, and v(A–E): 3, rules v(F,G), vi(A–C): 4, vi(D,E): 5, vi(F)–ix: 6, x–xii: 7, xiii–xiv. Signed by G. Bernard Shaw, W. B. Yeats, Seumas O'Sullivan, Oliver St J. Gogarty, F. R. Higgins, Lennox Robinson, Michael O'Donovan, and George Wm. Russell, Secretary. [Rule at foot] imprint: *Printed by Cahill & Co., Ltd., at Parkgate Printing Works, Dublin.* [8] blank: but registration copy note by AE: *Amendments which I have | indicated within appear to | be necessary. | George W. Russell | 12 Sept 1932.* Drafted by Russell. Registered on 12th September 1932, by H. M. Whitton (Registrar in Dublin) Reg. No. 1654. Issued in buff or blue-gray wrappers. 100 copies printed. 18.4 × 12.5 cm.

Yeats announced the Academy project at a dinner at Romano's (London), April 3, 1932. See *Part 12*, Gwynn, S. L. (1936: appdx): Yeats (1954) pp 801–3.

60D *Rules | of the | Irish Academy of Letters | Registered 12th September, 1932, as a Specially Authorised | Society under the Friendly Societies Act, 1896.* Pp [iv]+[10]: [i–ii] front cover lettered in black, as above, verso blank: [1]–8 text, [assented to by Seán O'Faolain, Brinsley MacNamara, Joseph O'Neill, Lennox Robinson, S. J. Waddell]: [9–10] formal *acknowledgment* of Registration of this "Complete Amendment of the Rules of the Irish Academy of Letters is registered [Register No. 1654 Dublin S.A.] under the Friendly Societies Act, 1896, this 14th day of April, 1938" by P. P. O'Donoghue, [with schedule of specific sections]: at foot of p [9] [rule] and imprint *Printed by Cahill & Co., Ltd., Parkgate Printing Works, Dublin.* [10] blank. End wrapper [iii–iv] blank. Issued in grass-green wrappers, twice stapled. 18.4 × 12.1 cm. [*Rules* 4, 5 (A–F: in orig. B–G), 6 (C,D), 11, 12, 13 unaltered from item 60C.]

PART 2

SYMPOSIA

61

Literary Ideals in Ireland. Articles by W. B. Yeats, AE, W. K.
Magee, and William Larminie. Dublin: May 1899. [Dublin]
61A *Daily Express.* Pp 88. [A] "Literary Ideals in Ireland", and
61B [B] "Nationality and Cosmopolitanism in Literature", by AE;
reprinted from the *Daily Express* (Dublin), November 12 and
December 10, 1898: at pp 49–56 and 79–88. [A] Alone reprinted in item 13. [A] and [B] both reptd in item 28. Item 61 published simultaneously in London, by T. Fisher Unwin. Reviewed by "Fiona MacLeod" in *The Bookman* (London) vol 16 pp 136–7 (August 1899). Full description in Wade's Yeats *Bibliography* (1958), p 267. 21.6 × 11.8 cm.

62

Ideals in Ireland. Edited by Lady Gregory. Articles by AE, Standish James O'Grady, W. B. Yeats, D. P. Moran, George Moore, and Douglas Hyde. London: January 1901. At the Sign of the Unicorn. Pp 107. "Nationality and Imperialism"
62A by AE, at pp 15–22. Reptd from [A] the *All-Ireland Review*
(Kilkenny: Dublin) April 28 and May 5, 1900. Reptd in item 28, and in *Irish Literature* (Chicago: 1904. De Bower Elliott Co.) vol 8 pp 2989–95. Full description in Wade (1958) pp 269–70. 19 × 12.6 cm.

63

The United Irishwomen, Their Place, Work and Ideals. Preface by the Rev T. A. Finlay. With articles by Ellice Pilkington and Sir Horace Plunkett. Dublin: May 1911. Maunsel and Com-
63A pany. Pp vi + 50. Second edition [A] Dublin: 1911. Maunsel.

"Ideals of the New Rural Society" by AE, at pp 36–50. Reptd in items 19 and 28. [Louisa E. B. Grattan Esmonde, Mrs Pilkington: 1871–August 24, 1936.] 18.2 × 13.2 cm.

64

The Fairy Faith in Celtic Countries, by W. Y. Evans-Wentz. London: November 1911. Oxford University Press. Pp 552. The replies printed anonymously on pp 59–66 were dictated to Dr Evans-Wentz by AE in Dublin. 22.8 × 14.8 cm.

65

Labour in Ireland, by James Connolly. Introduction by Robert Lynd. Dublin: May 1917. Maunsel and Company. Pp 383.
65A,B Reprinted [A] Dublin: 1920. Maunsel. Reprinted [B] Dublin: 1944. Irish Transport and General Workers' Union. In the *Appendix*, item 22 was reptd at pp 341–6. [Another view: *Disturbed Dublin: the Story of the Great Strike of 1913–14*, by Arnold Wright (London: 1914. Longmans Green).]
19 × 12.2 cm.

66

The Irish Home-Rule | Convention. New York: September 1917. The Macmillan Company. Pp iii + 183. This book contained: "A Defence of the Convention" by Sir Horace Plunkett: AE's *Thoughts for a Convention* [item 33A, including the appended letters from 33A] at pp 95–160. There was an editorial note on AE, by John Quinn, at pp 79–89: "An American Opinion" by John Quinn. Loosely inserted in some copies was a single leaf printed letter dated September 17, 1917, from Quinn, signed by him in ink. The book was issued in blue-gray cloth, lettered in gold on the front cover, title etc, enclosed in ornamental device: title etc lettered in gold on spine.
16.7 × 9.9 cm.

67

Secret Springs of Dublin Song, edited by Susan L. Mitchell. Dublin: July 1918. Talbot Press. Pp 62. [500 copies.] The verses were not signed. Mr John Irvine most kindly supplied the key to authorship. (Page 1) "Epigram to the authors" signed M.S. [Miss Kathleen Goodfellow, or "Michael Scot"; resided Dublin, 1959]: (2) "Spring in Dublin" [Oliver Gogarty]: (4) "A double ballad of Dublin" [Gogarty]: (6) "Il doit aller pour oyer des nouvelles chez les barbiers" ["Seumas O'Sullivan"]: (7) "The poet and his wife" [Lord Dunsany]: (9) "Johnny, I hardly knew you" [Robert Yelverton Tyrrell]: (11) "To Citizen Elwood in South America" [Gogarty]: (12) "Rondeau" [Gogarty]: (13) "The poet to the physician" ["O'Sullivan"]: (13) "The physician replies" [Gogarty]: (14) "The wild dog compares himself to a swan" ["O'Sullivan"]: (15) "Little Jack Horner" [Tyrrell]: (16) "To Carson, swimmer of Sandycove" [Gogarty]: (20) "The Isles of Greece" [Gogarty]: (24) "The Hermit" ["O'Sullivan"]: (25) "Ideal Poems (i) S.O'S." *and* (26) "Y - - - s" ["A.E."]: (27) "From 'The Queen's Threshold' " [Gogarty]: (28) "The old man refreshing himself in the morning" [Gogarty]: (29) "On the death of his aunt" [Gogarty]: (31) "Lugete veneres Cupidinesque" ["O'Sullivan"]: (33) "Ambition in Cuffe Street" ["O'Sullivan"]: (34) "Praise and Friendship" [(1) Gogarty, answered by "O'Sullivan"]: (35) "To the maids not to walk in the wind" [Gogarty]: (36) "The Hermit" [G. W. Redding]: (40) "Threnody on the death of Diogenes, the Doctor's dog" [Gogarty]: (43) "How would it be?" [Dunsany]: (44) "The pilgrimage to Plunkett House" [Gogarty]: (47) "A lament for George Moore" [Gogarty]: (49) "To George Moore on the occasion of his marriage" ["O'Sullivan" and Gogarty]: (51) "Fame" [Dunsany]. The "Epigram" (p 1) may have been written by Susan L. Mitchell.

24.9 × 17.1 cm.

68

The Voice of Ireland: a Survey of the Race and Nation, edited by William G. FitzGerald. Dublin and Manchester: June 1923.

John Heywood [publisher]. Item 43, revised and adapted
68A by AE, was printed at pp 92–8. A "Corrected edition" [A] Dublin and Manchester: April 1924. John Heywood [pp 636] in which item 43 was reprinted at pp 86–92. Another edition
68B [B] Dublin and London: 1924. Virtue and Company Ltd., [publishers], in which item 43 was reptd at pp 86–92. [None of these editions carried publication dates. Items 68A and 68B seem to differ only in the place and name of the publisher, on t/p.] 28.4 × 21.8 cm.

[W. George FitzGerald was unsuccessful in Dublin and emigrated to South America probably in the mid-1920's. He is believed to have died many years ago. In 1911, 1913, 1918, and 1933 books written by him were published under the pseudonym *Ignatius Phayre*. The Irish Free State Senator, Desmond FitzGerald (1889–1947) was his brother.]

69

The Freeman Book. Typical Editorials, essays, critiques and other selections from the eight volumes of The Freeman [New York] *1920–1924*, compiled by B. W. Huebsch. New York: ? October 1924. B. W. Huebsch [publisher]. Pp vi + 394.

69A "Lessons of the Revolution" by AE was reprinted from [A] vol 7 pp 466–68 (July 25, 1923).

69B The original article was off-printed [B] 1923, New York: unbound. [This compiler has not seen a copy.]
[69] 21.5 cm. *vertical*

PART 3

BOOKS PREFACED BY AE

70

[Anthology] *New Songs. A Lyric Selection | made by A.E. from poems by | Padraic Colum, Eva Gore-Booth, | Thomas Keohler, Alice Milligan, | Susan Mitchell, Seumas O'Sullivan, | George Roberts, and Ella Young. | Dublin: O'Donoghue & Co., | 31 South Anne St. | London: A. H. Bullen, | 47 Great Russell St. | Price, one and sixpence, net. | 1904. |* [*Second edition.*, printed in italic capitals, and appropriately *Third edition.*, at foot of t/p.] *Preface* by A.E. dated "Dublin, December, 1903.", at p 5. [Some of the poems in the collection had been first printed in *The United Irishman* (Dublin) and the *Celtic Christmas* special issues of the *Irish Homestead.*] Frontispiece "The Plougher" [woodcut?] drawn by Jack B. Yeats.

Pp [ii] + 58: [i–ii] fly-leaf: [1–2] blank, and verso the drawing printed in black only, by Jack B. Yeats: [3–4] t/p, verso blank: 5, [Preface]: [6] blank: [7] *Contents*: [8] blank: 9–56, text: [57] imprint enclosed in ornamental device, *Dollard | Printinghouse | Dublin | Limited.* | in centre of page: [58] blank.

Issued in mauve boards, with a white paper label stuck on upper right side of front cover, giving title and authors' names as on t/p, lettered in black. J. Quinn's copy inscribed, date 7.3.04. Published in March 1904. 500 copies.

19.5 × 13.3 cm.

70A Second edition, identical text and format: excepting only addition of *Second Edition.* at foot of t/p. Published perhaps in June 1904: also 500 copies.

70B Third edition, identical text and format: excepting only addition of *Third Edition.* at foot of t/p. Published perhaps in

October 1904: also 500 copies. This third edition may have been partly held over for issue in May 1905, without any alteration of the date on t/p. In a letter to T. B. Mosher, Russell alluded to this third edition having been lately issued, in May 1905. Reviewed by Oliver St. J. Gogarty in *Dana* (Dublin) vol 1 No 1 p 32 (May 1904). [F. York Powell (1850–May 8, 1904) read this book and most relished Susan Mitchell's poems.]

71

Shan F. Bullock, *Mors et Vita* [poems] With a *Foreword* by AE at pp 7–8. London: June 1923. T. Werner Laurie. 350 copies. Pp 63. [British Museum copy stamped: 15 Jun 23]
22.7 × 15 cm.

72

Edward Thomas Craig [1804–94], *An Irish Commune. Introduction* by G. W. Russell (AE), at pp iii–vii. With *Notes* by Diarmuid Coffey. Dublin: [n.d.: July 1920] Martin Lester Ltd. Pp vii + 178. 18.8 × 12.4 cm.

73

Oliver St John Gogarty, *Selected Poems. Foreword* "The Poetry of My Friend", by A.E. New York: ? December 1933. The Macmillan Company. Pp xxxvi + 177.

73A Re-issued [A] identical text and format, by the same company: 1943.

73B The English edition of item 73 was published as *Others to Adorn* [B] identical text: AE's *Foreword* at pp xi–xvi. London: April 1938. Rich & Cowan. Pp 222. 19.6 × 12.6 cm.

73C [C] *Collected Poems* by Oliver St John Gogarty. AE's *Foreword* to item 73 reptd, at pp ix–xiii. London: February 4, 1951. Constable & Co. [500 copies]. Pp xxvii + 212. 22 × 13.8 cm. [Other writing by AE concerned with Gogarty's poems:

a review of *The Ship and Other Poems*, in *Irish Homestead* vol 25 p 561 (August 24, 1918), unsigned.
Review of *An Offering of Swans*, in *Irish Statesman* vol 1 pp 436 and 438 (December 15, 1923), signed A.E.
Review of Gogarty's book *Wild Apples*, in *Irish Statesman* vol 13 pp 299–300 (December 14, 1929), signed Y.O. [See also item 59: AE's letter to Robert Bridges].

73D Another prose *Appreciation* of Gogarty by AE was printed on [D] a leaflet issued by The Pond Lecture Bureau [24 West 45th Street, New York, 19] advertising Gogarty's first lecture tour round America. That tour was made in January–March 1933. The pamphlet is a single large glossy sheet, folded once to make four sides. The paper is colored pale green, with lettering and photographs all printed in brown. On p [1] a photograph of "Fitte-Waters' bust of Dr Gogarty" with distinctive captions "Rodin's only pupil" etc. Pp [2–3] printed information concerning Dr Gogarty, the topics upon which he could be hired to talk, and a small photograph of Dr Walter Starkie, with Mr J. B. Pond and Dr Gogarty. P [4] the *Appreciation* of Gogarty, signed A.E., with a vignette photograph of AE at the top: his *Appreciation* occupies all p [4], printed in 2 columns. The pamphlet as folded measured: 20.6 × 20.2 cm.

Concerning the *Appreciation* by AE (which has not been elsewhere printed) Mr James Burton Pond [B. 1889] sometime Managing Director of the *Pond Lecture Bureau*, the lecturer, kindly wrote to this compiler: "I still have the hand-written manuscript, beautifully done by AE. I will sell it for $100.00. As to other details, I have them all. If I live I may write about this beloved person, but again I am not inclined to labor for love . . . What a treasure-house of material. You can find it no place except in my head."

74

Mrs J. R. Green [Alice Stopford Green], *The Government of Ireland. Foreword* by George Russell (Æ), at pp 1–2. London: 1921. Labour Publishing Company. [*Labour Booklet* No 5] Brit. Mus. copy stamped 9 Jun 21. Pp 16. 21.7 × 13.9 cm.

75

Irene Haugh, *The Valley of the Bells and Other Poems*. With an *Introduction* by A.E. at pp ix–x. Oxford: December 1933. B. H. Blackwell. Pp 52. 20.4 × 13.8 cm.

76

F. R. Higgins, *Island Blood*. *Foreword* by A.E. at pp ix–x. London: March 1925. John Lane, The Bodley Head. Pp 88. 19.4 × 13.4 cm.

77

Hugh Alexander Law, *Anglo-Irish Literature*. With a *Foreword*, pp xv–xvii by AE. London: January 1926. Longmans, Green and Co. Ltd. Pp 320. AE's review, item 99A, vol 7 pp 477–8 (January 22, 1927). 18.8 × 12.5 cm.

78

Hugh MacDiarmid [*pseudonym* of C. M. Grieve], *First Hymn to Lenin and Other Poems*. With an *Introductory Essay* by "AE" (George William Russell) at pp 1–7. London: December 1931. The Unicorn Press. Pp 44. [450 numbered copies.]
78A [A] The same contents printed on large paper: signed by the
78B author, [50 numbered copies]. Reprinted; Edinburgh: [B] 1957. Castle Wynd, Publishers. [78A] 22.8 × 14.6 cm.

79

Frank O'Connor [*pseudonym* of Michael O'Donovan], *The Wild Bird's Nest: Poems Translated from the Irish. With an Essay "On the Character in Irish Literature"* by A.E., at pp i–v. Dublin: July 12, 1932. Cuala Press. [250 copies] Pp 39. 21.6 × 15 cm.

80

Standish James O'Grady, *The Coming of Cuculain. Introduction* by A.E. at pp ix–xxiii. Dublin, and London: August 1919.

Talbot Press: T. Fisher Unwin. AE's *Introduction* was reptd
80A in items 81 and 81A. [New York: 1920. F. A. Stokes.] Also reptd item 28A,B, pp 12–21. 19 × 12.7 cm.

81

Hugh Art O'Grady, *Standish James O'Grady: the Man and the Writer*. A *Foreword* by A. P. Graves, and *A Tribute* by A.E. Dublin: November 1929. The Talbot Press. This edition included 8 poems by AE [item 21D, pp 37, 46, 47, 124, 129, 141, 194, and 197] wrongly attributed to Standish O'Grady. [See "An A.E. Curiosity" by Sir Henry McAnally in *The Book Collector's Quarterly*, (London) vol 3 pp 67–9 (June–August 1931).] This edition was withdrawn. Re-issued without the
81A AE poems [A] Dublin and Cork: February 1930. The Talbot Press. Pp 84. *A Tribute* by A.E. on pp 63–75. [1000 copies]. Reference to 2 other articles on O'Grady: see items 28 and 57. [As "The Last Champion of the Irish Aristocracy", rev sgd Y.O. in item 99A vol 13 pp 378–9 (Jan 11, 1930).]
22.8 × 14.8 cm.

82

Joseph O'Neill, *Land Under England*. With a *Foreword* by A.E. at pp 5–7. London: January 1935. Gollancz. [B.M. copy stamped: 23 Jan 35.] Pp 334. 19 × 13 cm.

83

Seumas O'Sullivan [*pseudonym* of J. S. Starkey], *Lyrics*. Selected and with a *Preface* by A.E. Reprinted from his review
83A of *Verses, Sacred and Profane* first printed in *Sinn Fein*, April 4, 1908. AE: pp [383]–[387]. Portland, Maine: November 1910. T. B. Mosher. [*The Bibelot* vol 16 No 11, pp 389–426]. Subscription copies only. The *Preface* reptd in item 28 p 30; item 28A p 55, line 6 to end. [Other reviews by AE of O'Sullivan's work: item 98 vol 24 pp 840–1 (Nov 17, 1917): vol 25 p 672 (Oct 12, 1918): item 99A vol 13 pp 418–9 (Jan 25, 1930).]
15.5 × 11.7 cm.

84

Seumas O'Sullivan, *Twenty-Five Lyrics*. With an *Introduction* by AE at pp i–iv. Flansham, Sussex: October 1933. The Pear Tree Press. [Printed in black and green. 150 copies.]
23.8 × 14.8 cm.

85

Odon Por, *Guilds and Co-operatives in Italy*. Translated by [Mrs] E. Townshend. *Introduction* by AE, pp vii–xi; and an *Appendix* by G. D. H. Cole. London: April 1923. Labour Publishing Company. [Mrs Townshend (*née* Gibson), 1849–1934] Pp 215. [See also item 98 vol 21 pp 81–3 (June 31, 1914) AE reference to Por, articles in *New Age*.] 18.4 × 12 cm.

86

Lionel Smith-Gordon *and* Laurence C. Staples, *Rural Reconstruction in Ireland*. With a *Preface* by A.E., pp v–vii. London: December 1917. P. S. King and Sons. Pp 261. [Sgd review by AE: item 98 vol 25 pp 20 and 22 (Jan 12, 1918).]
22.2 × 14.4 cm.

87

Katharine Tynan [Mrs Hinkson], *Collected Poems*. *Foreword* by A.E., pp vii–xiii. London: October 1930. Macmillan. Pp 382. The *Foreword* was reptd in item 57, pp 151–4 (abridged). 19.8 × 13.4 cm.

88

Sir Francis Fletcher-Vane, *Agin the Governments: Memories and Adventures*. With a *Foreword* by AE at p vii. London: September 1929. Sampson Low, Marston & Co. Ltd. [Sir F. Fletcher-Vane, F.R.G.S. (1861–June 10, 1934) first met by AE in 1916.] Pp 352. 24.2 × 15.8 cm.

89

John Butler Yeats, *Essays, Irish and American. With an Appreciation by A.E.*, at pp v–viii. Dublin: May 1918. Talbot
89A Press, Reptd [A] December 1918. Talbot Press. Pp 95. *Appreciation* was reptd in item 57, pp 149–51 (abridged). [Reviewed by AE in *Irish Homestead* vol 25 p 467 (July 13, 1918).] 19 × 13.9 cm.

90

Savel Zimand, *Living India. Introduction* by A.E. [George W. Russell] at pp ix–xii. [Dated: Dublin, 10th August 1928]. New York, London and Toronto: November 1928. Longmans, Green. [Brit. Mus. copy stamped: 19 Nov 28]. Reviewed in *Irish Statesman* vol 11 pp 320–1 (December 22, 1928) by D. A. MacManus; and see letter and editorial comment in vol 11 pp 355–6 (December 29, 1928). [S. Zimand, born at Iassy, Roumania, 1891. Resident in New York.] Pp 296.
20.8 × 13.8 cm.

PART 4

ORAL EVIDENCE TO PARLIAMENTARY COMMITTEES

91

Report to the Select Committee on Money Lending. Parliamentary Papers: Commons 1898, vol 10. Russell's submissions were made in London, Thursday March 31, 1898. Paragraphs 2121–2263: pp 109–15 (bound vol pp 237–43). London: H.M. Stationery Office. [Sir Patrick Hannon, in his ms. *Memoirs* notes: "The evidence we gave was so striking that the proceedings were abandoned for further consideration of the Bill then before the House of Commons."

92

Report by the Committee of Inquiry into the Work carried on by the Royal Hibernian Academy, and the Metropolitan School of Art, Dublin. Parl. Papers: Commons. 1906. Command 3256. Bound vol 31. Russell: heard in the Board Room, Leinster House, Dublin, Friday October 13, 1905. Para's 1243–75: pp 61–3 [Brit. Mus. bound vol: pp 885–7]. George Moore, Sir William Orpen and W. B. Yeats also testified. London: H.M. Stationery Office. [Quoted in Eglinton's *Memoir of AE* p 59.]

93

Department of Agriculture and Technical Instruction (Ireland): Departmental Committee of Inquiry. Parl Papers: Commons. 1907. Cmd. 3574. Bound vol 18. Russell: heard in 18 Lower Baggot Street, Dublin, Wednesday October 31, 1906. Para's 14442–81: pp 815–9. London: H.M. Stationery Office.

94

Royal Commission on Congestion in Ireland: Third Report. Parl Papers: Commons. 1907. Cmd. 3414. Bound vol 35. Russell testified in the Westminster Palace Hotel, London S.W. on Saturday November 3, 1906. Para's 14118–308: pp 53–63 [Brit. Mus. bound vol: pp 399–409]. London: H.M. Stationery Office.

95

Departmental Committee on Agricultural Credit in Ireland. Parl Papers: Commons. 1914. Cmd. 7376. Bound vol 13. Russell was questioned at 4 Upper Merrion Street, Dublin, Wednesday March 13, 1912. Para's 1885–2019: pp 60–6 [Brit. Mus. bound vol: pp 504–10]. London: H.M. Stationery Office.

PART 5

PERIODICALS WITH NUMEROUS CONTRIBUTIONS FROM AE

96

The Irish Theosophist (Dublin), 1892–7. [Volume and page numbers, followed by date of issue and reference to reprints. See also items 3, 4, 12, 16, 18, and *Daily Express* (Dublin) *The Path* (Hale).]

Vol 1 No 1 p 5 (October 15, 1892) poem sgd G.W.R. (item 21D p 101):

Vol 1 No 2 pp 9–10 (November 15, 1892) prose "A Word upon the Objects of the Theosophical Society", sgd G. W. Russell, F.T.S.: vol 1 No 3 p 25 (December 15, 1892) poem sgd G.W.R. (item 21D p 155):

Vol 1 No 4 pp 33–4 (January 15, 1893) "Jagrata, Svapna and Sushupti", sgd F., prose [edit note p 36, that article embodies some of Brother Russell's main points from the paper he read on December 28, 1892, "First Steps in Occultism".]:

Vol 1 No 5 p 40 (February 15, 1893) poem sgd G.W.R. (item 21D p 8): vol 1 No 5 pp 41–2, essay sgd F., "Concentration", continuation from January 1893 pp 33–4: vol 1 No 5 p 45 essay "The Hour of Twilight" sgd Æ:

Vol 1 No 6 p 56 (March 15, 1893) poem sgd G.W.R. (item 21D p 82): pp 57–8, essay contd "The Hour of Twilight", sgd Æ:

Vol 1 No 7 p 63 (April 15, 1893) poem sgd G.W.R. (item 21D, p 46): pp 67–8 story sgd Æ "The Mask of Apollo" (reptd item 12, etc):

Vol 1 No 8 pp 76–7 (May 15, 1893) essay "The Secret of Power" sgd Æ: pp 78–9 essay "The Element Language" sgd G.W.R. re-written from item 187: p 83 poem sgd G.W.R. (item 21D, p 10):

Vol 1 No 9 p 87 (June 15, 1893) poem sgd G.W.R. (item 21D, p 12): pp 89–90, essay contd from pp 78–9:

Vol 1 No 10 pp 99–101 (July 15, 1893) story "A Priestess of the Woods" sgd Æ (incldg first version of item 21D, p 89): pp 104–5, essay contd from pp 78–9:

Vol 1 No 11 p 113 (August 15, 1893) poem sgd G.W.R. (item 21D, p 22): pp 117–8, essay contd from pp 104–5:

Vol 1 No 12 pp 123–5 (September 15, 1893) story "A Tragedy in the Temple", sgd Æ; pp 125–7, essay concluded from pp 117–8: p 127, poems sgd G.W.R. (item 21D, pp 11, 13):

Vol 2 No 1 pp 4–6 (October 15, 1893) story "At the Dawn of the Kaliyuga" sgd Æ (incldg item 21D, pp 157, 151) [a versified repetition of this story was printed in item 21D, pp 86–8]: p 8 poem sgd G.W.R. (item 21D, p 9):

Vol 2 No 2 pp 13–4 (November 15, 1893) essay "The Ascending Cycle" sgd G.W.R.: pp 151–3 [misprint for pp 19–21] story "The Meditation of Parvati", sgd Æ, (reptd in item 12, etc): p 153 [p 21] poem sgd G.W.R. (item 21D, p 1) probably prompted by W. B. Yeats:

Vol 2 No 3 pp 33–5 (December 15, 1893) story sgd Æ, "A Talk by the Euphrates": p 36 poem sgd G.W.R., (item 21D, p 23):

Vol 2 No 5 pp 62–4 (February 15, 1894) story sgd Æ, "The Cave of Lilith" (reptd in item 12, etc): p 65, poem sgd G.W.R. (item 21D, p 91):

Vol 2 No 6 pp 78–80 (March 15, 1894) chapter 1 of story sgd Æ, "A Strange Awakening": p 84, poem sgd G.W.R. (item 21D, p 2):

Vol 2 No 7 pp 96–9 (April 15, 1894) story contd from pp 78–80: p 100, poem sgd G.W.R. (item 21D, p 294):

Vol 2 No 8 pp 108–110 (May 15, 1894) essay sgd R, "Comfort" (reptd in *The Path* (Hale)): pp 112–14, story contd from pp 96–9: (includes poem reptd in item 21D, p 66): p 118, poem sgd G.W.R. (item 21D, p 34):

Vol 2 No 9 pp 124–7 (June 15, 1894) story concluded from pp 112–14: p 136, poem sgd G.W.R. (item 21D, p 225):

Vol 2 No 10 pp 140–3 (July 15, 1894) story sgd Æ, "The

Midnight Blossom" (reptd in item 12, etc): p 151, poem sgd G.W.R. (item 21D, p 49):

Vol 2 No 11 pp 160–2 (August 15, 1894) story sgd Æ, "The Story of a Star" (reptd in item 12, etc): p 164, poem sgd R., "H.P.B. (*In Memoriam*)", not reptd:

Vol 2 No 12 pp 175–7 (September 15, 1894) essay sgd Æ, "A Doomed City": p 178, poem sgd G.W.R. (item 21D, p 84): [p 184, review of item 2, sgd G.A.H.B.]:

Vol 3 No 1 pp 8–12 (October 15, 1894) story sgd Æ, "The Mystic Night's Entertainment":

Vol 3 No 2 pp 29–32 (November 15, 1894) story contd from pp 8–12:

Vol 3 No 3 pp 44–7 (December 15, 1894) story contd from pp 29–32 (incldg poem reptd in item 21D, p 77):

Vol 3 No 4 pp 61–4 (January 15, 1895) story concluded from pp 44–7: p 68 poem sgd G.W.R. (item 21D, p 127):

Vol 3 No 5 pp 77–9 (February 15, 1895) essay sgd Æ, "On the Spur of the Moment": p 87, poem sgd G.W.R. (item 21D, p 186):

Vol 3 No 6 pp 101–3 (March 15, 1895) essay "The Legends of Ancient Eire", sgd Æ:

Vol 3 No 7 pp 119–22 (April 15, 1895) essay concluded from pp 101–3:

Vol 3 No 8 p 136 (May 15, 1895) poem sgd G.W.R. (item 21D, p 39):

Vol 3 No 9 pp 165–6 (June 15, 1895) review sgd Æ of *Lyrics* by R. H. Fitzpatrick (London: 1895) [that author may have been related to Eleanor Fitzpatrick, D. N. Dunlop's wife]:

Vol 3 No 10 p 177 (July 15, 1895) poem sgd R. (item 21D, p 55): pp 178–80, essay "A Basis for Brotherhood", unsigned, but probably written by Russell:

Vol 3 No 11 pp 189–92 (August 15, 1895) essay sgd Æ, "Yes, and Hope":

Vol 3 No 12 pp 221–3 (September 15, 1895) poem "Songs of Olden Magic No. 2" (item 21D, pp 215–17): [p 226, D. N. Dunlop quoted AE: "Give me seven mystics in earnest, and we will evoke the ancient spirit; we will bring back the old magic; the fires will burst forth and illuminate the land . . ."]:

Vol 4 No 1 pp 15–18 (October 15, 1895) essay sgd Æ, "Content" (incldg item 21D, p 296):

Vol 4 No 2 p 29 (November 15, 1895) poem "Songs of Olden Magic No. 4" (item 21D, p 90): pp 32–5 story "The Enchantment of Cuchullain", sgd Æ and Aretas: ["Aretas", pseudonym used by James Morgan Pryse (1859–1942), see note in item 59]:

Vol 4 No 3 pp 50–4 (Dec 15, 1895) story contd from pp 32–5:

Vol 4 No 4 pp 62–4 (January 15, 1896) Essay sgd Æ, "Shadow and Substance": pp 68–9, "Songs of Olden Magic, No 6", poem sgd Æ (item 21D, p 209): pp 72–5, story contd from pp 50–54:

Vol 4 No 5 pp 83–9 (February 15, 1896) story contd from pp 72–5: p 100, unsgd review of *From the Upanishads*, by Charles Johnston (Dublin: 1896. Whaley) [Probably by AE]:

Vol 4 No 6 pp 101–8 (March 15, 1896) story contd from pp 72–5 (including poem reptd in item 21D, pp 212–14):

Vol 4 No 7 p 121 (April 15, 1896) unsgd verses "W.Q.J." [died March 21, 1896] probably by AE (not reptd): pp 122–3, prose sgd Æ [Tribute to Judge]: pp 127–30, poem sgd Æ (reptd in item 5, pp 74–9, part reptd in item 21D, p 152):

Vol 4 No 8 p 146 (May 15, 1896) poem sgd Æ (item 21D, p 153): pp 150–2, essay sgd Æ, "Self Reliance": pp 156–7, essay sgd Æ "The Mountains" (incldg poem reptd in item 21D, p 222):

Vol 4 No 9 pp 169–71 (June 15, 1896) essay sgd Æ, "Works and Days": p 174, poem sgd Æ, "The King Initiate" (not reptd):

Vol 4 No 10 pp 190–2 (July 15, 1896) poem sgd Æ (item 21D, pp 108–10):

Vol 4 No 11 pp 210–12 (August 15, 1896) poem sgd Æ (not reptd):

Vol 4 No 12 pp 230–2 (September 15, 1896) poem sgd Æ (not reptd):

Vol 5 No 1 pp 6–8 (October 15, 1896) poem sgd Æ (its conclusion was alone reptd, in item 21D, p 105):

Vol 5 No 2 pp 24–7 (November 15, 1896) story sgd Æ, "The Childhood of Apollo" (reptd in item 12, etc): p 32, poem sgd Æ (item 21D, p 75):

Vol 5 No 3 pp 49–54 (December 15, 1896) poem sgd Æ (item 21D, pp 200–8):

Vol 5 No 4 pp 66–9 (January 15, 1897) prose sgd Æ, "The Awakening of the Fires" (reptd in item 3) [incldg item 21D, p 226]:

Vol 5 No 5 pp 85–9 (February 15, 1897) essay concluded from pp 66–9: p 91, poem sgd Æ (item 21D, p 52):

Vol 5 No 6 p 108 (March 15, 1897) poem unsigned (item 21D, p 132):

Vol 5 No 7 pp 127–31 (April 15, 1897) essay sgd Æ, "Priest or Hero?" (reptd in item 4):

Vol 5 No 8 pp 148–52 (May 15, 1897) essay concluded from pp 127–31: at pp 159–60 unsgd review (probably by AE) of *The Treasure of the Humble* by Maurice Maeterlinck (1897. George Allen):

Vol 5 No 9 pp 168–70 (June 15, 1897) essay sgd Æ, "The Age of the Spirit":

Vol 5 No 10 pp 181–5 (July 15, 1897) essay sgd Æ, "A Thought along the Road":

Vol 5 No 12 pp 221–5 (September 15, 1897) essay sgd Æ, "The Fountains of Youth" (incldg item 21D, p 197).

[For illustrations by AE in *Irish Theosophist* see Part 15, p 236, below.] [October 15, 1892–September 15, 1897. Edited by D. N. Dunlop (1868–1935).] 23.4 × 17.8 cm.

97

The Internationalist (Dublin, October 1897–March 1898). [See also items 12, 16, and *The Green Sheaf* (London) and *The Path* (Hale).]

Vol 1 No 1 pp 10–13 (October 15, 1897) story sgd Æ, "A Dream of Angus Oge" (reptd in item 12, etc):

Vol 1 No 2 pp 24–6 (November 15, 1897) essay sgd Æ, "The Hero in Man": pp 35–8 prose sgd G.W.R. "On the March":

Vol 1 No 5 pp 91–3 (February 15, 1898) essay sgd Æ, "Transformation" (incldg poem reptd in item 21D, p 19):

Vol 1 No 6 pp 103–7 (March 15, 1898) essay "In the Shadow of the Gods" (incldg poems reptd in item 21D, pp 73, 106, 289) sgd AE. [October 15, 1897–March 15, 1898. Edited in Dublin by Russell, in London by H. A. W. Coryn.]

23.4 × 17.8 cm.

98

The Irish Homestead (Dublin [1897]–1923). Russell's contributions to this periodical were very numerous. He was appointed its editor, in succession to H. F. Norman (1868–1947), probably in August 1905. Thereafter the editorials and weekly notes were written by Russell. With a few exceptions reference to those prose articles is not listed: see reference in item 30. This list gives only reference to AE's poems: the numbers in parentheses refer to item 21D pagination.] [CC *for* Celtic Christmas] [vol 4 p 54 (January 15, 1898) "Co-operative Banks", AE's first prose article in *The Irish Homestead*]: CC December 1897 p 24 (197): CC December 1897 p 10 (218): CC December 1898, pp 8–9, story "A Dream of Angus Oge" reptd from item 97: CC December 1898, p 14 (106): [vol 4 p 239 (March 12, 1898) quotes item 21D, p 128 in reference to item 2]: vol 5, CC December 1899 pp 10–11 (112): vol 6, CC December 8, 1900 p 16 (28 and 63): vol 7, CC December 1901, p 20 (105): vol 8, CC December 1902 pp 4–11 (item 9B), and p 15 (298): vol 9 p 694 (August 22, 1903) (173): vol 9, CC December 1903 [illustrations by AE]: vol 10, CC December 3, 1904 p 15 humorous verses by A.E., (not reptd): vol 11, CC December 2, 1905 p 13 (106), and p 23 poem "The Climbers" sgd A.E., reptd from item 96 vol 3 p 8: vol 12, CC December 1, 1906 p 1 (21): vol 14, CC December 7, 1907 pp 1–2 (reptd from item 96 vol 4 p 210): vol 15, CC December 5, 1908 [illustrations by AE]: vol 16, CC December 11, 1909 p 10 (291): vol 17 p 731 (September 3, 1910) unsigned "Notes of the Week" includes comment on aviation; see item 21D, pp 183–5: vol 20 pp 922–3 and 942–3 (November 8, 15, 1913) Russell's avowal of item 22 etc as being statements only of personal opinion, not connected with I.A.O.S. policy. [See also items 25, 26, 29, 31, 36, 38, and 40.] [March 9, 1896–September 8, 1923.] 33.4 × 21 cm.

99

The [*First*] *Irish Statesman* (Dublin) vol 1 p 622 (December 20, 1919) (item 21D, pp 358–69: see also item 37). [June 28, 1919–June 19, 1920. Edited by Warre B. Wells (1892–1956).]

99A *The* [*Second*] *Irish Statesman* (Dublin). [As with item 98 AE's contributions to this paper were so numerous that a list would fill a volume. This compiler's analysis of the prose printed in item 57 is his sole attempt here to list AE's articles in the *Irish Statesman*. For prose and verse Russell used several pseudonyms, A.E., G.A.L., O.L.S., Querist, L.M.E., R.I.E., and Y.O.] [Verse by AE printed in the *Irish Statesman* but excluded from his *Collected Poems*: vol 2 p 9 (March 15, 1924): vol 4 p 202 (April 25, 1925): vol 4 p 751 (August 22, 1925): vol 5 p 42 (September 19, 1925): vol 5 p 297 (November 14 1925): vol 5 p 330 (November 21, 1925).]

Poems by Russell printed in item 99A: [volume followed by page number, with page reference to item 21D in parentheses]: 3, 430 (340): 12, 469 (382): 1, 75 (348): 3, 169 (352): 2, 585 (351): 11, 431–2 (384): 3, 495 (309): 3, 108 (320): 2, 687 (308): 9, 176 (400): 2, 817 (337): 11, 68 (395): 1, 460 (324): 7, 425 (408): 11, 492 (394): 7, 617 (377): 3, 267 (315): 10, 489 (413): 4, 75 (330): 2, 201 (329): 7, 248 (393): 8, 420 (380): 2, 687 (322): 3, 751 (346): 3, 430 (314): 4, 333 (334): 2, 201 (312): 6, 388 (388): 12, 430 (379): 2, 521 (303): 3, 267 (306): 3, 751 (327): 2, 521 (319): 6, 514 (373): 2, 817 (304): 10, 428 (410): 13, 89 (424): 2, 817 (328): 13, 10 (387): 3, 495 (323): 13, 108 (399): 3, 782 (356): 4, 751 (417): 10, 208 (376): 13, 511 (405): 12, 107 (411): 6, 514 (373): 5, 42 (332): 7, 225 (374): 4, 456 (331): 2, 687 (305): 13, 373 (404): 2, 201 (350): 12, 188 (415): 6, 232 (392): 2, 521 (311): 14, 67 (item 53, p 69): 3, 430 (340): 3, 72 (316): 10, 387 (414): 10, 386 (423): 4, 11 (339): 3, 267 (307). [See also items 201, 202, 204.] [September 15, 1923–April 12, 1930. Edited by G. W. Russell.] 33.4 × 21 cm.

100

The Dublin Magazine (Dublin). [See items 50A, 58, and 117.] vol 1 No 5 p 367 (May 1926) a poem reptd only in item 117, p 212 and in Part 123 item CCXX: [Numbers in parentheses refer to item 53] vol 9 No 2 p 1 (47): 8, No 4 p 1 (71): 7 No 4 p 3 (48): 9 No 1 p 1 (78): 7 No 4 p 2 (44): 7 No 4 p 4 (88): 7 No 4 p 4 (87): 7 No 4 p 3 (60): 8 No 1 p 1 (74): 8 No 1 p 2 (41): No 3 p 1 (40): 8 No 1 p 2 (72): 7 No 2 p 2 (79): 7 No 4 p 1 (39): 7 No 4 p 2 (70): 9 No 3 p 1 (42): 10 No 4 p 8 (item 58A): 7 No 2 p 1 (69) (also reptd in items 209 and 99A, vol 14 p 67): 9 No 2 p 1 (73) [1926–58. Edited by J. S. Starkey, "Seumas O'Sullivan".] 24 × 17.8 cm.

101

The New English Weekly (London). [1933–4] vol 1 No 1 (April 21, 1932) a brief letter from AE to the editor, A. R. Orage (1873–1934): [volume followed by page numbers: references in parentheses to pagination in item 53.] 4, 205 (64): 4, 22 (81): 5, 252 (45): 4, 321 (66): 4, 469 (19): 4, 293 (61): 4, 580 (31). [See also item 122.] 30.6 × 20.4 cm.

PART 6

SOME ARTICLES BY AE, PRINTED IN PERIODICALS OTHER THAN THOSE WHICH HE EDITED, NOT REPRINTED BY AE

102

"The Art of John Hughes" in *New Ireland Review* (Dublin) vol 10 pp 162–5 (November 1898). Signed A.E.

103

"The Application of Co-operation in the Congested Districts" [Text of a paper read in Dublin, Tuesday, December 19, 1899] in the *Journal of the Statistical and Social Inquiry Society of Ireland* (Dublin) vol 11 part 80 pp 517–27 (August 1900) (pubd. Sealy, Bryers and Walker). Signed Geo. W. Russell.

104

"An Irish Sculptor—John Hughes, R.H.A." in *Journal and Proceedings of the Arts and Crafts Society of Ireland* (Dublin) vol 1 No 3 pp 243–8 (1901). Signed A.E. [An expanded version of item 102.]

104A To be reprinted in this compiler's survey of Hughes' life and sculpture.

105

"The Rt Hon Horace Plunkett" in *The Gael* (New York) March 1902: pp 81–2. Signed "A.E."

106

"Britannia Rule-the-Waves. A Comedy (in one act and in prose)." Printed in *Sinn Fein* (Dublin) February 9, 1907: p 3 cols 3–5. Unsigned. [A parody of W. B. Yeats' *Kathleen-*
106A *ni-Houlihan.*] Reptd in *Nationality* (Dublin) vol 1 No 33 (Saturday, January 29, 1916) pp 5–6. [See also item 107.] Both papers edited by Arthur Griffith. [Yeats' retort, "To a Poet . . .", first printed in *The Green Helmet* (1910. Cuala Press): reptd in his *Collected Poems* (1950) p 105.]

107

"On the Degeneration of the Drama", a sonnet printed in *Sinn Fein* (Dublin) February 16, 1907: p 3 col 3. Unsigned. Evidently another attack on Yeats.

108

"Jack B. Yeats" in *The Book-Lover's Magazine* (Edinburgh) [formerly *The Book of Book-Plates*] vol 8 part 3 pp 132–8 (dated 1908–9). Signed AE. [This article may have been written as response to the paintings by Jack Yeats exhibited *circa* May 10 to June 1909 at the Leinster Lecture Hall, Dublin. Or perhaps the exhibition in Walker's Galleries, London, "Pictures of Life in the West of Ireland", closing February 29, 1908.]

109

"The Other Irish Question" in *The Round Table* (London) No 7 pp 447–71 (June 1912). Unsigned.

110

"The Co-operative Movement" in *The New Statesman* (London) vol 1 No 14 (July 12, 1913), in the *Supplement On the Awakening of Ireland* inserted between pp 448–9, with separate pagination. Signed A.E. [A.E., pp 2–5. Other authors: Bernard Shaw, J. M. Hone, C. H. Walsh, May C. Starkie, E. A. Boyd, George A. Birmingham, and one unsigned.]

111

"How to Protect Ourselves from the Peace which Threatens Us" in *Better Business* (Dublin) vol 1 pp 16–25 (October 1915). [*Better Business* pubd by Maunsel & Co.: edited at the I.A.O.S. by Miss Florence Marks (died *circa* 1955, aged over 80).] Signed George W. Russell.

112

"The Self-supporting Community". Part 1 in "Four Years of Irish Economics, 1914–18", in *Studies* (Dublin) vol 7 pp 301–6 (June 1918). Signed George Russell (A.E.). [The other authors: (2) E. J. O'Riordan, (3) Edward E. Lysaght, (4) Andrew E. Malone: at pp 306–27.]

113

"Conditions of an Irish Settlement" in *Pearson's Magazine* (New York) vol 47 No 3 pp 102–6 (September 1921). Signed. ["An Irish Fairy Tale" by Violet Russell was printed in the Christmas issue, vol 47 No 7 pp 307–10.]

114

"Irish Anticipations" in *Survey Graphic* (New York) vol 47 pp 291–4 (November 26, 1921). Signed A.E. [Between pp 287–347 in vol 47 Sir Horace Plunkett, Savel Zimand, Erskine Childers and others also answered the editorial question "What would the Irish do with Ireland?"]

115

"Address to the Thirtieth Annual Dinner of the American-Irish Historical Society" (delivered January 28, 1928), in the

Journal of the American-Irish Historical Society (New York) vol 27 (for 1928). Signed.

116

"The Censorship in Ireland", in *The Nation and Athenæum* (London) vol 44 pp 435–6 (December 22, 1928). Signed A.E.

117

"Twenty-five Years of Irish Nationality", in *Foreign Affairs* (New York) vol 7 No 2 pp 204–20 (January 1929). Signed
117A "A.E." Off-printed [A], January 1929: pp 17. [A.E. amended his own copy: p 205, 14 lines up, "move *the mightier of* his": p 206, 11 lines down, "Cuchulain of Muirthem*ne*".] Poem on p 212 reptd from item 100 vol 1 p 367.

118

"Is America Dollar-bound?" in *Forum and Century* (New York) vol 83 pp 32–6 (January 1930). Signed.

119

"The Philosophy of Rural Civilisation" in the *Bulletin of the State Board of Agriculture* (Jefferson City, Missouri), vol 28 No 11 pp 4–13 (November 1930). Signed George W. Russell, "AE". [Address delivered October 28, 1930, at the Missouri Farmers' Week.]

120

"Building a Rural Civilisation", in the *Journal of the National Education Association* (Washington, D.C.) vol 20 p 65 (February 1931). Signed.

121

"An Irish Poet on American Agriculture", in the *Co-operative Marketing Journal* (Washington, D.C.) vol 5 No 2 pp 33–6

(March–April, 1931). Signed George Russell. [See also a 'portrait' of A.E. in *Literary Digest* (New York) vol 107 p 20 (October 11, 1930), "Poet to the Farmers".]

122

"Memories of A. R. Orage", in the *New English Weekly* (London) vol 6 pp 97–8 (November 15, 1934). Signed A.E. [That issue included other articles commemorating Orage, written by Bernard Shaw, G. K. Chesterton, T. S. Eliot, Herbert Read, and others.] See also: Philip Mairet, *A. R. Orage: A Memoir* (London: 1936. Dent).

[In item 98 throughout the second decade of this century AE made frequent editorial comment on Orage's articles in the *New Age* (London). His keen analysis of Orage's methods in controversy was printed in item 98 vol 19 p 253 (March 30, 1912). See also the two letters to Orage in item 59.]

Violet Russell (A.E.'s wife) wrote *Heroes of the Dawn* [stories] with illustrations by Beatrice Elvery, (Dublin: December 1913. Maunsel. Second edition: 1922. Maunsel). Mrs Russell's stories were also printed in magazines (see item 113). In *Sinn Fein* (Dublin) September 26, 1908, some of her verses were printed.

PART 7

SOME POEMS BY AE, SET TO MUSIC

123

Bantock, Granville R. In *Three Songs for Children* the second poem by AE, "Frolic" [item 21D, p 21] at pp 5–7. The first and third poems were written by Alfred Hayes. (London: 1923. Joseph Williams Ltd): set for voice with pianoforte accompaniment.

124

Bantock, Granville R. *Carrowmore* [item 21D, p 106], for voice and pianoforte: pp 8. (London: 1926. Swan & Co., Music Publishers, Ltd).

125

Bantock, Granville R. *The Gates of Dreamland* [item 21D, p 106], for voice and pianoforte. (London: 1930. F. Williams).

126

Bax, Arnold E. T. *Parting* [item 21D, p 72]. (London: 1921. Murdoch & Co). (Now published by Chappell & Co., London).

127

Edmonds, John. *The Lonely*, [item 21D, p 346], for voice and pianoforte. Pp 5. [31 cm.] (New York: 1948. C. Fischer. [*Modern Art Songs*, No 5.]) [J. Edmonds, born in U.S.A., 1913.]

128

In *Songs of Praise*, edited by Percy Dearmer, Ralph Vaughan Williams and Martin Shaw (London: O.U.P.) No 122 by A.E., "When the unquiet hours depart" [item 5, p 54: not the shortened reprint in item 21, p 192]. Tune "From *Magdalen Hymns*, c. 1760".

129

Fox, C. Milligan. "The Gates of Dreamland" [item 21D, p 106] set for voice and pianoforte. Printed in item 98 vol 11, *Celtic Christmas* supplemental issue (December 2, 1905) p 13. Reptd in Charlotte M. Fox's *Songs of Irish Harpers* (?1910. Bayley & Ferguson). [C. M. Fox (born 1864; died in London, February 1916). Mrs Fox was the originator of the Irish Folk Song Society. She was sister of Alice L. Milligan.]

PART 8

SOME OTHER PERIODICALS IN WHICH PROSE AND POEMS BY AE WERE PRINTED

[*Volume and page numbers followed in parentheses by page numbers item 21D*]

130

All-Ireland Review (Kilkenny, later Dublin: January 1900–December 1906). [See items 9 and 62.] Vol 1 No 1 p 1 (item 21D, p 227): 1, 8 p 6 (item 10 p 27: not in 21): 1, 21 p 5 (37): 1, 23 p 2 (59): vol 2 p 143 (89, 139): 2, 150 (106): vol 3 p 672 (112, 114): vol 4 No 2 p 21 (231). *Prose:* vol 1 No 29 p 2 (July 21, 1900) review sgd A.E. of *The Divine Adventure* by "Fiona MacLeod": vol 1 No 33 p 1 (August 18, 1900) letter from A.E. replying to "Fiona MacLeod's letter in issue No 31: vol 2 pp 237–8 (October 12, 1901) 2 letters from A.E. to the editor, Standish O'Grady: [vol 3 No 38 p 632 (November 22, 1902) editorial note: a series of reviews of Celtic literature was current in *L'Humanité Nouvelle* (Paris)]: vol 5 No 3 p 30 (January 16, 1904) review sgd A.E. of *Myths* by Ethel Longworth Dames: vol 5 No 14 p 160 (April 2, 1904) a letter, several signatories included Russell, "A Rural Library Association" (item 59): vol 5 No 18 p 209 (April 30, 1904) editorial note that A.E. had written an article about him "in the American press" [not traced; probably in *The Reader* (New York: Indianapolis) or *Criterion* (New York)]: [vol 6 No 20 pp 236–7 (May 20, 1905) editorial reply to a correspondent, perhaps significantly akin to the quest AE adopted after the insurrection in Dublin: "I too am looking for one man, but think of him more as a hero than a saint; but a saint too, in the sense that the world will have no hold upon him, that he will look through the world and know it for the cowardly, hypocritical, blood-sucking, soul-and-body devouring old devil that it is . . ."]:

131

American Federationist (New York) vol 34 p 548 (May 1927) (item 21D, p 342): vol 38 p 223 (February 1931) (item 21D, p 149).

131A

[*Appreciation* (London: New York: *subsequently* Dublin) the "Journal of the Threefold Movement" issued vol 1 Nos 1, 2, 3 as *Calamus*: No 4 as *Appreciation* (October 1929). The letter which AE wrote supporting this association, dated August 6, 1930 (printed in item 59) may have been printed in *Appreciation*: this compiler has not seen issues later than January 1930. Russell may have been invited to support this association of religious faiths, by his friend Sir John Woodroffe, or by Sir Francis Younghusband.]

132

The Athenæum (London) vol 105 p 12 (January 5, 1899) (item 21D, pp 6 and 9).

133

A Broad Sheet (London) "Remembrance" [poem] (item 21D p 166) illustrated by Jack B. Yeats, in color. Published in February 1903 by Elkin Mathews Ltd.

134

Current Literature (New York) vol 37 pp 527–8 (December 1904) (item 21D, p 261): vol 46 p 452 (April 1909) (21D, p 86).

135

Current Opinion (New York) vol 56 p 383 (May 1914) (item 21D, p 97): vol 78 p 225 (February 1925) (21D, p 306).

136

Daily Express (Dublin). [See item 61.] Issue September 10, 1898, a letter sgd Geo. W. Russell, "Art in Ireland" (p 3 col 2): ["The Poetry of AE" by W. B. Yeats, in issue September 3, 1898]: November 26, 1898 review sgd A.E. of *Poems* by Eva Gore-Booth (London: Longmans) (p 3 col 8): December 26, 1898, letter sgd by Russell and W. G. Strickland as joint honorary secretaries of the Committee arranging an Art Loan Exhibition in Dublin: January 28, 1899, "The Irish Literary Drama", review sgd A.E., of Edward Martyn's *The Heather Field* and *Maeve* (p 3 col 2): February 25, 1899 "Politics and Character", sgd A.E. (p 3 cols 2–3): April 22, 1899, "The Spiritual Influence of Art", sgd A.E. (p 3 cols 3–4): June 17, 1899, rev. sgd A.E. of *The Dominion of Dreams* by "Fiona MacLeod" (London: Constable) (p 3): July 1, 8, 15, 22, and 29, 1899, "The Mask of Apollo", "The Cave of Lilith", "The Childhood of Apollo", "The Meditation of Parvati", "The Midnight Blossom", stories reptd from item 96 (reptd in item 12) (all on p 3): August 5, 1899, humorous verses "A Railway Journey" sgd R. (p 3 col 2), perhaps by Russell: September 23, 1899, "The Story of a Star", sgd A.E. (p 3 cols 2–3) reptd from item 96 (reptd in item 12). [*Daily Express* then controlled by Plunkett: editor, T. P. Gill.]

137

Daily News (London) "Ulster: An Open Letter to Rudyard Kipling" was printed in the issue April 15, 1912. [Kipling's verses had been printed in *The Morning Post* (London) April 9, 1912: reptd in his book *The Years Between* (1919) and in his *Complete Poetry*.] AE's "Open Letter" was reptd by Darrell Figgis in his *Æ* (1915); by AE, slightly altered, in item 28; also reptd in *The Recorder* (New York: American Irish Historical Society) January 2, 1939: partly reptd by M. J. MacManus in an article printed in *The Sunday Press* (Dublin) March 26, 1950, and reptd *Irish Press* (Dublin) December 24, 1951, and in MacManus' book *Adventures of an*

Irish Bookman (Dublin: 1952. Talbot Press). This letter was admired as exemplary invective by Herbert Read and Bonamy Dobrée. They sought A.E.'s permission to include it in their *London Book of English Prose* (London: 1932. Eyre & Spottiswoode), but AE asked them to exclude it, having grown to dislike even righteous indignation. [*Proverbs*, xv, 23.] T. M. Kettle also wrote a retort to Kipling's verses, as "Kipling's Banjo Strings". [Compare Kipling's "Recessional" to AE's poem "To the New Gods" in *Collected Poems* (1919 ed) pp 256–7.]

138

Dana (Dublin) vol 1 p 105 (August 1904) (item 21D, p 119): vol 1 p 61 (June 1904) (21D, p 111). [See also item 28.]

139

Dial (Chicago) vol 24 p 326 (May 16, 1898), (item 21D, pp 18, 129).

139A

Dublin Saturday Post (Dublin) November 8, 1913: p 2 col 7, a quotation from item 24, above.

140

Ethical Echo (Dublin). Mr Percy Muir kindly showed this compiler some copies of this periodical with contrib's by Charles Weekes: vol 1 No 3 [prose] "Tendency and sin": vol 1 No 3 [verse] "The Rev Gyles Wrestler": vol 2 No 3 [prose] "Word and theory. A rejoinder to G. W. Russell" (October 1893). Russell contributed prose and verse to three issues. [A complete file may be found in the AE collection, Indiana University Library, Bloomington.]

141

Fortnightly Review (London) vol 71 p 38 (January 1899) (item 21D, pp 9 and 54).

142

Freeman (New York). [See items 38B and 69.] Quotations made in editorials, issues dated November 29, 1922: February 21, 1923: July 4, 1923: July 25, 1923, from AE's articles in item 98. Editorial welcome to *Irish Statesman* in issue October 17, 1923. Quotation from an AE article in item 99A, in issue November 7, 1923.

143

Freeman's Journal (Dublin). [See items 7B, 34B, and *Portraits of A.E.* No 2; p 244 below.]

144

The Gael (New York). [See item 105.] Issue December 1901 an article "Modern Art in Ireland" quotes from AE's review in *Freeman's Journal* (Dublin) October 21, 1901, on p 362: October 1903, p 330, quotes from AE's article on W. B. Yeats, from "The New York *Reader*", sgd A.E.: November 1903, p 370, poem sgd A.E., "Connla's Well" (item 21D, p 158) reptd from item 8: April 1904, pp 153–4, "A Dream of Angus Oge", sgd A.E. reptd from item 96, and reptd in item 12. [December 1904, p 406, a note, *The Mask of Apollo* "shortly will be issued by Whaley's."] [Edited by Stephen J. Richardson.]

145

Golden Book Magazine (New York) vol 12 p 34 (December 1930) (item 21D, p 141).

146

The Green Sheaf (London). [See below Part 15, p 236: and item 9.] Number 3 (1903) p 8, poem sgd A.E., "Reconcilement reptd from item 98 (December 1902) reptd in item 21D, p 298:

Number 4 (1903) pp 4–7, "A Dream of Angus Oge", sgd A.E., reptd from item 97, reptd in item 12. [*The Green Sheaf* edited by Pamela Colman Smith.]

147

Ireland (New York) vol 1 No 52 p 11 col 3: (December 30, 1916): a quotation from item 30 p 68 (4 lines up) to p 69. But misquotation *ideals*, where item 30 has *ideas*. Vol 2 No 10 p 9 col 2 (March 10, 1917), text of a "Memorial" sent to the Trustees of the National Gallery, Dublin, by artists all of whom had presented work to the Gallery. The letter concerned Hugh Lane's pictures. The signatories included: Sir John Lavery, George Atkinson, Mary Barton, Max Beerbohm, Mildred A. Butler, D. Y. Cameron, George Clausen, Mark Fisher, Nathaniel Hone, John Hughes, Augustus John, Gerald Kelly, W. J. Leech, Sir William Nicholson, Dermod O'Brien, Sir William Orpen, Sir William Rothenstein, George W. Russell, Charles Shannon, Oliver Sheppard, P. Wilson Steer, Wm. Young, Henry S. Tuke and Jack B. Yeats. [*Ireland* edited by J. C. Walsh and Sir J. A. Shane Leslie.]

148

Irish Citizen (Dublin) vol 1 No 33 p 262 col 3 (January 4, 1913) reprints a letter from Russell to Miss C. Pankhurst, first printed in *The Suffragette* (London).

149

Irish Industrial Journal (Dublin) vol 7 No 155 pp 879–80 (December 21, 1912) quotes from AE's article in item 98 vol 19 (December 14, 1912). The *Irish Industrial Journal* vol 7 pp 765–6 (November 2), pp 813–4 (November 23) had included attacks on the I.A.O.S. and on Russell: their spokesman Mr William Field M.P., was unsympathetic to the co-operative movement. Russell had taxed him with the challenging reproach "amateur economist". He bit back vituperatively.

150

The Irishman (Belfast) vol 1 No 1 p 5 (January 15, 1916): a letter dated Dublin, December 3, 1915, from AE to the editor, A. Newman. [Expressing interest in the new paper, and his hope for impartial presentation of facts. "I find no paper, either Nationalist or Unionist with the slightest interest in telling the truth. They cannot tell the truth either about themselves or their enemies, and as I get older I have lost interest in sentimental causes . . ."]

151

Irish Opinion (Dublin). [Edited by Andrew E. Malone: *new series* edited by Cathal O'Shannon.] Vol 1 No 36 pp 2 and 4 (February 17, 1917) quotation from a leaflet circularised in Dublin advertising a lecture "The Heroes of Gaelic Literature" to be delivered in the Trades' Hall, Capel Street on Monday evening February 19, 1917, for the *Gaelic League*: NS vol 1 No 26 p 274 (May 25, 1918) a brief paragraph in Irish, "A.E. agus Lucht Oibre": NS vol 1 Nos 29, 30, 31, 32, 33 (June 15, 22 and 29, July 6 and 13, 1918) one sentence as page-heading above "Co-operative Notes" on pp 297, 305, 313, 321 and 329, "It is a great adventure, the Building up of a Civilisation," "Our feebleness arises from our economic individualism," "Our task is truly to Democratise civilisation," "We should aim at a Society where people will be at harmony with their economic life": (from item 98 vol 25 pp 493–4 [July 27, 1918]) NS vol 1 No 36 p 352, article "Agricultural Labour and the Land", sgd A.E. (item 98, as "The Problem of Agricultural Labour") (August 3, 1918): NS vol 1 No 52 pp 498 and 502 (November 23, 1918) a letter dated 14th November 1918 to William O'Brien (Secretary of the Irish Labour Party) "On the New Order in Russia". [The *new series* was sub-titled *The Voice of Labour*.]

152

The Irish People (Dublin) November 18, 1899 (a letter to the editor).

153

Irish Review (Dublin) vol 1 p 430 (November 1911) (264): 2, 460 (November 1912) (61): 3, 228 (July 1913) (30).

154

Irish Times (Dublin). Letters printed in the issues dated: January 5, 1905: October 7, 1913 (item 22): December 17, 1917 (reptd in item 28B): December 27, 1917: December 29, 1922 (reptd in the *New York American*, March 4, 1923. This "Open Letter to Irish Republicans" provoked the editor of the *Irish Republican Daily Bulletin* in Dublin, to address an *Open Letter to Mr George Russell* in that paper, December 30, 1922): November 15, December 3, 8, and 13, 1932. [See item 33.]
Also: March 14, 1921 (p 12 col 5) a quotation from item 98 (March 12, 1921).

155

Irish Worker (Dublin). [See item 22B.]

156

Kilkenny Moderator (Kilkenny). [See item 13C.]

157

Leader (Dublin). [See item 11.]

158

Literary Digest (New York) vol 49 p 1022 (November 21, 1914) (236): 56, 37 (February 23, 1918) (see item 32): 67, 38 (October 9, 1920) (354): 81, 36 (April 19, 1924) was reptd in item 100 vol 1 No 5 p 367, also reptd elsewhere: 83, 33 (November 8, 1924) (320): 84, 38 (March 14, 1925) (340): 90, 41 (August 21, 1926) (373): 97, 42 (April 7, 1928) (408): 99, 36 (was reptd from *Living Age* December 15, 1927) (October 27, 1928): 104, 27 (February 15, 1930) (404): 110, 22 (August 22, 1931) (?356): 117, 33 (February 24, 1934) (item 53 p 64).

159

[*Littell's*] *Living Age* (Boston, Mass.) vol 216 p 778 (March 19, 1898) (49): 217, 2 (April 2, 1898) (136): 241, 576 (May 28, 1904) (37): 242, 64 (July 2, 1904) (95): 242, 128 (July 8, 1904) (37): 242, 256 (July 23, 1904) (?117): 242, 640 (September 3, 1904) (266): 260, 450 (February 20, 1909) (86): 260, 642 (March 13, 1909) (124): 260, 658 (May 1, 1909) (124): 272, 130 (January 20, 1912) (?160): 280, 194 (January 24, 1914) (37): 280, 258 (January 31, 1914) (95): 283, 578 (December 5, 1914) (49): 283, 624 (December 12, 1914) (236): 284, 322 (February 6, 1915) (?73 or 11): 284, 578 (March 6, 1915) (75): 285, 2 (April 3, 1915) (136): 285, 258 (May 1, 1915) (192): 286, 322 (August 7, 1915) (22): 286, 386 (August 14, 1915) (128): 286, 770 (September 25, 1915) (21): 288, 258 (January 29, 1916) (146): 288, 450 (February 19, 1916) (3): 288, 642 (March 11, 1916) (150): 289, 2 (April 1, 1916) (97): 289, 322 (May 6, 1916) (?55): 289, 450 (May 20, 1916) (266): 291, 2 (October 7, 1916) (47): 304, 421–7 (February 14, 1920) (see item 37): 319, 238 (November 3, 1923) (348): 324, 444 (February 21, 1925) (?): 324, 572 (March 7, 1925) (?): 326, 670 (September 26, 1925) (337): 327, 464–6 (November 28, 1925) (item 99A, vol 5 pp 176–7): 329, 464–6 (May 29, 1926) (item 99A, vol 6 pp 154–5): 329, 620 (June 19, 1926) (402): 331, 63 (October 1, 1926) (373): 331, 269 (November 1, 1926) (332): 331, 339 (November 15, 1926) (420): 333, 1114–5 (December 15, 1927) (400): 337, 378 (November 15, 1929) (422, 387): 337, 636 (January 15, 1930) (399).

160

London Mercury (London) vol 23 p 599 (April 1931) (item 21D, p 387).

161

Lucifer (London) vol 3 No 16 pp 339–41 (December 15, 1888): vol 3 No 17 pp 437–8 (January 15, 1889): [letters to the editor, H. P. Blavatsky]: both reptd in item 59: vol 16 pp 68–9 (March 15, 1895), a letter dated February 16th 1895, sgd Geo. W. Russell (see also item B 2 p 49).

162

Manchester Guardian (Manchester). [See items 34A and 42A].

163

Nation (New York) vol 117 p 589 (November 23, 1923) "Hunger strike in Ireland".

163A

National Democrat (Dublin). [Edited by F. Sheehy-Skeffington and F. Ryan.] [*Not seen by this compiler.*]

164

Nationality (Dublin). [See item 106A.]

165

Nationist (Dublin). [Edited by T. M. Kettle.] [*Not seen by this compiler.*]

166

New Age (London). [See item 33E.]

167

New Ireland Review (Dublin). [See item 102]: vol 10 p 101 (October 1898) (reptd in item 21D, p 271): vol 10 pp 333–8 (January 1899), review sgd A.E. of *The Cuchullin Saga in Irish Literature* by Eleanor Hull: (1898: Nutt) vol 10 p 165 (November 1898) (reptd in item 21D, p 139).

168

New Republic (New York) vol 44 p 143 (September 20, 1925) (poem "To set that soaring joy": reptd only in *The Best Poems of 1926*, ed. L. A. G. Strong: see below, item 203).

169

Observer (London) July 12, 1931, p 5 cols 3–4. A review sgd "A.E." of *Snow* [poems] by Humbert Wolfe [1885–1940] (London, 1931. Gollancz).

169A

Oriel Review (New York). [See item 59: letters to M. L. Wilson.]

170

Orpheus (London) [formerly *Transactions of the Theosophical Art Circle*, of which issue numbered 2 has not been seen by this compiler]: Nos 6 and 7, pp 29–33 and 53–6 (April and June 1909) reptd AE's article "Art and Literature" from *The Shanachie* (Dublin) vol 1 No 2 pp 102–15 (Winter 1906), again reptd in item 28: No 14, frtspce (April 1911) monochrome repro of painting by AE, and below, his poem "Frolic" (item 21D, p 21) reptd from item 98 vol 12 (Dec 1906) "Celtic Christmas" issue, p 1: No 15, frtspce (opp. p 295) mono repro of AE ptg "Aengus the Harper" (July 1911): No 16, frtspce (opp. p 327) (October 1911), mono photo of AE's painting "Sea-Vision".

170A

Ourselves (Bow, London, E.) [*Editor*, C. H. Collings, F.T.S.; *sub-editor*, Howard H. Birt, F.T.S.] The magazine of the Bow lodge of the Theosophical Society. The honorary secretary of that lodge was Walter H. Box, 108 Tredegar Road, Bow.] In vol 1 No 1 (April 6, 1895) at p 6, "Those from whom we quote", prose signed G.R. which included mention that a short sketch of Epictetus will be published in *Ourselves*, soon.

Vol 1 No 2 (May 4, 1895) pp 13–14, prose "The Great Object of the T.S.", sgd Violet North (later AE's wife): followed by a prose article sgd Sidney G. P. Coryn. Vol 1 No 7 (May 1896) pp 84–5, prose review of *Among the Gnomes* by Franz Hartmann (London, 1896. T. Fisher Unwin), sgd G.R. [This magazine, issued on the first Saturday in each month was later amalgamated with *Crusader* (London).]

171

Overland (New York) [new series] vol 69 p 331 (April 1917) (item 21D, p 47).

172

The Path (Hale, Cheshire: *later* London) vol 1 No 2 pp 22–3 (July 1910) "Content", prose reptd from item 96 vol 4 No 1 pp 15–18 (October 15, 1895), incldg item 21D p 268:

Vol 1 No 4 p 80 (October 1910) review sgd Æ of *The High Deeds of Finn* by T. W. H. Rolleston (London: Harrap):

Vol 1 No 5 pp 81–2 (November 1910) "Comfort", prose sgd R., reptd from item 96 vol 2 No 8 pp 108–10 (May 15, 1894):

Vol 1 No 6 pp 103–4 (December 1910) "The Hour of Twilight", prose reptd from item 96 vol 1 Nos 5 and 6, at pp 45, 57–8 (February 15, March 15, 1893) [with an early photograph of AE, as a vignette]:

Vol 1 No 7 pp 133–4 (January 1911) "At the Dawn of the Kaliyuga" story sgd A.E. (incldg item 21D, pp 157, 151) reptd from item 96 vol 2 No 1 pp 4–6 (October 15, 1893):

Vol 1 No 7 pp 142–4 (January 1911) "Instead of an Editorial", sgd Y.O., abridged from item 98 vol 17 pp 1033–6 (December 17, 1910) "A Christmas Sermon for Rural Cooperators":

Vol 1 No 8 pp 155–7 (February 1911) review sgd Y.O. of *The Christ Myth* by Arthur Drew (London: 1910. T. Fisher Unwin):

Vol 1 No 9 p 173 (March 1911) poem "Over the hill-tops" (reptd in story "A Dream of Angus Oge" in item 12, etc) from item 97 vol 1 No 1 p 11 (October 15, 1897) sgd A.E.:

Vol 1 No 9 pp 175–8 (March 1911) prose "The Secret of Power" reptd from item 96 vol 1 No 8 pp 76–7 (May 15, 1893), sgd A.E.:

Vol 1 No 10 pp 206–7 (April 1911) "Instead of an Editorial", sgd G.W.R., adapted from item 98 vol 18 pp 184–5 (March 11, 1911) "A Good Example for the World Generally":

Vol 2 Nos 1–4 (July–October 1911) pp 30–2, 58–60, 85–8, 117–21, prose "The Element Language", reptd from item 96 (details listed in item 187) sgd G. W. Russell:

Vol 3 No 3 pp 101–3 (September 1912) prose "Instead of an Editorial" reptd from item 98 vol 19 pp 677–8 (August 24, 1912):

Vol 3 No 7 pp 279–80 (January 1913) "On the Labours of the next Prophet", reptd abdgd from "The Labour of the next Prophet" in item 98 vol 19 p 996 (December 7, 1912):

Vol 3 No 10 pp 379–82 (April 1913) "The Village Fifty Years Hence" prose reptd from item 98 vol 20 pp 167–8 (March 1, 1913):

Vol 4 No 2 pp 41–2 (August 1913) poem "Transformations" sgd A.E., "What miracle was it" [probably its first publication: C. A. Weekes asked Russell to write that poem] reptd subsequently in item 21D p 283:

Vol 4 No 11 pp 406–8 (May 1914) "The Excuse for Civilisation", prose from item 98 vol 20 pp 1047–8 (December 20, 1913):

Vol 4 No 12 pp 455–7 (June 1914) "Are Economic Forces Non-moral" reptd from item 98 vol 21 pp 344–5 (May 2, 1914).

173

Pearson's Magazine (New York) [see items 41A and 113.]

174

The Pioneer (Dublin) vol 1 No 2 pp 75–6 (March 1911) review sgd G.W.R. of [Sir] Norman Angell [Lane]'s *The Great Illusion* (London: 1910. Heinemann) as "Peace or War?". In *After All. The Autobiography of Sir Norman Angell* (London: 1951. Hamish Hamilton) he notes the confusion into which his accumulated correspondence had been thrown by bomb-damage in the 1939 war. Sir Norman Angell advised this compiler that he has no trace of any letters from AE: he corresponded with and met so many people then his memory has blurred. [*The Pioneer* edited by James H. Cousins, P. L. Pielou, F. Sheehy Skeffington, and others as a board.]

175

Poet Lore (Boston, Mass.) vol 16 No 4 pp 83–6 (December 1905) (item 21D, pp ?129, 117 and 273).

176

Quarterly Review (London) vol 266 p 310 (April 1936) (item ?53 p 88).

176A

The Quest (London) vol 2 No 1 pp 161–2 (October 1910) poem "The City" later reptd in *Irish Review*, and in item 21D, p 30. [Editor, G. R. S. Mead.] Rev of item 21 in vol 5 No 4 pp 799–800 (July 1914) sgd. See Mead's unsgd reviews of: item 35 (vol 10 No 2 pp 273–5, Jan 1919): item 43 (vol 14 No 4 pp 563–7, July 1923): item 45 (vol 17 No 1 p 137, Oct 1925) he refers to his continuing friendship with AE.

177

The Reader (New York). [See items 13, 28, and 198.] Vol 2 No 3 p 216 (August 1903) editorial note quoting AE's poems "Forgiveness" and "A Woman's Voice" (item 21D, pp 67, 68): vol 2 No 3 pp 249–50 essay "The Poetry of William Butler Yeats" sgd A.E. [Reptd in items 13, 28.] also quoted in item 144: Vol 3 No 3 pp 230–3 (February 1904) editorial note gives a brief biography of AE (p 231 repro a drawing of him by J. B. Yeats the Elder) quotes 2 stanzas from poem "Love" (item 21D, p 153) and the "Epilogue" to item 10 (item 21D, p 293): also quotes from an AE letter a message for W. B. Yeats (then lecturing there); AE has read some Yeats poems in a Sligo village, exciting the community with them so much that the community donated £7 towards a fund to buy books for a new library. Russell had frequently advocated support for the *Rural Libraries' Association*. Finally on p 233 AE's poem "The Silence of Love" (item 21D, p 117).

177A

Reedy's Mirror (St Louis, Missouri). Issue dated February 4, 1904: poem signed AE, first printed in item 10, p 36. Reptd in item 21, p 117.

178

The Round Table (London). [See item 109.]

179

Samhain (Dublin). [See item 13B.]

180

Saturday Review of Literature (New York). [See item 57, pp 174–8]: vol 4 p 605 (February 18, 1928) ("Deepness of earth") (item 21D, p 421).

181

Scholastic (Pittsburgh) vol 27 p 8 (September 28, 1935) (?162): vol 31 p 23 (October 16, 1937) (2, 358 and 304).

182

Sewanee Review (Sewanee, Tenn.) vol 15 p 158 (April 1907) (47): 15, 161 (April 1907) (124).

183

The Shanachie (Dublin). [See item 28]: vol 1 pp 75–6 (item 21D, pp 64, 35), (Winter 1906).

184

Sinn Fein (Dublin). [See items 28, 83, 106, 107.] Poem in issue November 14, 1908, sgd Æ (item 21D, p 229).

184A

Speaker (London). [Lady Gregory referred to contribs by AE, *circa* 1898. Not yet identified by this compiler.]

185

The Suffragette (London) vol 1 No 11 p 162 col 3 (December 27, 1912): a letter reptd in *The Irish Citizen.*

186

Sufi Quarterly (Geneva). [Edited by Ronald A. L. Mumtaz Armstrong]: vol 5 No 4 pp 190–1 poem "Krishna" sgd A.E. (item 21D, pp 61–2), with an interesting edit *Foreword* to that poem, quoting a recent AE letter. Vol 7 No 4 pp 226–30, editorial article, introducing ref to item 50: quotes AE's *Preface* to item 21: repts item 48 p 14 (item 21D, p 384) from item 50 p 97: followed by poem "The Heroes" at pp 230–2 (item 21D, pp 79–81: from item 50 pp 88–9). Vol 7 No 4 p 259 (March 1932) poem sgd A.E. "The Vesture of the Soul" (item 21D, p 89).

187

The Theosophist (Adyar, Madras: and Bombay) [Edited by H. P. Blavatsky] vol 9 No 99, pp 171–6 (December 1887). Prose, "The Speech of the Gods", sgd C. Johnston, F.T.S. [and] Geo. Russell. The copy of that magazine once owned by "Seumas O'Sullivan" (Dr J. S. Starkey) was probably given to him by AE. That copy is now owned by The Lilly Library, Indiana University, Bloomington. Corrections marked almost certainly by AE: p 172 (6 lines up) a marginal letter *N*, perhaps implying "new paragraph": although unnecessary. P 173 (21 up), *for* cancelled: corrected to: "as in *far*),". P 173 (17 up), *five* cancelled: corrected to: "the *fire* elements". P 174 (6 up), punctuation corrected: "light of the sky", [inverted commas displaced]. P 175 (12 down), "in Pak, to *comb*, and Pik,". P 175 (16 up), *combination* cancelled: *continuation* inserted. P 175 (14 up), *late* corrected to *lake*. P 175

(12 up), *Gea* corrected to *Gel.* P 175 (5 up), *Cuk* corrected to *Luk.*

[Russell alone re-wrote this article as "The Element Language", for publication in the *Irish Theosophist*: vol 1 pp 78–9, 89–90, 104–5, 117–18, 125–7 (May, June, July, August, and September 15, 1893). They were reprinted in *The Path* (Hale), see above. In an early letter to C. C. Rea he expounded similar linguistic theories. See also *The Candle of Vision*, chapter 14, pp 120–7, "The Language of the Gods".]

The Theosophist (Adyar) vol 56 No 9 p 266 (June 1935) reprints from *Collected Poems*, p 35.

187A

Theosophy in Ireland (Dublin). Several poems by AE reptd from *Collected Poems* during the decade 1950–9.

188

The Times (London) [see items 23A, 27]. September 2, 1920, p 11 (item 21D, p 354). May 13, 1915, prose "Sun and Wu", not reptd (facts corrected by another correspondent, May 25). August 23, 1920 (letter protesting at the destruction of Irish creameries). March 28, 1921 (letter: "Irish Finance"). April 2, 1921 ("Irish Finance" second letter). [*Note*: The sonnet addressed to Terence MacSwiney, Lord Mayor of Cork (Sept 2, 1920). A ms copy of it is now in the National Library of Ireland, (Ms 7392) captioned "Brixton". At the foot of the page Russell noted: "Daniel Corkery wrote to me about this as MacSwiney's true friend. Terence sent me a message from his prison after reading it."]

188A

The Times Literary Supplement (London). March 31, 1921 (letter, concerning Hugh Lane's testamentary intentions). May 19, 1921 (letter, "On the Quality of Sound" in verse).

189

Ulad (Belfast) vol 1 No 2 p 8 (February 1905) "A Prayer", sgd A.E. (item 21D, p 187).

190

The Ulsterman (Belfast). Vol 1 No 4 p 30 (July 1933), two sentences quoted from item 30.

191

United Irishman (Dublin). [See items 13B, 28.] A poem "Ireland (July 21st 1903)", comment on King Edward VII's "forthcoming visit to Dublin", printed in the issue dated July 18, 1903.

192

The Vâhan (London). [See item B 2 p 49.]

192A

Vox Studentium (Geneva) vol 3 No 3 pp 11–12 (January 1926) unsgd prose quotn from unsgd note in item 99A vol 5 p 326 col 2 and p 327 col 1 (November 21, 1925) "Education in the Free State".

192B

The Watchword and Voice of Labour (Dublin) vol 1 No 47 (new series) p 1 columns 3–4 and p 3 col 2 (August 21, 1920): reprinted AE's editorial leader from the previous week's *Irish Homestead*, captioned "Whom the Gods wish to destroy".

192C

The Worker (Dublin). This compiler has only seen vol 1 Nos 3, 4, and 5 (Saturdays, January 9, 16, and 30, 1915) in which there were no contributions from AE.

192D

192C *World Theosophy* (Hollywood) vol 1 No 1 pp 74–5 (1931) reported an interview with AE by Gladys Baker, originally printed in the *News-Age-Herald* (Birmingham, Alabama).

193

Yale Review (New Haven, Conn.) vol 18 (ns), pp 28–30 (September 1928), poems reptd in item 21D, pp 376, 400, and 418.

PART 9

OTHER BOOKS CONTAINING ARTICLES IN VERSE OR PROSE BY AE

194

[Anonymous editor] *An Ulster Garland* (Belfast: 1928. The Hospital for Sick Children), p 9 AE's poem reptd in item 21D, p 418: illustrated with a wood-cut by John F. Hunter.

195

A Treasury of Irish Poetry compiled by Stopford A. Brooke and T. W. H. Rolleston (London: 1900. Smith, Elder. 2nd ed, 1905) in which A.E. wrote the note on William Larminie, pp 476–7. AE poems at pp 487 *et seq*. Reptd in item 21D, at pp 54, 37, 47, 129, 197, 194, 46, 141, and 124.

196

Let Labour Lead. A May-Day Manifesto by the Dublin United Trades' Council and Labour League (Dublin: May 1, 1918) [18.3 × 12.1 cm], to which A.E. contributed some notes: p 4 (at top), quotn, source not given: "It requires great intellectual and moral qualities to bring about a great revolution. A rage at present conditions is not enough.": p 5 the prose note sgd "A.E.", "Labour's own cause is the highest": p 11 (at top) another quotation in prose, by AE, source not given, "The ideal Labour should set before itself is not a transitory improvement in its wage, because a wage war never truly or permanently improves the position of Labour." A copy of this pamphlet is in the Colby College Library, at Waterville. The note on p 5 was written by AE at Wm. O'Brien's request.

197

William J. Maloney, *The Forged Casement Diaries* (Dublin: 1936. Talbot Press). Quotations from some letters written by AE, at pp 24, 227, and 250. They are presumed by the Director of the National Library of Ireland to be among the Maloney papers bequeathed to the Library during the 1930's, still under seal. [The Casement diaries were released for public inspection in the Public Record Office, London, from August 10, 1959. Newspaper reports by scholars offering various opinions as to the likelihood of interpolations, were printed in *Sunday Times* (London) August 16, 1959, and the *Irish Times*, August 14, *etc.*]

198

Irish Literature: Selections in Prose and Verse, editorial Board under chairmanship of Justin M'cCarthy, M.P. (Chicago and Philadelphia: 1904. De Bower Elliott Co.: *and* John D. Morris and Company), 10 vols. Vol 5 p 1866, a quotation from AE's article on William Larminie, first printed in *A Treasury of Irish Poetry*, by Brooke and Rolleston [see above]. Vol 7 pp 2737–40, "Standish O'Grady", sgd A.E. reptd from *The Reader* (New York). Vol 8 pp 2989–95, reprints "Nationality and Imperialism" from item 62. Vol 4 pp 2996–3004, reprints poems by A.E., subsequently reptd in item 21D at pp: 139, 218, 23, 106, 54, 37, 47, 129, 158, 194, 46, 141, 124, 3, 9. Vol 9 pp 3651–3, reptd AE's article on W. B. Yeats, first printed in *The Reader* (New York), and subsequently reptd in item 28. [See also *Portraits of A.E.* No 5.] AE was a Member of the Editorial and Advisory Board.

199

The Cabinet of Irish Literature selected and edited by Charles A. Read revised edition edited by Katharine Tynan Hinkson (London: 1902–3. Gresham Publishing Co. 4 vols). AE poems in vol 4, pp 260–1 subsequently reptd in item 21D, pp 23, 106, 139, 218.

200

The Portable Irish Reader, compiled by Diarmuid Russell (New York: 1946, 1956. Viking Press) reptd poems by AE at pp 667 and 669 (from item 21D, pp 303, 320). For prose reptd from AE, see item 30.

201

The Best Poems of 1924, selected by L. A. G. Strong (Boston, Mass.: 1924. Small, Maynard & Co.) poems by AE: p 3, reptd from item 99A, vol 1 p 75 (September 29, 1923) reptd in item 21D, p 348. And p 4, reptd from 99A, vol 2 p 9 (March 15, 1924), omitted from all collections.

202

The Best Poems of 1925, selected by L. A. G. Strong (Boston: 1925. Small, Maynard & Co.) poems by AE: pp 1–2, reptd from item 99A, vol 2 p 521 (July 5, 1924), reptd in item 21D, pp 311, 303.

203

The Best Poems of 1926, selected by L. A. G. Strong (New York: 1926. Dodd, Mead & Co.) pp 1–2, reptd from *New Republic* (New York) vol 44 p 143 (September 20, 1925), omitted from all collections.

204

The Best Poems of 1927, selected by L. A. G. Strong (New York: 1927, Dodd, Mead & Co.) pp 15–16, reptd from item 99A, vol 7 p 617 (March 5, 1927), reptd in item 21D, pp 377–8. And p 17, reptd from item 99A, vol 6 p 514 (July 17, 1927), reptd in item 21D, p 373.

205

Wayfarer's Love, chosen by Millicent Fanny S. Leveson Gower, the Duchess of Sutherland (Westminster: 1904. Archibald Constable). AE's poem, from item 21D, p 120. [The Duchess of Sutherland died 1955, aged 88.]

206

Roger Casement, by Geoffrey de C. Parmiter (London: 1936. Arthur Barker). Perhaps AE drafted the letter to Herbert Asquith which was printed at pp 349–50?

207

Sri Aurobindo Came to Me, by Dilip Kumar Roy (Pondicherry, India: 1952. Sri Aurobindo Ashram) includes a letter to the author, dated January 6, 1932, from AE at pp 91–8, with commentary on it by Sri Aurobindo Ghose (1872–1950). [Mr Roy trans (? Bengali) "in an Indian journal," item 21D, p 61.]

208

The Five Hundred Best English Letters chosen and edited by the First Earl of Birkenhead [F. E. Smith (1872–1930)] (1931. Cassell) pp 902–3: without addressee's name printed a letter to C. A. Weekes [December 6, 1926], in which AE commented on item 21D, pp 195, 312, and 320. The letter is in item 59.

209

The Golden Book of Tagore edited by Ramananda Chatterjee (Calcutta: 1931. The Golden Book Committee). P 221, poem "First Love" ("What treasure would I not have poured") sgd A.E. (George Russell). AE wrote to Sir William Rothenstein ["Friday": ?mid-May 1931]: ". . . I have not written a line since [*Vale*]. I hunted through my manuscripts and found a lyric which somehow escaped my memory when I was making up *Vale* and I send it to you to forward to your Indian correspondent. Will you tell him I was out of Ireland, and his letter about the *Golden Book* never reached me . . . I wish I had something first class to send as I have a great admiration for Tagore whom I never met . . . if the verses are suitable send them on. If not put them in [the] waste paper basket . . ." AE's poem had been printed in item 99A, vol 14 p 67 (March 29, 1930) sgd O.L.S. Reprinted in item 100 vol 7 No 2 p 1 (April 1932). Reptd in item 53 p 69. [Issued to commemorate Rabindra Nath Tagore's 70th birthday.]

PART 10

INSTITUTIONAL COLLECTIONS OF LETTERS FROM AE, MANUSCRIPTS, AND COLLECTIONS OF ASSOCIATION COPIES OF HIS OWN BOOKS, OR OF RARE PAMPHLETS BY AE

Armagh. The County Museum, The Mall, Armagh. Letters to: Charles A. Weekes, Caroline Clements Rea (*later* Mrs R. E. Coates): Susan L. Mitchell: Dermod and Mabel O'Brien: A. de Blacam, and others. A notebook with poems written by Susan Mitchell, illustrated by AE, with water-colors. Another notebook containing poems by AE, written out for Susan Mitchell by AE. An early notebook containing the outline of a play, etc, by AE. Some of his drawings, and some rare pamphlets.

Buffalo. The Lockwood Memorial Library, The University of Buffalo, New York. Letters to C. M. Grieve ("Hugh MacDiarmid"), etc. Some letters to Oliver St J. Gogarty, and others.

Cambridge. The Houghton Library, and the Widener Library, Harvard University, Cambridge, Mass. Letters to T. B. Mosher, George Roberts, and others. Some rare pamphlets, and letters concerning the Irish National Theatre Society in Dublin.

Dublin. The National Library of Ireland, Kildare Street, Dublin. Letters to R. I. Best, S. L. Gwynn, E. MacLysaght, Maurice Moore, Joseph O'Neill, Sarah Purser, and others. Some rare pamphlets, mss poems by AE, etc.

Dublin. Department of Manuscripts, Trinity College, Dublin. Letters to Edward Dowden, Joseph King, M.P. Some rare pamphlets and periodicals.

Indiana. The Lilly Library, University of Indiana, Bloomington. Through the courtesy of the Librarian the list of holdings of letters from and to AE were listed for this book. The collection includes about 100 books with autograph inscriptions from their authors to AE (many from the late J. S. Starkey's collection). One of the most extensive AE collections in existence.

MANUSCRIPTS DIVISION

(Letters from and to AE in the collections)

Letters from AE

To Sinclair, Upton Beall, Oct 2, 1914
To Solomons, Edwin M., Sept 17, 1932; June 1, Aug 9, 11, 15, 16, 17, 18, 24, Oct 3, 1933; Jan 16, 1934 (all copies)
To Starkey, James Sullivan, June 2, 1905; July 12, 1932

Letters to AE from

Bax, Sir Arnold Edward Trevor, one undated letter
Bax, Clifford, one undated letter
Blunt, Wilfrid Scawen, July 18, 1902
Brooks, Van Wyck, Jan 8, 1932
Buckton, Alice Mary, May 24, 1921, and one undated letter
Bullock, Shan F., Jan 13, 1923, and 3 undated letters
Campbell, M. W., Jan 5, 1931
Campbell, Richard, May 5 and June 18, 1930
Childers, Erskine, Feb 28, 1920, and one undated letter
Clarke, Austin, 4 undated letters
Colum, Mrs Mary (Maguire), [1922]
Colum, Padraic, [1906], Apr 28, 1908; Jan 1, 1918; Apr 14, 1930; Apr 3, 1933
Curtis, Edmund, Apr 16, 1930
Donald, Sir Robert, June 27, 1912
Duke, Sir Henry Edward, July 11, 1917
Figgis, Darrell, Dec 26, 1913
Flower, Robin, Apr 1, 1924, and Jan 24, 1929
Fremantle, Mrs Anne (Jackson), one undated letter
Gibbon, Monk, June 7, 10 (postcard), 1926; Apr 14, 1930; Dec 1931
Gregory, Isabella Augusta (Persse) Lady, 3 undated letters and one undated card
Grieve, Christopher Murray, Oct 6, 1931

Guthrie, James Joshua, Apr 12, 1906
Hackett, Helen, Nov 27, 1929
Hargrove, Constance, one undated letter
Hart, Charlotte I., one undated letter
Higgins, Frederick Robert, Apr 14, 1930
Hinkson, Mrs Katharine (Tynan), June 6, 1915
Hunt, B., one undated letter
Jefferies, Bertha Starr, Jan 13, 1933
Johnston, John, Dec 14, 1918
Koenig, Mrs Eleanor Constance (Sheehan), Apr 14, 1930
Little, Philip Francis, one undated letter
Lowenfels, Walter, Jan 6, 1933
Lytton, V. A. G. R. Bulwer-Lytton, 2nd Earl of, Jan 1, 1903
McDonagh, Thomas, Aug 23, 1907
MacKenna, Stephen, Jan, [May 8], 1909; [1913]; Oct, Dec, 1932; [1932] (2 letters); and 4 undated letters
Mathew, Frank, Oct 23, 1915
Milligan, Alice, one undated letter
Moore, George, 1906, and one undated letter
Mumford, Lewis, Nov 9, 1926
Nevinson, Henry Woodd, May 5, 1930
O'Grady, Standish, 189–; May 2, 1916; and 3 undated letters
Olds, Leland, July 11, 1930
Oliver, Frederick Scott, Apr 16, 1912
Phibbs, Geoffrey, one undated letter
Prokosch, Frederic, Nov 21, 1931; [1931]; Sept 7, 1932
Pryse, James Morgan, Feb 19, 1925
Rowe, Charles J., Apr 29, 1930
Rumsey, Mrs Mary (Harriman), July 23, 1928 (2 letters); June 12, 1930; and one undated letter
Sharp, Mrs Elizabeth A., Dec 25, [1905]
Sharp, William, June 17, 1899; [1899]; June 15, 1900; and 2 undated letters, one of them being enclosed with Sharp, Mrs Elizabeth A. to AE, Dec 25, [1905]
Shaw, Mrs Charlotte Frances (Payne-Townshend), Oct 6, 1921
Sitwell, Edith, Apr 2, 1932
Stephens, James, July 28, Oct 1, 1913; Feb 19, 1914; July 19, 1915

Strong, Leonard Alfred George, May 31, 1927
Tobias, Matthew, June 1, 1905
Trench, Herbert, Mar 27, 1923
Waddell, Helen Jane, Apr 9, 1930
Warren, Mrs Maude Lavinia (Radford), one undated letter
Wells, James Ray, Dec 10 and 14, 1929
Wilson, Robert Noble Denison, Nov 19, 1927
Yeats, William Butler, Feb 8, [1889]; [?1889]; [Nov 15 and Nov ?, 1891]; 2 letters, [1897]; Jan 12, 22, Feb 8 and Mar 27, [1898]; (2 letters) [?1898]; [Mar 6 and Aug 27, Nov 1899]; [May, 1900]; Oct 18, [1902]; [1902]; Feb 21, May 14, [June 17, July 2, 17], Dec 18, 1903; [?1903]; Apr 8, 1904; [Apr], Jan 3, [8], Aug 3, 7, Sept 3, 7, 17, 19, 1906; (2 letters) [?1906]; [Apr], June 28, [1919]; Jan 12, Mar 14, 29, July 1, [1921]; [1921]; Mar 30, [?1922]; Apr 13, [1930]; Oct 29, [1931]; [1932]; and 2 undated letters
Zimand, Savel, Apr 29, 1930

Some of the Yeats letters have been published in *The Letters of W. B. Yeats, ed. by Allan Wade* (London, 1954. Rupert Hart-Davis). Some of the Yeats letters also appear in "Some passages from the letters of W. B. Yeats to AE" *Dublin Magazine* vol 14 No 3 pp 9–21 (July–Sept 1939).

Two letters from Stephen MacKenna to Russell, [1913] and [?1932] are published in *Journal and Letters of Stephen MacKenna, ed. with a memoir by E. R. Dodds . . .* (New York, [1937]: Morrow), pp 137–9 and pp 301–3.

OTHER AE MANUSCRIPTS IN THE LILLY LIBRARY

Theosophical Diary, July 18, 1895, to July 27, 1896. [pp 33]

The Interpreters (1922). Holograph ms of Chapter 10 [pp 7], and typescript of the entire book [pp 147].

Voices of the Stones (1925). Folder i, with title "The Grey Stones" [pp 38]. Folder ii, typescript with holograph revisions [pp 62]. Folder iii, Printer's copy, typescript [pp 61]. Folder iv, Printer's copy, carbons [pp 13].

The Sunset of Fantasy (?1930). With notes for lectures for an American tour. Typescript with holograph revisions. [pp 37].

The *Foreword* to item 87, above [pp 3].

A Note on Seumas O'Sullivan (1932?) [pp 3]. Probably the *Introduction* to item 84 above.

Review [pp 2] of *The City Without Walls* by Margaret Cushing Osgood (Nov 1932: Cape).

Songs and their Fountains (1932). Holograph ms, [pp 115]. Typescript carbon of holograph ms, [pp 115]. Holograph ms of later draft of chapter xiv [pp 5]. Typescript carbon of holograph ms of later draft of chapter xiv [pp 5].

The Avatars (1933). Holograph ms, [pp 132]. Partial typescript [pp 7]. Typescript printed as chapters i–xi, [pp 68]. Typescript, printer's copy [pp 180]. Typescript carbon, printer's copy [pp 177].

Black Jesus [not dated]. Typescript [pp 8].

Enid [n.d.]. Holograph [pp 76].

On a True Foundation for a Rural Community [n.d.]. Holograph [pp 2].

Sunset of Fantasy [n.d.]. A fragment, holograph and typescript [pp 22].

Two poems on one leaf of paper [n.d.].

Ulster and Irish Trade Policy [n.d.]. [pp 6].

Four *Sketch-books* [n.d.]. [pp 458].

Kansas. University of Kansas, Lawrence. Library of the late P. S. O'Hegarty.

London. The British Museum Library, Department of Manuscripts. Letters from AE to A. J. Balfour (and valuable correspondence between Horace Plunkett and Balfour), and Bernard Shaw. The Department of Printed Books includes a useful selection from AE's rare pamphlets: and his own copy of *Gods of War*, besides a complete file of the *Irish Theosophist* and *The Internationalist*.

London. The Plunkett Foundation for Co-operative Studies Library. Letters to Horace Plunkett from AE, and a carbon copy of the letter to David Lloyd-George. Plunkett's personal diaries (as yet unpublished), with a typed transcript of selection made by the Secretary, Miss M. Digby, O.B.E., for reference during composition of her biography of Plunkett. The library includes an almost perfect set of the *Irish Homestead* and the *Irish Statesman.*

London. Theosophical Society in Gt Britain, 50 Gloucester Place, W.1. Rare theosophical periodicals.

New York. The H. W. and A. A. Berg Collection, New York Public Library, Fifth Avenue and 42nd Street, New York 18. Letters from AE to John Quinn, and some rare AE pamphlets.

Oxford. The Bodleian Library. Rare AE pamphlets.

Texas. The University of Texas Library, Austin, Texas. The J. M. Hone collection.

Washington, D.C. The Library of Congress. In 1939 AE's younger son Mr Diarmuid C. Russell presented to the Library of Congress a notebook through which AE had written in pencil drafts of poems, many as yet unpublished. [Permission to scrutinise this notebook, or to order a photographic copy, must be obtained from Mr D. C. Russell. Permission yet to be granted to this compiler.]

Waterville, Maine. The Library, Colby College, Waterville, Maine. The James A. Healy collection: mss, letters, pamphlets and books by Irish writers. The AE holdings were listed by Dr Carlin T. Kindilien in the *Colby Library Quarterly*, series 4 No 2 (May 1955). Among the letters are many to the late Judge Richard Campbell and E. A. Boyd: others to James Stephens, W. B. Yeats, Wm. Byrne ("Wm. Dara"). Additionally Mr D. C. Russell informed this compiler he gave a collection of AE letters and copy letters to the Library at Colby College "several years ago". He could not recall either their extent, condition, or any other details. Prompted by Oliver St J. Gogarty the children of the late Mrs Mary Harriman Rumsey also gave some sketches and letters to that Library. Access to the collection, or permission to purchase copies is granted solely to "Colby Scholars."

Yale University Library, New Haven, Conn. Some AE letters, to J. C. Squire, W. L. Phelps, Mary Sutliffe, and mss of some AE poems, etc.

PART II

PUBLIC SALES INCLUDING MANUSCRIPTS, LETTERS OR VALUABLE ASSOCIATION COPIES OF AE's BOOKS

The John Quinn Library Sale. New York, Anderson Galleries, 1923–4. The AE items numbered 8312–8381 in the printed *Catalogue* were sold on Weds., February 13, 1924. Included, ms of items 12, 35 and 37 in this book. And inscribed copies of items: 12 (with page proofs), 14 (with poem, item 21D, p 275) inscribed by AE on fly-leaf), 19, 35, 37, 42, 44. Also copies of items: 3, 4, 11, 22, 24, 24A, 32, 33, 35, 36, 39, 41, 108. Priced *Catalogue* in British Museum Library and National Library of Ireland.

On Monday, November 11, 1935, books "The Property of the late Dr G. W. Russell ("AE")" were sold at Messrs Sotheby & Co's auction rooms, London, "by order of his executor". *Catalogue* pp 3–4 lots 12–26.

Lot 12 R. W. Emerson, *The Conduct of Life*. 1st ed. Boston: 1860. Ticknor.

13 O. St J. Gogarty, *Wild Apples*, with Preface by W. B. Yeats; and with pencil portrait of the author by G. W. Russell, signed "Geo. W. Russell, A.E.", and "Oliver St. J. Gogarty". Dublin: 1930. The Cuala Press. Original boards. Lady Gregory, *Gods and Fighting Men*. Original cloth. 1904.

14 F. R. Higgins, *Arable Holdings*. Limited edition. Dublin: 1933. Cuala Press. Orig. boards. "Seumas O'Sullivan", *Twenty-five Lyrics*, 1933. Austin Clarke, *Pilgrimage*, 1929, *The Bright Temptation*, 1932. Padraic Colum, *Wild Earth*, 1907. First editions. And 63 others, mostly signed presentation copies.

15 [G. W. Russell] *Some Irish Essays*, 1906. *The Renewal of*

Youth, 1911. *Michael*, 1919. F. R. Higgins, *Island Blood*, 1925. All first editions; and others.

16 G. B. Shaw, *Back to Methuselah*, 1921. First edition. Presentation copy inscribed by the author on half-title, and with G. W. Russell's signature on fly-leaf. Orig. cloth.

17 P. B. Shelley, *Poems*, 1880. Orig. cloth. Signatures of Aneurin Williams [1859–January 20, 1924. A friend of Horace Plunkett: first editor of *Co-partnership* (London), author of *Co-partnership and Profit-sharing* (London: 1913. O.U.P.) originator, with his article on a Society of Nations, in the *Contemporary Review* (London), October 1914, of the concept of the League of Nations.], Ralph Hodgson (the poet), and G. W. Russell. A. E. Housman's *Last Poems* (1922) inscribed and signed by H. W. Nevinson. Orig. cloth.

18 James Stephens, *Insurrections*, Dublin: 1909. Maunsel. Orig. quarter-cloth. Presentation copy to the dedicatee inscribed "To AE a Master from J. Stephens an Apprentice. May 1909".

19 James Stephens, *The Hill of Vision*, Dublin: 1912. Maunsel. 1st ed. presentation copy inscribed: "AE from James Stephens Feb xii –,".

20 James Stephens, *The Crock of Gold*, 1st edition inscribed: To Æ from James Stephens 3rd October 1912. Orig. cloth.

21 James Stephens, *The Insurrection in Dublin*, presentation copy inscribed by the author, 1916. *Reincarnations* with 5-line inscription from Stephens to AE, 1918. Both first editions; orig. cloth.

22 James Stephens, *Deirdre*. Inscribed: With love and thanks to my dear Æ. Had he not been where would this book be. James Stephens Sep 1923. Orig. cloth.

23 James Stephens, *In the Land of Youth*, presentation copy inscribed and signed by the author, 1924. *Etched in Moonlight*, inscribed: George Russell. Dear Æ this is not my latest, but my last. Tis rather depressing, and need not be read. This is but a gesture from me to a better man. James Stephens, 1928. *Strict Joy*, inscribed: Dear Æ: Here is another book, and my love. James Stephens, 1931. All first editions; orig. cloth.

24 W. B. Yeats: [The presentation copies are inscribed and, all

except one, signed by the author; the others bear the signature of G. W. Russell on the fly-leaf.] *The Wanderings of Oisin*, 1889. *The Secret Rose*, prestn. copy, 1897. *The Wind Among the Reeds*, prestn. copy, 1899. *The Shadowy Waters*, prestn. 1900. *The Celtic Twilight*, prestn. copy, 1902. *In the Seven Woods*, Dundrum, 1903. *Poems, 1899–1905*, prestn. copy, 1906. *Responsibilities*, 1916. *Reveries over Childhood and Youth*, 1916. *Per Amica Silentia Lunae*, 1918. *Later Poems*, 1922. *Plays and Controversies*, 1923. *Essays*, 1924. *Early Poems and Stories*, 1925. *Autobiographies*, 1926. *The Tower*, 1928. *The Winding Stair*, prestn. copy, 1933.

25 Geoffrey Chaucer, *The Works*. Edited by T. Speght [Black Letter], 1687, wanting frontispiece. Calf.

26 Plotinus, *The Enneads*, translated from the Greek by Stephen MacKenna. 5 vols. Limited edition. Orig. boards. 1917, etc. Signature of George Russell on fly-leaf of vols 1 and 4; presentation inscriptions from the translator in vols 2, 3, and 5—on inside upper front cover. [One of these inscribed vols was owned in 1954 by Mrs Sophie Jacobs, of London.]

The 1935 sale lots were bought as follows: lot 12, 13, 14, 15, 22, 25, and 26 bought by 'Goodfellow', prices: £1, £5, £7, £4 10s., £11, £3 10s., £5 5s. [Probably bought by Miss K. Goodfellow, a witness to AE's last Will. Pseudonym: "Michael Scot".]

Lots 16–19, and 21 and 23 were bought by Walter Hill of Chicago (since deceased, and the business discontinued). Prices, £9, £5 5s., £14 10s., £5 10s., £9, £14 10s.

Lot 10 was bought by the Ulysses Bookshop (Mr Jacob Schwartz, of Brighton), for £24.

Lot 24 was bought by Messrs Pickering & Chatto of London, for £32.

[AE's son gave several of AE's books to Dr Hector Munro. Among them H. P. Blavatsky's *The Secret Doctrine* (Los Angeles: 1925. Theosophical Publishing Co.) was heavily scored throughout in crayon, apparently by AE. That copy is now owned by Mrs William Sitwell. Mrs Sitwell also owns AE's copy of Mabel Collins' *Idyll of the White Lotus*, and *The Chaldean Oracles of Zoroaster* (see Part 8), Mrs Pamela Travers (London) owns other books once AE's property.]

On Tuesday, April 9, 1957, letters, manuscript, etc, the property of Mrs George Roberts, sold at Messrs Sotheby & Co's auction rooms, London. *Catalogue*, lots 445, 446, 447 included AE items. The other lots from the papers of the late George Roberts 448–58 inclusive, were mainly letters concerning the Abbey Theatre.

Lot 445 Irish National Theatre Society. Draft of the *Rules* of the Society, in AE's handwriting; 7 leaves quarto. The printed *Rules* [item 60 in this *Bibliography*]. Statement of the aims of the Society [wrappers], 1903. Notes taken by G. Roberts at meetings of the Reading Committee, June 29, 1904, to October 29, 1905; his notes for the A.G.M., May 25, 1906. The mailing list of the Society. [Purchased for £40 by Mr I. Kyrle Fletcher. Now owned by the Theater Collection, The Houghton Library, Harvard University.]

446 Programs of performances of the Irish National Theatre Society, including program of the first performance of W. B. Yeats' *Kathleen ni Houlihan*, with AE's *Deirdre*, in the hall of St Teresa's Total Abstinence Association, Dublin, on April 2, 1902. [Fletcher, £48. Houghton Library.]

447 Five autograph letters signed from AE to George Roberts including the letter resigning from the I.N.T.S. (not dated). Letters to Roberts from Thomas MacDonagh (2), J. M. Hone (8), and other letters from Edward Martyn, J. S. Starkey, W. G. Fay, Gavan Duffy, Thomas Kettle, Harry Clarke, Maire Walker, and others. [Fletcher, £22. Houghton Library.]

448, 449, 450–3 all purchased by Mr Fletcher (letters from Lady Gregory, Miss A. E. F. Horniman, W. B. Yeats, etc). Other papers stored in a Dublin warehouse since about 1924 were sold after Roberts' death, by the warehouse proprietor: Roberts had not paid their rent for storage. His widow learned of those papers after the trunks had been displayed on the Dublin quays, and combed by Dublin's book-collectors.

On Monday, December 8, 1958, printed books and manuscripts "from the Library of the late Seumas O'Sullivan" were sold at auction by Messrs Christie, Manson & Woods, Ltd., London.

Lot 243 A.E., *Collected Poems*. Presentation copy inscribed to

Seumas O'Sullivan, dated 1913; with autograph letter signed, to O'Sullivan, corrected proof and typescript of two poems by AE. A.l.s. from W. B. Yeats to AE, thanking him for the above book which "has brought back many memories", referring to the dedication and discussing Irish matters: 4 pages. [£22 bought by Myers & Co., for a private client.]

244 A.E., *Enchantment*, with ink inscription on t/p and 5 typed letters from the book's publisher in New York, 1930. *Vale*, 1931. *Song and its Fountains* presentation inscription to O'Sullivan and his wife, Mrs J. S. Starkey, and containing 7 original colored crayon drawings by AE in the text, 1932. *The House of the Titans*, presentation inscription to O'Sullivan and a.l.s. to him declaring this to be his last book, 1934. *Selected Poems*, inscribed to O'Sullivan by AE's younger son, Diarmuid Russell, 1935; with 2 a.l.s. from AE, and 3 holograph mss poems, a corrected proof of a poem, and a photograph all loosely inserted. The proofs probably from item 100. [£30. Myers & Co., London.]

245 A.E., *Homeward, Songs by the Way*, 1st ed., 1894. With author's signature on t/p. The same, 2nd ed, 1895, with author's note inserted. Another ed, with mss poem in AE's handwriting on title; Portland Maine. *The Earth Breath*, 1897. *Ideals in Ireland*, 1901. *The Divine Vision*, 1903; presentation inscription from AE to O'Sullivan. *The Mask of Apollo*, 1904, with a.l.s. from AE to Starkey (pp 2), and typed letter inserted. *Enchantment*, 1930. And 3 others by AE; in all, 11 vols in original bindings. (In *Enchantment* 5 original mss poems in AE's hand, and a letter from AE to O'Sullivan.) [£29. Dr Jacob Schwartz, of Brighton.]

246 A.E., *Ideals in Ireland*, with a.l.s. AE to J. Starkey and corrected proof of poems from item 100. *The Interpreters*, presentation inscription to O'Sullivan, with 2 a.l.s. to him and typescript of 3 poems with corrections in AE's writing, loosely inserted. *Vale*, inscribed by AE "For Seumas O'Sullivan I have dedicated these songs"; New York, 1931. *Vale* contained 15 colored crayon drawings by AE. [£18. Mr Frank Hollings of London. Subsequently sold in America—probably to the University of Texas.]

247 A.E., *Gods of War*, 1915. *Imaginations and Reveries*, 1915. *The National Being*, 1916. *The Candle of Vision*, 1918. Inscribed by AE to O'Sullivan. *The Interpreters*, 1923 with a small crayon drawing on the t/p by AE and loosely inserted is a corrected proof of AE's poem printed in item 100 (vol 1 p 367), "Sackville Street, 1917", and a typescript of an unpublished poem "Artists and Ecclesiastics" (perhaps prompted by Russell's controversial correspondence in the *Irish Times*, 1932). Also orig. holograph ms of "The Honourable Enid Majoribanks, M.P.," (pp 37). All in orig. bindings. [£38. Mr F. Hollings; subsequently sold in America.]

248 A.E., *The Nuts of Knowledge*, 1903; *blue morocco, gilt edges*, Dun Emer Press: another copy in original boards. *The Earth Breath*, 1897; orig. boards. *Midsummer Eve*, 1928; orig. boards. Six pamphlets [not listed in *Catalogue*] and 2 others also by AE; with corrected proof of "The House of the Titans", with letter handwritten by AE presenting the proof to O'Sullivan, and four other a.l.s. AE to him, and an original ms poem and a typescript, and a copy of Part 12B CLXII. [£38. Mr F. Hollings; subsequently sold in America.]

250 G. B. Shaw, *Man and Superman*, 1903; *John Bull's Other Island*, 1907: both first editions, cloth bound, with Russell's signature on [?] fly-leaf. Inserted is a long typed letter sgd by Shaw, to AE, referring to politics, dated 1921; and an autograph postcard from Shaw to AE (1917). James Joyce, *Ulysses*, 1922; wrappers, bound-in. [£12. Maggs Bros., London. Purchased on commission for a private customer.]

261 W. B. Yeats, *The Celtic Twilight*, 1st ed, 1893. Inscribed: George Russell from W. B. Yeats December 1893. Contains a few small corrections in ink, by Yeats. [£38. Myers & Co., London.]

263 W. B. Yeats, *Four Years*, 1921. *Early Memories*, 1923. *Estrangement*, 1926. Orig. boards, Cuala Press. Russell's signature on fly-leaf of *Early Memories*. [£6. Messrs Quaritch, London.]

264 W. B. Yeats, *The Hour Glass and Kathleen ni Houlihan*, 1904; orig. half-boards. Inscribed by Yeats on fly-leaf: George

Russell from his friend the writer, March 1904. [£34. Myers & Co., London.]

266 W. B. Yeats, *The King's Threshold and On Baile's Strand*, 1904: orig. half-boards. Inscribed by Yeats on the fly-leaf: W. B. Yeats from W. B. Yeats March 1904. Russell struck out Yeats' name and substituted his own as recipient. [£36. Myers.]

267 W. B. Yeats, *Michael Robartes and the Dancer*, 1920. *Further Letters of John Butler Yeats*, selected by Lennox Robinson, 1920: orig. boards. Russell's signature on fly-leaf of both books. [£4. Mr Francis Edwards, 83 Marylebone High St, W1.]

269 W. B. Yeats, *Poems*, 1895: orig. cloth gilt (loose). Inscribed: To my friend George Russell on August 26th 1895, W. B. Yeats. [£75. Myers.]

275 W. B. Yeats, *Stories of Michael Robartes and his Friends*, 1931. Inscribed to Seumas O'Sullivan by Russell. [With 3 other Yeats books, not inscribed.] [£8. Mr F. Hollings.]

276 W. B. Yeats, *Stories of Michael Robartes and his Friends*, 1931. Pasted on end-paper is an inscription: To George Russell from W. B. Yeats, Feb. 8th., 1932. [AE's wife had died on February 3, 1932.] [£11. Mr F. Hollings.]

277 W. B. Yeats, *Stories of Red Hanrahan*, 1904: Dun Emer Press. Inscribed on first blank leaf: To Violet Russell with the thanks of the printers 1905. *Discoveries*, 1907. *Poetry and Ireland* (with Lionel Johnson), 1908. [£6. Mr F. Hollings.]

278 *Twenty-one Poems by Lionel Johnson*, selected by W. B. Yeats, 1904: Dun Emer Press. Inscribed on fly-leaf: To Violet Russell with the gratitude of the printer of Dun Emer, Feb. 21st 1905. [With 3 others.] [£10. Private buyer, "Dean."]

279 W. B. Yeats, *Where there is Nothing*, New York 1903. Inscribed: To George Russell from his friend the writer May 1903. [£28. Myers.]

280 *Some Passages from the Letters of AE to W. B. Yeats*, 1936: and 3 other Cuala Press books. [£8. Messrs Quaritch, London.]

285 William Blake, *The Book of Thel* and *America a Prophecy:* 2 vols, engraved throughout. Brown paper wrappers. Both

vols inscribed by W. B. Yeats to Russell, dated November 9th 1891. W. B. Yeats' autograph signature and address at April 1891 inside the front cover of both volumes. [£18. Mr Frank Hollings.]

The remainder (and bulkier portion) of Dr Starkey's library was (1) bequeathed to the Library of Trinity College Dublin (Wesleyan Methodist hymn-books) and (2) bought by Messrs Elkin Mathews Ltd of Bishop's Stortford. From (2) copies inscribed by AE to Starkey included items numbered in this list of AE's writings: 9C (inscribed to "Constance Markiewicz 'Lavarcam', with the kind regards of the author [sgd] 13.12.07"), 40B, 41, 36, 70 (with a letter, 1905 "I can at last declare a dividend on *New Songs*: O'Donoghue has given me a bill for £10." Enclosing three cheques, each £1. 5s., for O'Sullivan, Keohler, and Roberts), 20 (with a small text correction by AE); but not inscribed), item 187 (with 8 corrections pencilled-in by AE). Additionally copies of items: 7, 7A, 34, 34A, 11, 19, 24, 3, 27 (50 copies), 4, 69B, 44, 37, 13, 33A, 22, 23, 51, 67: and 3 letters to Seumas O'Sullivan (1905, 1925, 1935). Copies of: Standish O'Grady's *The Coming of Cuculain* (1894. Methuen) with AE's signature and notes; signed presentation copy O'Grady to AE of *The Departure of Dermot* (Dublin: 1917. Talbot Press); John B. Yeats' *Letters to his son W. B. Yeats* (1944. Faber) with 2 autograph letters signed from J. B. Yeats to AE (New York, 1912–13) and one letter to Starkey concerning a portrait of AE; a collection of Jack B. Yeats' plays etc, including *The Scourge of the Guelph* (1901. Elkin Mathews) inscribed by author to George Russell, Dec 1903; with the Jack Yeats' collection was a copy of item 7C; item 61 inscribed Hermetic Society Dublin; Arthur Kingsley Porter's *The Crosses and Culture of Ireland* (New Haven: 1931. Yale University Press) with AE's signature. These were bought variously by: Sir Geoffrey Keynes; The Huntington Library; the Newberry Library; the Houghton Library, Harvard University; the Lockwood Memorial Library, University of Buffalo; and others to Mr Feldmann; The House of Books (New York); and the majority to the Indiana University Library, Bloomington at the instigation of Professor David A. Randall. Five pages (quarto) notes of AE's conversation (1905) written down by Seumas O'Sullivan included criticism of Yeats' *The Shadowy Waters* (Harvard). This compiler sadly learned too late about the sale, and arrived in time only to purchase W. B. Yeats' selection from Blake's *Poems* (1893. Lawrence & Bullen) inscribed by AE "To Violet (Alter Ego) from George, Xmas 96".

On Thursday, February 25, 1960, at Messrs Hodgson & Co.'s auction rooms, London: lot 168. 19 autograph letters, and 7 typed letters signed from AE to E. H. W. Meyerstein (1889–September 1952), and one a.l.s. "to Mrs Pilkington"; comprising 37 closely written pages in fragile condition, and 8½ pages typed. Purchased for immediate re-sale, probably to an American institutional collection, by the expert London dealer Frank Hollings (Mr A. Miller), for £65. The underbidder was Mr Bertram Rota.

On Thursday, March 24, 1960, at Messrs Hodgson & Co.'s auction rooms, London: "The Library of Miss Helen Waddell, sold by order of the Official Solicitor". Lot 200 comprised books by AE: item 49A inscribed on fly-leaf "To dear Helen A.E.". Item 49 inscribed on fly-leaf "For Helen Waddell | The verses you liked are | in this book. May I give | it to you in memory of | a delightful afternoon. | AE". Item 52 inscribed on title-page "For Helen Waddell | from A.E. 4/10/33" and with a sketch of a mountain, in colored crayon and ink also on t/p and signed Geo. W. Russell "AE", and loosely inserted (not cataloged) a brief covering letter, undated, from AE at 41 Sussex Gardens, enclosing *The Avatars*. Item 53 inscribed on fly-leaf "For | Dear Helen | from | AE". Item 54 inscribed on fly-leaf to O[tto]K[ylmann] from AE's younger son Diarmuid Russell. This compiler bid up to £6. The lot was eventually bought by the London dealer Mr M. H. Mushlin, 123 New Bond Street, London, W.1, at the remarkable price—commercially daring—of £17 10s.

In an undated and unnumbered *Catalogue of First Editions, association copies, autograph letters and manuscripts* circulated to clients by House of Books Ltd (18 East 60th Street, New York 22) in the Spring, 1960, AE items as follows were offered for sale. Item 1 (this list item 2) presentation copy from the publisher, \$35.00; item 2 (21) AE's inscription to Seumas O'Sullivan, \$25.00; item 3 (48) inscribed "For Seumas O'Sullivan in memory of a long friendship. A.E." (with 5 letters from the publisher, James R. Wells, to AE), \$45.00; item 4 (49) with a snapshot laid-in, on rear, "AE at croquet Grange Ho Sept. 1931" (Starkey's home), \$20.00; 5 (54) inscribed on front end-paper to Seumas O'Sullivan from Diarmuid Russell, with 2 a.l.s. from AE to O'Sullivan, March 16 and March 31, 1935 (3 pp quarto) "regarding his illness, expects he will be all right in a month's time. Mentions that he is working on a volume of selected poems and the books from which he is making the selection. Asks for various dates, etc, as his own books are crated." $35.00; item 6, poem 99 lines "Wood Magic" in ink, sgd at top with corrections, deletions etc, $30.00; item 7 poem "A Mountain Tarn" 18 lines in ink sgd at end, $25.00: item 8 poem "Eros" typescript 12 lines, corrected in ink, sgd at end, $25.00; item 9 poem "Dawn Magic" proof of 15-line poem, corrections in ink (in title *Dawn* crossed out, etc), $17.50; item 10, untitled mss poem "Not in *Collected Poems*", 9 lines in ink, unsigned, $20.00; item 479, W. B. Yeats' *The Celtic Twilight* (London, 1893) inscribed to George Russell and dated same month as publication, some corrections in Yeats' hand on seven pages, (? *which*) $175.00; item 480, W. B. Yeats' *Poems* (London, 1895) inscribed "To my friend George Russell on August 26th, 1895. W. B. Yeats" (the book was not published until October), $225.00; item 485, W. B. Yeats' *Where there is Nothing* (New York, 1903) first American public edition, inscribed on front end-paper "George Russell from his friend the writer May 1903"—enclosed in half-morocco slip-case, $85.00; item 486 W. B. Yeats' *The Hour Glass* (London, 1904) inscribed "George Russell from his friend the writer March 1904", $75.00; item 48, W. B. Yeats' *The King's Threshold, and On Baile's Strand* (London, 1904) inscribed in error "W. B. Yeats from W. B. Yeats, March 1904" with AE's correction, having crossed out author's name in the inscription and substituted his own, Geo. W. Russell, $115.00; item 489, a.l.s. from W. B. Yeats to G. W. Russell, from Coole Park, October 21 [no year] "probably 1913, reference to AE's *Collected Poems*", 3½ pages 8vo (about 275 words), "My dear Russell... You and I are alike in one thing that we must always have a 'household' . . . a party, though neither you or I will have anything to do with the sort of party that founds itself on 'principles' . . . I have little to say of the poems I have not said years ago and the old favourites remain undisturbed. I think our common vocabulary has suffered much from the collapse of the romantic movement. The mischief is that I can no longer endure in your work any of the fine things I once loved . . .", $75.00.

PART 12A

BOOKS KNOWN TO AE IN HIS YOUTH. A SELECTION

I Arnold, Edwin. *Indian Idylls.* 1883, Trübner.

II —— *The Light of Asia.* 53rd edition, 1889, Trübner. [Book 8 p 234: compare with AE item 21D, p 377.]

III —— *The Song Celestial.* 7th ed, 1885, Trübner.

IV Arnold, Matthew. *Early Poems. Narrative Poems, etc.* 1885, Macmillan.

V —— *Literature and Dogma.* 1883, Smith Elder. [Popular ed, 2/6.]

VI —— *Lyric and Elegiac Poems.* 1885, Macmillan.

VII Bellamy, Edward. *Looking Backward: 2000–1887. A Romance.* 17th ed, [1889], W. Reeves.

VIII Besant, Annie. *The Case Against W. Q. Judge.* 1895, Annie Besant, publisher.

IX —— *Why I Became a Theosophist.* 1889, Freethought Publg Co.

X *The Bible, authorised version.* [In a letter to C. C. Rea, probably written in early October 1887, Russell wrote: "Read the *New Testament*, the *Psalms*, *Job* and the Prophets: leave *Genesis* alone, at least as far as believing it goes."]

XI Blake, William. *Poems.* 1885, Walter Scott [1/–].

XII Blavatsky, Helena Petrovna. *Isis Unveiled*, in 2 vols. New York, 2nd ed, 1877, J. W. Bouton.

XIII —— *The Secret Doctrine.* Los Angeles, 1888. New ed, 1939, Theosophy Co.

XIV —— *The Voice of the Silence and other Chosen fragments from the Book of the Golden Precepts.* Translated and annotated by "H.P.B." New York, 1893: *The Path.* London, 1893, Theosophical Publg Co. [One copy seen by this compiler was inscribed: "James Stephens from his friend Æ". Below that inscription, and impressed in purple wax the diphthong pseudonym, surrounded by a laurel wreath. That seal was designed, and made in gold, by Lord

Dunsany, as a gift to Russell. Stephens' copy (pp 108) was bound in limp red leather.]

XV Boehme, Jacob. *Forty Questions*. 1891, Kegan Paul.

XVI [——] *His Life and Teaching*, by H. L. Mortensen. 1891, Hodder.

XVII [——] *Jacob Behmen, an appreciation*, by A. Whyte. 1890.

XVIII Browning, Elizabeth Barrett. *Poems*. 1887, Routledge. [1/–].

XIX Browning, Robert. *Selected Poetical Works. Series 1 and 2*. 1884, Smith, Elder. [3/6].

XX Carpenter, Edward. *Towards Democracy*. [2nd ed] Manchester, 1885, John Heywood.

XXI *Chaldæan Oracles* [of Zoroaster]. Edited and revised by Sapere Aude. 1895, Theosophical Publishing Society. [AE. marked his own copy at numbers: 80, 84, 85, 88, 103, 107, 111, 129, 150, 152, 155, 157–9, 160, 164–5, 172–4, 176, 179, 180–5, 187, 198–9, and pp 53–4.]

XXII Collins, Mabel [Mrs Keningale Cook]. *Idyll of the White Lotus* [n.d.] George Redway, publisher. [Another edition: 1884. G. Reeves.]

XXIII Curry, Eugene [*afterwards* O'Curry]. *On the manners and customs of the ancient Irish. A series of lectures* . . . Edited, with an Introduction, appendices, etc, by W. K. Sullivan. 3 vols London and Edinburgh, 1873, Williams and Norgate.

XXIV Dante. Translated by Henry Wadsworth Longfellow: *The Divine Comedy*. [Morley's Universal Library]. 1885, Routledge. [1/–].

XXV Darwin, Charles Robert. *Descent of Man and Selection in Relation to Sex*. New ed, 1887, John Murray. [7/6].

XXVI —— *The Origin of Species by Natural Selection*. New ed, 1888, John Murray. [6/–].

XXVII De Quincey, Thomas. *Confessions of an English Opium-eater*. 1883, Routledge. [6d.]

XXVIII Emerson, Ralph Waldo. *Conduct of Life*. 1886, Ward, Lock. [3d. or 6d.]

XXIX —— *Essays*. 1886, Ward, Lock. [3d. or 6d.]

XXX —— *Poems*, with prefatory notice by Walter Lewis. 1885, Walter Scott. [1/–].

XXXI —— *Select Writings*. Introduction by Percival Chubb. 1888, W. Scott. [1/–].

XXXII Epictetus. *Enchiridion*, with notes by T. W. H. Rolleston. 1881, Kegan Paul. [3/6].

XXXIII Epictetus *Teaching*, *Enchiridion*, *Dissertations*, *etc*. 1888, W. Scott. [1/–].

XXXIV FitzGerald, Edward. *The Rubáiyát of Omar Khayyám*.[Various editions published during the decade 1880–90 by Quaritch.]

XXXV Gore, Charles [1853–1932], *and others*. *Lux Mundi. Studies in the Religion of the Incarnation*. 1889, John Murray.

XXXVI Haeckel, Ernst Heinrich Philipp August. *The History of Creation*. 4th ed, translated from the 8th German edition by E. Ray Lankester. 1892, Kegan Paul.

XXXVII Hartmann, F. *The Life and Doctrines of Jacob Boehme*. 1891.

XXXVIII Higgins, Godfrey [1773–1833]. *Anacalypsis, an attempt to draw aside the veil of the Saïtic Isis; or an Inquiry into the origin of languages, nations and religions*. 1836. 2 vols, Longmans.

XXXIX Ibsen, Henrik. *Pillars of Society, and other plays* [including *The Doll's House*] trans. and edited by Havelock Ellis. 1888, Walter Scott. [1/–].

XL Johnston, Charles. *The Awakening to the Self. Translated from the Sankara Acharya*. New York, 1897.

XLI —— *From the Upanishads*. [Translations]. Dublin, 1896, Whaley. [The copy presented by Johnston to his Mother is inscribed with date "Xmas 1895". The book has a long dedicatory letter addressed to Russell.]

XLII —— *Useful Sanskrit Nouns and Verbs in English Letters*. 1892, Luzac & Co.

XLIII Keats, John. *Poetical Works*, ed Wm. T. Arnold. 1888, Kegan Paul.

XLIV Landor, Walter Savage. *Imaginary Conversations*. Introduction by Havelock Ellis. 1886, Walter Scott. [1/–].

XLV *Lucifer* (London), 1887–97. Continued as *The Theosophical Review*, 1897–1909, edited by Annie Besant and G. R. S. Mead.

XLVI Marcus Aurelius Antoninus. *Meditations*, translated by Jeremy Collier. 1887, Walter Scott. [1/–].

XLVII Mead, George Robert Stow. *Thrice-Greatest Hermes*. 3 vols. 1906, Theosophical Publishing Co.

XLVIII —— [*editor*] *The Vâhan. A Vehicle for the Interchange of Theosophical Opinions*. (London), 1891–[1900].

XLIX —— *and* Jagadîshâ Chandra Chattopahyâya. *The Upanishads*, [translated]. 2 vols. 1896, Theosophical Publg Co.

L Morris, William. *Earthly Paradise*. 1886, Reeves and Turner.

LI Müller, Friedrich Max. [editor, and in part translator of] the *Sacred Books of the East* (31 vols), 1881–9, O.U.P.

LII Neander, Johann August Wilhelm. [*General*] *History of the Christian Religion and Church*. Trans from the German by Torrey and Morrison, 1850–8, Bohn's Library.

LIII Niemand, Jasper [*pseudonym of* Mrs Julia Wharton Lewis Ver-Planck (*née* Campbell)]. *The Vow of Poverty and Other Essays*: various editions. [Reptd, 1904, Thomas Green, publr.] [See reference by AE in a letter to Mrs Constance Sitwell in item 59 (June 17, 1935).]

LIV O'Grady, Standish James. *History of Ireland. Vol 1: Heroic Period. Vol 2: Cuculain and his Contemporaries*. 1878, 1880, Sampson, Low.

LV —— *The Flight of the Eagle*. 1897, Lawrence and Bullen.

LVI Plato. *Crito, Phaedo and Protagoras*. 1888, G. Bell.

LVII —— *Crito and Phaedo*. 1888, Cassell.

LVIII *Apology and Crito*. ed W. Wagner. 1887, G. Bell.

LIX —— *Easy Selections*, ed A. Sidgwick. 1888, Rivingtons.

LX Scott, Sir Walter. *Ingoldsby Legends*. 1885, Ward, Lock.

LXI —— *Scottish Minstrelsy*. 1885, Ward, Lock.

LXII Shakespeare, William. The *Albion* edition (?). 1881, Warne. [3/6]. [But AE's friend the late Osborn Bergin, wrote to this compiler in 1950: "I found him weak as regards Shakespeare . . . I lent him Raleigh's book on Shakespeare, which he read twice, and after that I think he really began to study Shakespeare . . ." (March 17, 1950).]

LXIII Shelley, Percy Bysshe. *Early Poems*. 1888, Routledge. [1/–].

LXIV Spencer, Herbert. *Education: Intellectual, Moral and Physical*. New ed, 1883, Williams and Norgate. [2/6].

LXV Swinburne, Algernon Charles. *Selected Poems*. 1887, Chatto.

LXVI Tennyson, Alfred. *Poems*. 2 vols, 1883, Kegan Paul. [12/–].

LXVII Thoreau, Henry David. *Walden*, with an Introduction by Will H. Dircks. 1886, Walter Scott. [The Camelot Classics series: 1/–].

LXVIII Tyndall, John [1820–93]. *Fragments of Science for Unscientific People*. 1st ed, 1871. Augmented 6th ed, in 2 vols, 1879.

LXIX Walker, Edward Dwight. *Reincarnation: A Study of Forgotten Truth*. 1888, Ward Lock.

LXX Ward, Mrs Humphry [Mary Augusta Arnold]. *Robert Elsmere*. 1888, Smith, Elder. [In this novel Mrs Ward expressed her belief in the social implications of Christianity having more relevance to current problems than mere musing upon the miraculous. Mrs Ward was an active opponent of women's franchise.]

LXXI Whitman, Walt. *Democratic Vistas.* 1888, Walter Scott. [Camelot Classics: 1/–].

LXXII —— *Leaves of Grass.* [Selection from] ed Ernest Rhys. 1886, Walter Scott. [Camelot Classics: 1/–].

LXXIII Wordsworth, William. *Selected Poems.* 1885, Ward, Lock.

LXXIV Yeats, William Butler. *The Celtic Twilight.* 1893, Lawrence and Bullen. [AE was characterised in chapter 3 as "A Visionary". In a letter written during February 1894 to Elkin Mathews (quoted in a booksellers catalog—the letter lost), Charles Weekes wrote his opinion of that characterisation, "Not exactly a true one". Although Yeats did not name Russell he printed on page 21, in full, a poem subsequently reprinted by AE in item 2 p 20. AE, pp 17–25.]

Note—Russell was Librarian in the Dublin lodge of the Theosophical Society during the decade 1890–9. He may have had leisure and opportunity to read many obscure theosophical books. That lodge's *Catalogue* has not yet been located by this compiler. Russell was observed throughout life as a voracious reader. For leisure he read thrillers.

See below, books by W. Q. Judge, F. S. Oliver, and A. P. Sinnett.

PART 12B

BIOGRAPHICAL AND CRITICAL ALLUSIONS TO AE AND TO SOME AMONG HIS ASSOCIATES AND CONTEMPORARIES

LXXV Amery, Leopold C. M. S. *My Political Life. Volume 1: 1896–1914*. 1953, Hutchinson. [AE: p 398].

LXXVI Anderson, Robert Andrew. *With Horace Plunkett in Ireland*. 1935, Macmillan.

LXXVII Andrews, Charles Freer. "An evening with AE" in *Visva-Bharati Quarterly* (Calcutta, and Santiniketan, Bengal) new series, vol 1 part 2 pp 91–2 (August 1935).

LXXVIII Bantock, Raymond. *Thoughts for the Year*, an 8-page pamphlet (18.1 × 11.6 cm) privately printed and circulated as a Christmas card in 1934. The 37th (of 38) "Thoughts" was a remark made to Mr Bantock by AE: "Sin is anything which limits you".

LXXIX Bax, Arnold Edgar Trevor. *Farewell my Youth*. 1943, Longmans, Green.

LXXX Bax, Clifford. *Inland Far*. 1925, Heinemann.

LXXXI —— *Ideas and People*. 1936, Lovat Dickson. [AE: pp 231–40].

LXXXII —— *Rosemary, For Remembrance*. 1948, Frederick Muller.

LXXXIII —— *Some I Knew Well*. 1951, Phoenix House. [AE: pp 77–96].

LXXXIV Beasley, Pieras [*or* Piers]. *Michael Collins and the Making of the New Ireland*. 1927, Harrap.

LXXXV —— *Michael Collins, Soldier and Statesman*. Dublin and Cork, 1937, Talbot Press.

LXXXVI Becker, M. L. "Reader's Guide: Visit to Dublin", in *Saturday Review of Literature* (New York) vol 4 p 587 (February 11, 1928). Reprinted in [A] *Outlook* (New York) vol 148 p 256 (February 15, 1928).

LXXXVII Besant, Annie. *An Autobiography, With an additional survey of her life by George S. Arundale*. Adyar, Madras, 1939, Theosophical Publishing House.

LXXXVIII Bhattacharyya, Mohinimohan. In the *Calcutta Review* (Calcutta) vol 56 pp 257–70 (September 1935).

LXXXIX Biens, Friedrich. [*See* Part 15: 1934.]

XC Binyon, Laurence. "Tradition and re-action" in *Modern Poetry*. April 1926: p 15.

XCI Birmingham, George A. [*pseudonym* of Rev. J. O. Hannay]. "The Literary Movement in Ireland", in *Fortnightly Review* (London) vol 82 pp 947–57 (1907).

XCII —— *Pleasant Places*. 1934, Heinemann. [AE: p 172].

XCIII —— *General John Regan* [a novel]. 1913, Hodder and Stoughton. [Plot told to Hannay by AE, and to St. J. Ervine—play *William John Mawhinney* revised as *Ballyfarland's Festival*.]

XCIV Blavatsky, H. P. *The Letters of H. P. Blavatsky to A. P Sinnett, etc.*, ed. *A. T. Barker*. 1925, T. Fisher Unwin.

XCV —— *The Collected Writings*, edited by her nephew Mr Boris de Zirkoff. Los Angeles, 1950 [—in progress]: Philosophical Society.

XCVI Bodkin, Thomas. *Hugh Lane and his Pictures*. 1932. Revised edition. Dublin, 1956, Stationery Office.

XCVII —— *and* O'Hegarty, P. S. "A.E. or Æ" in *The Times Literary Supplement* (London), January 4, 1936: p 15.

XCVIII Bonn, Moritz Julius. *Die englische Kolonisation in Irland*. 2 vols. Stuttgart and Berlin, 1906: Cotta.

XCIX —— translated by T. W. H. Rolleston. *Modern Ireland and her Agrarian Problem*. Dublin, 1906: Hodges, Figgis.

C —— *Wandering Scholar*. New York [1948]: John Day. London, 1949: Cohen and West.

CI Bose, Abinash Chandra. *Three Mystic Poets: Yeats, AE, and Tagore*, Kolhapur, 1945.

CII Bowen, Gilman Beamish ["Pat"]. "Æ: Theosophist", in *Canadian Theosophist* (Hamilton, Ontario) vol 16 No 6 p 162 (August 15, 1935).

CIII —— In *The Aryan Path* (Bombay) vol 6 No 12 pp 722–6.

XIV Boyd, Ernest Augustine. *Ireland's Literary Renaissance*. Dublin, 1916: Maunsel. *Second ed.*: New York, 1922.

CV —— *Appreciations and Depreciations*. Dublin, 1917: Talbot Press. New York, 1918: John Lane. [Reprints "AE, mystic and economist" from the *North American Review* (Boston, Mass.) August 1915: pp 251–61.]

CVI —— *Portraits, Real and Imaginary*. New York, 1924: Doubleday, Doran. [AE: reprinted from *Dial* (New York) vol 66 pp 31–3 (January 11, 1919).]

CVII Bragdon, Claude [born 1866]. *Merely Players*. New York, 1929: Knopf.

CVIII —— "Footnote on Æ" in *Dial* (New York) vol 86 pp 575–8 (July 1929).

CIX Bramsbäck, Birgit [*formerly* Bjersby]. *James Stephens: a Literary and Bibliographical Study*. Upsala (Lundequistska); Dublin (Hodges, Figgis); Cambridge, Mass. (Harvard University Press): 1959.

CX Brooks, Sydney [1872–1937]. A "Pen Portrait" of AE in *The Irish Booklover* (London) vol 4 No 1 p 20 (August 1912).

CXI —— *Aspects of the Irish Question*. Dublin, 1912: Maunsel.

CXII *Canadian Theosophist* (Hamilton, Ont.) vol 16 No 6 (August 15, 1935). That issue contains memorial tributes to AE, from G. B. Bowen, James M. Pryse, and others.

CXIII Carty, James [died 1959]. *Bibliography of Irish History: vol 1, 1870–1911*. Dublin, 1940: Stationery Office.

CXIV —— *Bibliography of Irish History: vol 2, 1912–1921*. Dublin, 1936: Stationery Office.

CXV *Catholic Bulletin* (Dublin), ed Fr. Timothy Corcoran, S.J. (1872–1943). Vol 17 Nos 5 and 6 (May, June 1927): vol 18 No 10 pp 988–9 (October 1928) [an attack on James Joyce, Yeats, and AE]: vol 20 No 5 pp 424–6 (May 1930): vol 20 No 10 pp 907–11 (October 1930): vol 22 No 1 pp 4–5 (January 1932): vol 22 No 5 p 322 (May 1932), from which this sentence indicates the general level of Dr Corcoran's taste (Plunkett had died on March 26, 1932), "The double spirit of malicious mouthing that was so characteristic of the defunct *Irish Statesman*, the spirit of Russell and of Plunkett, of Yeats and O'Flaherty, manifests itself against the general character of the Irish people on our Irish land." [*James*, chapter 3 verse 10. *ii Corinthians*, 13, 8. *Matthew*, 6, 23–24. *Matthew*, 5, vv 22 and 37. *Matthew*, 10, 12. Evidently the learned Father had forgotten the merciful spirit informing scripture: he was a celibate priest.]

CXVI Chaturvedi, Benarsidas *and* Sykes, Marjorie. *Charles Freer Andrews*. (*Foreword* by M. K. Gandhi). 1949, Allen and Unwin.

CXVII Churchill, Winston Spencer. *The World Crisis*. 5 vols 1923–31, Thornton Butterworth.

CXVIII Clarkson, Jesse Dunsmore [born 1895]. *Labor and Nationalism in Ireland*. New York, 1925: Columbia University Press.

CXIX Clyde, William McCallum. *A.E.* Edinburgh, 1935 : The Moray Press. [Reprinted from item 100 vol 10 No 3 pp 8–30 (July 1935), with an added *Foreword* by "Seumas O'Sullivan".] An attempt at critical assessment which seemed to this compiler to serve mainly as an expression of Mr Clyde's failure to appreciate Mr T. S. Eliot's poetry.

CXX Coates, *Mrs* Caroline Clements [*née* Rea]. "Some Passages from the Early Letters of AE", in item 100 vol 15 Nos 1 and 2 (January and April, 1940) pp 9–15 and 14–24. Partly reptd in item 59.

CXXI —— *Some Less-known Chapters in the Life of A.E. (George Russell).* [A lecture delivered in Belfast during November 1936]. Duplicated on 14 foolscap sheets (one side only). [A] The same text, privately printed by Alex Thom & Co., in Dublin: pp 11. [Copies of both texts are in the County Museum, Armagh.]

CXXII Collis, Robert. *The Silver Fleece: an Autobiography.* 1936, Nelson. [An extremely interesting account of AE: pp 263–72.]

CXXIII Colum, Mary Catherine Maguire. "Æ" in the *Saturday Review of Literature* (New York) vol 12 pp 11–12 (July 27, 1935).

XCCIV —— *From these Roots*, London and New York, 1937: Scribners.

CXXV —— *Life and the Dream.* 1947, Macmillan.

CXXVI Colum, Padraic, and Colum, Mary. *Our Friend James Joyce.* 1959. Gollancz.

CXXVII —— "Poet's Impression of A.E." in *World Review* (Chicago, and Mount Morris, Ill.) vol 6 p 117 (March 19, 1928).

CXXVIII —— "Æ and his Poetry" in *New Republic* (New York) vol 87 p 23 (May 13, 1936).

CXXIX —— "Faith and Works of Æ" in *New Republic* (New York) vol 94 pp 228–9 (March 30, 1938): a review of item 57 and of *A Memoir of . . . AE* by 'John Eglinton'.

CXXX —— [A lecture delivered to the University of Miami during 1936: unpublished. Mr Colum kindly permitted this compiler to copy the text of that lecture.]

CXXXI —— "Darrell Figgis" in item 100 vol 14 No 2 (April 1939). [A] Item 100 vol 24 No 4 pp 11–17 (October 1949) and vol 25 No 1 pp 18–25 (January 1950) "Early Days of the Irish Theatre". [B] "Arthur Lynch" in item 100 vol 19 No 3 pp 10–14 (July 1944). [C] "Tom Kettle" in item

100 vol 24 No 3 pp 28–35 (July 1949). [D] "James Stephens as a prose Artist" in item 100 vol 26 No 3 pp 38–46 (July 1951).

CXXXII —— *Arthur Griffith* [a biography]. Dublin, 1959: Browne and Nolan.

CXXXIII A commemorative article in *Consumer's Co-operation* (New York) vol 21 pp 159–60 (September 1935).

CXXXIV Cousins, James Henry Sproull. "AE: poet of the spirit" in *The Theosophist* (Adyar) vol 56 No 12 p 596 (September 1935).

CXXXV —— *and* Cousins, Margaret E. *We Two Together*. Madras, 1950: Ganesh & Co.

CXXXVI Cronin, Alice Beatrice *and* Horsley, Sydney Eleanour. *The Irish Collection of Books and Paintings at the University of Wisconsin*, Madison, Wisc., 1915: The University.

CXXXVII Cumberland, Gerald [*pseudonym of* Charles F. Kenyon, 1879–1926]. *Written in Friendship*. New York, 1924: Brentano's.

CXXXVIII Cummins, Geraldine. *E. Œ. Somerville: a Biography*. 1952, Andrew Dakers.

CXXXIX Curran, Constantine Peter. In *Studies* (Dublin) vol 24 pp 366–78 (September 1935).

CXL —— [His *Memoirs*, awaiting publication.]

CXLI Curtis, Edmund [1881–1943]. *A History of Ireland*. 6th ed, 1950: Methuen.

CXLII Davidson, D. "Two Views of the World State, Æ and H. G. Wells", in *American Review* (New York) vol 7 pp 225–48 (June 1936).

CXLIII Davison, Edward Lewis [b. 1898]. *Some Modern Poets*. London and New York, 1928: Harper Bros. ["Three Irish Poets", Yeats, AE and Stephens, at pp 173–96.]

CXLIV de Blacam, Aodh [*or* Hugh]. "Æ" in the *Catholic World* (New York), vol 142 pp 99–101 (October 1935). Also printed [A] in *Irish Monthly* (Dublin) September 1935: and [B] in *Modern Review* (Calcutta) vol 58 p 688 (December 1935).

CXLV —— "Talks with AE" in *Irish Bookman* (Dublin, and Tralee) vol 1 pp 13–19 (February 1947).

CXLVI de Lury, Alfred Tennyson. In the *Canadian Theosophist* (Hamilton, Ont.) vol 16 No 6 p 167 (August 15, 1935).

CXLVII Desmond, Shaw. *The Drama of Sinn Fein*. New York, 1923: Scribners.

CXLVIII Dodds, Eric Robertson. [*editor*] *The Journal and Letters of Stephen MacKenna*. 1936, Constable.

CXLIX Dowden, Edward. A review of item 2 in *Illustrated London News* (London) vol 105 No 2885 p 142 (August 4, 1894).

CL [——] *The Letters of Edward Dowden and his Correspondents*. Edited by 'John Eglinton'. 1914, Dent.

CLI [Dowden, Hester (*Mrs* Travers Smith)]. See *Far Horizon* by Edmund Bentley. 1951, Rider & Co.

CLII Drury, T. W. E. *and* Figgis, T. F. *Rathmines School Roll, 1858–1899*. Dublin, 1932: Privately printed. [Copy in the British Museum.]

CLIII Dunlop, Daniel Nicol. *British Destiny: the Principles of Progress*. 1916, Path Publishing Co.

CLIV —— *The Path of Attainment*. 1916, Path Publishing Co.

CLV —— *The Science of Immortality*. 1918, Path Publishing Co.

CLVI Dunsany, *Lord*. *My Ireland*. 1937, Jarrolds. [AE: pp 1–9].

CLVII —— *The Sirens Wake*. 1945, Jarrolds. [AE: pp 26–9].

CLVIII [——] See *Dunsany the Dramatist*, by Edward H. Bierstadt. (New York, 1919).

CLIX [——] See *Lord Dunsany: King of Dreams* by Hazel G. Littlefield Smith (New York, 1959: Exposition Press).

CLX Dwyer, Arthur William. Interview reported in *Niagara Falls Gazette* (New York), October 22, 1930. [Mr Dwyer had been a member of the Dublin lodge of the Theosophical Society.]

CLXI Eglinton, John [*pseudonym of* William Kirkpatrick Magee]. *Irish Literary Portraits*. 1935, Macmillan. [AE: pp 39–61. Re-states his article "AE and his story" from *Dial* (New York) vol 82 pp 271–81 (April 1927).]

CLXII —— *A Memoir of G. W. Russell (A.E.)*. 1937, Macmillan. Re-issued, 1943 in a "Cheap edition". [Despite factual errors the *Memoir* remains the sole indispensable source-book for students of AE's life. Discussing his book with this compiler, in 1950, Dr Magee admitted errors of judgment in the book. Some re-considerations he wrote out in item 100 vol 16 No 1 pp 17–20 (January 1941), "A Note on AE's Fantasy *The Avatars*". Secondly, "The Poetry of AE", in item 100 vol 26 No 3 pp 5–9 (July 1951). Dr Magee was AE's anonymous obituarist in *The Times*. That obituary notice offended some readers by the tone of somewhat condescending appraisal. Mrs Pamela Travers, for one, sweated angrily when reminded of it, in 1950. Charles Weekes had been invited to write the obituary article during AE's lifetime. He was too fond of Russell, as he declared, to undertake such a task.] Dr Magee wrote the article in the *D.N.B.*

CLXIII Ellis-Fermor, Una Mary. *The Irish Dramatic Movement.* [1939]. 2nd ed, 1954: Methuen.

CLXIV Ellmann, Richard. *Yeats, the Man and the Masks.* 1949, Macmillan.

CLXV —— *The Identity of Yeats.* 1954, Macmillan.

CLXVI —— *James Joyce* [the biography]. 1959, O.U.P.

CLXVII Ervine, St John Greer. *Sir Edward Carson and the Ulster Movement.* Dublin, 1915: Maunsel. [pp 49–50, a letter from AE to Mr Ervine, is quoted.]

CLXVIII —— *Some Impressions of my Elders.* New York, 1922: Macmillan. London, 1923: Allen & Unwin. Reptd, 1924. [AE: pp 31–63. Also in *North American Review* (Boston, Mass.) vol 212 pp 238–49 (August 1920).]

CLXIX —— *Craigavon, Ulsterman.* 1949, Allen & Unwin.

CLXX —— *Bernard Shaw, his Life, Work and Friends.* 1956, Constable.

CLXXI Evans-Wentz, Walter Yeeling. *The Tibetan Book of the Dead.* 1927, O.U.P.

CLXXII —— *Tibetan Yoga and Secret Doctrines.* 1959, O.U.P.

CLXXIII Fallon, P. P. [Attorney-at-Law, New York]. "George Russell's Poetic Philosophy", in *Ireland-American Review* (Dublin) vol 1 No 3 (December 1938).

CLXXIV Fay, Gerard. *The Abbey Theatre.* 1958, Hollis & Carter.

CLXXV Fay, William G. *and* Carswell, Catherine. *The Fays of the Abbey Theatre.* 1935, Rich & Cowan.

CLXXVI Feld, R. C. "The Opinions of AE", in *Century Magazine* (New York), November 1921: pp 3–9. [In *Bookman* (New York) November 1925: pp 267–70 Russell was reported to have said "No such interview was granted or took place. The opinions are about half mine."]

CLXXVII Ferrar, W. J. "Some Aspects of AE". *Quarterly Review* (London) vol 150 pp 232–40 (October 1928).

CLXXVIII Figgis, Darrell Edmund. *Æ (George W. Russell). A Study of a Man and a Nation.* Dublin, 1915: Maunsel. New York, 1916: Dodd Mead. [AE described this book to Messrs Macmillan & Co. as factually worthless. Among AE's surviving friends several expressed to this compiler their amusement at Figgis's book. Figgis was unlucky in his personal life. The book contains some excellent literary criticism.]

CLXXIX Fingall, Elizabeth M. M. Plunkett, *Countess of. Seventy Years Young. Memories told to Pamela Hinkson.* 1937, Collins. [AE: pp 233 and 241–3. A fine photograph of AE facing p 242, and an interesting letter to Sir Horace Plunkett (dated 23.7.99) on p 242, in which AE refers to item 6: "I regret to say that the Organising pamphlet is still in mss. It needs to be touched up in reference to creameries . . ."]

CLXXX Finlay, Thomas Aloysius, *Father*. A memorial tribute in *Co-operative News* (Manchester) No 3347, p 5 (July 27, 1935): reptd in item 100 vol 10 No 4 (October 1935).

CLXXXI FitzPatrick, Edward A. *McCarthy of Wisconsin.* New York, 1944: Columbia University Press. [Charles McCarthy, 1873–1921.]

CLXXXII Flaccus, Kimball. "Poet and Patriot", in *Voices* (New York?), No 85 pp 36–9 (Spring 1936).

CLXXXIII Ford, Julia Ellsworth. [*See* Part 17 No 10.]

CLXXXIV Fox, R. M. *Jim Larkin: the Rise of the Underman.* 1957, Lawrence and Wishart.

CLXXXV Freeman, John. "The Poetry of AE". *Bookman* (London) vol 68 pp 243–4 (1925).

CLXXXVI Gallagher, Patrick. *Paddy the Cope.* 1939, Cape. New York, 1942: Devin-Adair.

CLXXXVII Garnier, Charles-Marie. "Tagore et George Russell, AE", in *Revue Anglo-Americaine* (Paris) vol 7 pp 97–112 and pp 231–46 (December 1929 and February 1930). The poems by AE, in this essay, are mis-quoted. The essay was off-printed [A] as a pamphlet, in 1930.

CLXXXVIII Gibbon, William Monk, *Dr.* "Childhood and early youth of AE" in item 100 vol 31 Nos 2 and 3 at pp 6–14 and 8–17 (April, July, 1955).

CLXXXIX —— "Æ—the years of mystery", in item 100 vol 32 No 1 pp 8–21 (January 1956).

CXC —— "Æ and the Household", in item 100 vol 34 No 2 pp 23–31 (April 1958). [In 1952 Dr Gibbon advised this compiler that he had written a thesis concerning AE's early life, for which he had been awarded a Ph.D. degree from Dublin University. "I have only shown it to a Frenchman"—not named. The foregoing three articles may have been adapted from that thesis, which this compiler has not seen.]

CXCI Gleeson, Evelyn. [*See* Part 13 (1903).]

CXCII Glenavy, *Lady* [*née* Beatrice Elvery]. [*Memoirs*—awaiting publication.]

CXCIII Gogarty, Oliver St John. *As I Was Going Down Sackville Street*. 1937, Rich & Cowan. [New York, 1937: Reynal & Hitchcock.]

CXCIV —— *Mourning Becomes Mrs Spendlove, and other Portraits, Grave and Gay*. New York, [1948]: Creative Age Press. [AE: pp 103–22].

CXCV —— In the *Colby Library Quarterly* (Waterville, Maine, series 4 No 2 pp 24–8 (May 1955)): an excerpt from Dr Gogarty's chapter on AE in his then unpublished book *Nine Worthies*.

CXCVI Gore-Booth, Eva. *Selected Poems*, edited with a memoir, by Esther Roper. 1933, Longmans, Green.

CXCVII Greene, David H. *and* Stephens, Edward M. *J. M. Synge, 1871–1909*. New York and London, 1959: The Macmillan Co.

CXCVIII Gregory, Isabella Augusta, *Lady*. *Lady Gregory's Journals 1916–1930*, edited by E. S. Lennox Robinson. 1946, Putnam. [New York, 1947: Macmillan.]

CXCIX —— *Our Irish Theater*. 1st ed, 1913. [New York, 1914: Putnam.—AE letters quoted, pp 31–2 and 99.] New ed, revised by E. S. Lennox Robinson: 1939, Macmillan.

CC —— *The Image* [a play]. Dublin, 1910: Maunsel. [Based on the same story as "George Birmingham's" novel *General John Regan*.] [See *Lady Gregory: a Literary Portrait* by Elizabeth Coxhead (1961, Macmillan).]

CCI Grieve, Christopher Murray ["Hugh MacDiarmid"]. A review of item 50, in item 101 vol 3 pp 591–3 (October 5, 1933), "AE and Poetry". That article was reprinted by Mr Grieve in his book *At the Sign of the Thistle* (London, 1934: Stanley Nott). Mr Grieve owns a copy of that book which was presented by AE to A. R. Orage, and on the fly-leaf is the inscription: "Dear Orage. This is the book I spoke about. I would like to know what you think about the psychology. I will come round next week to hear your opinion if you have time to read. Yours ever AE."

CCII —— *Lucky Poet*. 1943, Methuen. [AE: pp 75, 99, etc.]

Hunt-Grubb, H. T. [See below: items CCXCVII *and* CCCXIII.]

CCIII Gwynn, Denis. *Edward Martyn and the Irish Revival*. 1930, Cape.

CCIV Gwynn, Denis. *The Life of John Redmond.* 1932, Harrap.

CCV —— [*editor*] *Tribute to Thomas Davis by W. B. Yeats. With an Account of the Thomas Davis Centenary Meeting held in Dublin on November 20th., 1914, including Dr Mahaffy's prohibition of the "Man called Pearse", and an unpublished protest by "AE".* Cork and Oxford, August 1947: Cork University Press, and B. H. Blackwell. [AE's letter to W. B. Yeats, at pp 20–2.] [Professor Denis Gwynn's numerous scholarly books should be consulted by students of modern Ireland.] 21 × 14 cm.

CCVI Gwynn, Stephen Lucius. *Experiences of a Literary Man.* [1926], Thornton Butterworth. [AE: pp 200–4].

CCVII —— *Irish Literature and Drama.* 1936, Nelson. [Useful appendix on the formation of the Irish Academy of Letters.]

CCVIII Harvey, [*Rt. Rev. Dr. T.*] Arnold. "Memories of Coole" in the *Irish Times* (Dublin), November 23 and 24, 1959.

CCIX Haugh, Irene. "Study of AE", in *Ireland-American Review* (Dublin), vol 1 No 1 pp 36–49 (September 1938).

CCX —— "A Visit to our National Gallery" in the *Irish Monthly* (Dublin) vol 60 No 713 pp 693–8 (November 1932).

CCXI Hayakawa, S. I. "AE's Golden Age". *Poetry* (Chicago) vol 48 pp 290–2 (August 1936).

CCXII Henderson, Fred. "AE, an Appreciation and a Remembrance", in *Eastern Daily Press* (Norwich, England) Friday, July 19, 1935: p 8 col 6. [Councillor Henderson traveled on the *Aurania* from New York. On that boat he first met AE: they were constantly together throughout the 13-day trip (left New York, March 1, 1935). That spontaneous tribute is among the most heartfelt of any known to this compiler.]

CCXIII Henn, Thomas Rice. *The Lonely Tower.* 1950, Methuen.

CCXIV Hinkson, Pamela. In the *Observer* (London) July 21, 1935.

CCXV Höpf'l, Heinz. *AE: Dichtung und Mystik.* Bonn, April 1935: Peter Hanstein. [pp 77].

CCXVI —— *AE, Dichter und Mystiker.* Leipzig, 1936: in the *Neuphilologischer Monatsschrift*, vol 7 No 1.

CCXVII Hone, Joseph Maunsell. *The Life of George Moore.* 1935, Gollancz.

CCXVIII —— *The Moores of Moore Hall.* 1939, Cape.

CCXIX —— *W. B. Yeats: 1865–1939.* 1942, Macmillan.

CCXX Howarth, Herbert. *The Irish Writers 1880–1940. Ireland under Parnell's Star.* 1958, Rockliff.

CCXXI —— "Whitman and the Irish Writers" in *Proceedings of the ICLA Congress in Chapel Hill, N.C.*, edited by W. P. Friederich. Chapel Hill, N.C., 1959: University of North Carolina Press.

CCXXII Hume, Ernest Robert. *The Thirteen Principal Upanishads. With a List of recurrent and parallel passages by George C. O. Haas.* 2nd ed, 1931. O.U.P. (Indian branch).

CCXXIII Jackson, P. E. "Recollections of Old Dublin Lodge" in *Theosophy in Ireland* (Dublin) vol 17 Nos 3 and 4 (July, October, 1938) and vol 18 Nos 1 and 2 (January, April, 1939). [Copy preserved in the present Dublin lodge of the Theosophical Society.]

CCXIV Jameson, Grace Emily. *Mysticism in AE and Yeats in Relation to Oriental and American Thought.* Pp 184. [An unusually brilliant doctoral dissertation: presented to Ohio State University in 1932. Abstract No 9 in the printed *Abstracts of Doctoral Dissertations in Ohio State University, 1932*, at pp 144–51.]

CCXXV —— "Indebtedness of G. W. Russell and W. B. Yeats to Blake" in *Proceedings of the Modern Language Association of America*, June 1938: pp 575–92.

CCXXVI Jeffares, A. Norman. *W. B. Yeats: Man and Poet.* 1949, Kegan Paul.

CCXXVII Johnston, Charles. *The Crest Jewel of Wisdom, and other writings* translated from Sankara Acharya. Covina, Calif., 1946: Theosophical University Press.

CCXXVIII —— *The Great Upanishads. Isha, Kena, Katha and Prashna Upanishads.* Vol 1 only, published. New York, 1927: Quarterly Book Store.

CCXXIX —— *Ireland through the Stereoscope.* New York, [1907]: Underwood and Underwood.

CCXXX —— *Kela-bai. An Anglo-Indian Idyll.* New York, 1900. Doubleday & McClure.

CCXXXI —— *The Yoga Sutras of Patanjali, translated.* London, 1949: John M. Watkins. New York, 1949: Quarterly Book Dept.

CCXXXII —— [translator of] *The System of the Vedanta* by Paul Deussen. Chicago, 1912: Open Court Publishing Co.

CCXXXIII Jones, E. D. "Evening with AE", in *Christian Century* (New York) vol 55 pp 491–3 (April 20, 1938).

CCXXXIV Joy, Maurice. "Ireland's Modern Mystic" in *New York Herald Tribune* (New York), February 6, 1938: section 9 p 4 cols 1–4. [Review of Eglinton's *Memoir . . . of AE.*]

CCXXXV —— [*See* Part 13 (1906).]

CCXXXVI Joyce, James A. *Ulysses.*

CCXXXVII —— *The Letters of James Joyce* vol 1 ed by Stuart Gilbert (New York and London, 1957: The Viking Press, and
CCXXXVIII Faber and Faber). Vol 2 ed Richard Ellmann. (London and New York, 1961. Same publishers.)

CCXXXIX Joyce, Stanislaus. *My Brother's Keeper*, ed Richard Ellmann. New York and London, 1958: The Viking Press, Faber and Faber.

CCXL Judge, William Quan. *Echoes from the Orient.* New York, 1890: The Path.

CCXLI —— *The Ocean of Theosophy.* New York, 1894: The Path.

CCXLII —— *The Bhagavadgita*, translated. Los Angeles, [11th ed] 1928: The Theosophy Co.

CCXLIII Lawrence, T. E. [1888–1935]. *The Letters of T. E. Lawrence*, ed by David Garnett. 1938, Cape. [pp 688–9: a letter to Frederic Manning (1882–1935), dated May 2, 1930, mentions AE.]

CCXLIV Letts, Winifred M. "Some Dublin Characters", in *Fortnightly Review* (London) vol 171 [n.s. 165] pp 55–61 (January 1949).

CCXLV Lynd, Robert. *I Tremble to Think.* 1936, Dent. [AE: pp 28–35].

CCXLVI Lyons, Dr F. S. L. "Edwardian Dublin", in *Irish Times* (Dublin), July 20, 21, 22, 23, 24, 25, 27, 28, 29, and 30, 1959.

CCXLVII Lysaght, Edward E. *Sir Horace Plunkett and his place in the Irish Nation.* Dublin, 1916: Maunsel.

CCXLVIII Lyttelton, Edith. "Æ" in the *Spectator* (London) vol 155 p 190 (August 2, 1935).

CCXLIX Lytton, E. R. B. [*Earl of*]. In [Littell's] *Living Age* (Boston, Mass.) July 22, 1899: vol 222, pp 254–60. [That article was checked by the late Sir Edward Marsh: see Christopher Hassall's biography of Marsh (1959, Cassell).]

CCL McArdle, Dorothy Margaret C. [died 1958]. *The Irish Republic.* 4th ed Dublin, 1951: Irish Press. [1st ed, London, 1937: Gollancz.]

CCLI MacBride, Maud Gonne. *A Servant of the Queen.* 1938, Gollancz.

CCLII MacCarthy, Desmond. "Memories of Æ", in the *Sunday Times* (London), July 28, 1935: p 6 columns 3–4. That article prompted Mr C. P. Curran, S.C., to write to the *Sunday Times* a letter sharply objecting to MacCarthy's assertion that AE did not intend to return to Ireland: letter, issue dated August 4, 1935: p 8 col 6. Issue August 11th Mr Maurice Healy (p 10 col 5) complaining at Mr Curran's 'wounding phrase' concerning 'Irish tame geese' abroad. In issue August 18th Hugh A. Law wrote (p 10 col 7) supporting Mr Curran's correction of MacCarthy.

MacDiarmid, Hugh. [*See* Grieve, C. M.]

CCLIII MacDonagh, Thomas. *Literature in Ireland.* Dublin, 1916: Talbot Press.

CCLIV MacLiammoir, Micheál. *All for Hecuba. An Irish Theatrical Autobiography.* 1946, Methuen.

CCLV MacLysaght, Edward. *Master of None.* [Unpublished: Ms 4750 in National Library of Ireland.]

CCLVI MacManus, L. *White Light and Flame. Memories of the Irish Literary Revival and the Anglo-Irish War.* Dublin and Cork, 1929: Talbot Press.

CCLVII MacManus, Michael Joseph. *Eamon de Valera.* Chicago, 1946: Ziff-Davis Publg Co. [Dublin, 1947: Talbot Press.]

CCLVIII —— In *Sunday Press* (Dublin) March 26, 1950, quoted from item 63 pp 36–50.

CCLIX —— *The Green Jackdaw.* Dublin, 1925: Talbot Press. [At p 35 verses parody AE's. Again quoted in *Irish Press* (Dublin) December 24, 1951.]

CCLX MacManus, Seumas. *We Sang for Ireland.* [Poems by the editor, Ethna Carberry and Alice L. Milligan.] Dublin, 1950: M. H. Gill.

CCLXI MacNamara, Brinsley [*pseudonym of* A. E. Weldon]. *Abbey Plays 1899–1948.* Dublin, 1949: Abbey Theatre [*printed* At The Sign of the 3 Candles.]

CCLXII MacNeice, Louis. *The Poetry of W. B. Yeats.* 1941, O.U.P.

CCLXIII Malone, Andrew E. *The Irish Drama.* 1929, Constable.

CCLXIV Mansergh, Nicholas. *Ireland in the Age of Reform and Revolution.* 1940, Allen & Unwin.

CCLXV Massingham, Harold John. *Remembrance: an Autobiography.* 1941, Batsford. [AE: p 23].

CCLXVI Merchant, Francis. *A.E. an Irish Promethean.* Columbia, South Carolina, 1954: Benedict College Press. [pp vi + 242 + iv.] Dr Merchant's book, a doctoral thesis, has some interesting appendices in which are printed letters from Mr J. B. Priestley, Mr Séan O'Casey, Sir J. A. Shane Leslie, Bt., Mr St John Ervine, and others. Additionally Mr Merchant printed from a carbon copy (preserved in the Plunkett Foundation for Co-operative Studies, in London) AE's letter to David Lloyd George, (February 18, 1918) at pp 241–2.

CCLXVII Meyerstein, E. H. W. [1889–1952]. "Æ to E. H. W. Meyerstein" by Vera Watson. In *English* (London) vol 12 No 71 pp 220–5 (Autumn 1959). [Includes extracts from several interesting letters from AE to Meyerstein.]

CCLXVIII Milligan, Alice Letitia. "An Agriculturist," verses addressed to AE, in *Sinn Fein* (Dublin) July 10, 1909.

CCLXIX —— *Poems*, edited by Henry Mangan. Dublin, 1954: M. H. Gill. AE selected her [A] *Hero Lays* (Dublin, May 1908: Maunsel).

CCLXX —— In item 100 vol 10 No 4 (October 1935).

CCLXXI Mitchell, Susan Langstaff. [*See* Part 17 No 13. Reptd, 1913.]

CCLXXII —— *George Moore*. Dublin, 1916: Maunsel.

CCLXXIII Moore, George Augustus. *Hail and Farewell.* [*Ave* (1911), *Salve* (1912), *Vale* (1914). Heinemann. Frequently reprinted.]

CCLXXIV —— *Evelyn Innes*. 1898, T. Fisher Unwin. [AE was portrayed as Ulick Deane: see pp 147, 218, 302 *et seq*, 338.]

CCLXXV —— *Sister Teresa* [sequel to the foregoing]. 1901, T. Fisher Unwin. [AE as Ulick Deane: pp 24, 49–50, 65–6.]

CCLXXVI —— *The Making of an Immortal.* [A play]. New York, 1927: Bowling Green Press (Wm Edwin Rudge). [Based on a story told to Moore by AE—but never written by AE.]

CCLXXVII —— *Letters of George Moore, edited by John Eglinton, to whom they were written.* Bournemouth (Hants), 1942: privately distributed by Messrs Sydenham Ltd. Surplus stocks bought by Messrs Quaritch, *circa* 1944, from Dr Magee. [Reviewed in the *Irish Times* (Dublin), November 14, 1942: p 2 col 7.]

CCLXXVIII —— *Letters 1895–1933 to Lady Cunard*, edited by Rupert Hart-Davis. 1957, Hart-Davis.

CCLXXIX [——] A *Bibliography*, by Edwin Gilcher, is in active preparation.

CCLXXX Morris, Lloyd. *The Celtic Dawn.* New York, 1917: Macmillan. [See his article on AE in *Columbia University Quarterly* (N.Y.) vol 18 pp 332–44 (September 1916).]

CCLXXXI —— *A Threshold in the Sun.* New York and London, 1943: Harper Bros. [AE: pp 149–57.]

CCLXXXII In the *Nation* (New York) vol 112 pp 221–2 (February 9, 1921), "Protest from Æ"—not seen by this compiler: may refer to some earlier article?

CCLXXXIII Nevinson, Henry Woodd. *Changes and Chances.* 1923, Nisbet & Co.

CCLXXXIV —— "AE the mystical farmer" in *Week-end Review* (London), September 13, 1930: pp 340–1.

CCLXXXV Norman, Harry Felix. In item 100 vol 10 No 4 (October 1935).

CCLXXXVI —— In *Theosophical Forum* (New York) vol 8 (February 1936).

CCLXXXVII —— In *Yearbook of Co-operation, 1936.* London, 1936: P. S. King. [A] Off-printed and circulated as a pamphlet.

CCLXXXVIII North, Jessica Nelson. [*See* Part 16: North.]

CCLXXXIX In the *Northern Whig* (Belfast), editorial leader "Lest We Forget" attacking AE: Thursday, December 20, 1917: p 4 cols 6–7.

CCXC O'Brien, Conor Cruise. *Parnell and his Party, 1880–1890.* Oxford, 1957: Clarendon Press.

CCXCI —— [*editor*] *The Shaping of Modern Ireland.* 1960, Kegan Paul.

CCXCII O'Brien, James Howard. *Theosophy and the poetry of George Russell (AE), W. B. Yeats and James Stephens.* [Unpublished typescript: pp 366. "A Thesis submitted . . . for the degree of Doctor of Philosophy in the University of Washington. 1956." A copy was presented to the National Library of Ireland, by the author: pressmark, IR 82104. 02. Source: English Dept., Western Washington College, Bellingham, Washington, U.S.A.]

CCXCIII O'Casey, Séan. *Inishfallen, Fare Thee Well.* 1949, Macmillan. [AE: "Dublin's Glittering Guy", pp 208–31.]

CCXCIV O'Connor, Frank [*pseudonym of* Michael O'Donovan]. "Two Friends: Yeats and AE", in *Yale Review* (New Haven) vol 29 No 1 pp 60–88 (September 1939).

CCXCV —— "AE—a Portrait", in *The Bell: a Survey of Irish Life* (Dublin) vol 1 No 2 pp 49–57 (November 1940).

CCXCVI O'Connor, Ulick, *S.C.* [A biography of the late Oliver St John Gogarty: in active preparation.]

CCXCVII [In the *Occult Review* (London), July 1935: pp 161–72] "The Religious and occult philosophy of AE", by H. T. Hunt-Grubb.

CCXCVIII O'Dea, D. "Irish Mystic", in *Virginia Quarterly Review* (Charlottesville, Va.) vol 2 pp 210–21 (April 1926).

CCXCIX O'Faolain, Séan. "The Humanity of AE", in *Inisfail* (Dublin) vol 1 No 1 (March 1933). The sole issue of that magazine launched as an advertising stunt by Arks Advertising Agency, Dublin.

CCC —— "Æ" in the *London Mercury* (London) vol 32 No 190 pp 361–4 (August 1935).

CCCI —— "Æ and W.B." in the *Virginia Quarterly Review* (Charlottesville, Va.) vol 15 No 1 pp 41–57 (January 1939).

CCCII O'Hegarty, Patrick Sarsfield. *A History of Ireland under the Union, 1801–1922*. 1952, Methuen.

CCCIII —— In item 100 vol 10 No 4 (October 1935).

CCCIV Oliver, Frederick Scott. *The Life of Alexander Hamilton*. 1906, Constable.

CCCV Orage, Alfred Richard. *Readers and Writers, 1917–1921*. London, 1922: Allen & Unwin. [New York, 1922: Knopf.] [AE: pp 117–34.]

CCCVI O'Sheel, Sheamus. "Two Irishmen". *New Republic* (New York), vol 54 pp 14–16 (February 22, 1928).

CCCVII O'Sullivan, Seumas [*pseudonym of* James Sullivan Starkey]. *Essays and Recollections*. Dublin, 1944: Talbot Press.

CCCVIII —— *The Rose and the Bottle*. Dublin, 1946: Talbot Press.

CCIX Phelps, William Lyon. *Autobiography*. N.Y. and London, 1939: O.U.P. [AE: pp 827–35.]

CCCIX (A) Phillips, [Walter] Alison. *The Revolution in Ireland 1906–1923*. 1923, Longmans. [Probably the most fair summary.]

CCCX Plass, Martin [born 1913]. *Mystische Lyrik und Politische Prosa im Werke G. W. Russell* (AE). [pp 109]. Würzburg-Aumühle, 1940: K. Triltsch.

CCCXI Plotinus, translated by Stephen MacKenna. *The Enneads*. [5 vols: 1917, 1921, 1924, 1926, 1930]. Revised ed, by B. S. Page. 1956, Faber.

CCCXII Plunkett, Sir Horace. *Ireland in the New Century*. 1904, John Murray.

CCCXIII [In *Poetry Review* (London) January 1938: pp 39–53] "AE: Poet, Painter and Mystic" by H. T. Hunt-Grubb.

CCCXIV Pogson, Rex. *A. E. F. Horniman and the Gaiety Theatre*. 1952, Rockliff.

CCCXV Power, Arthur. *From the Old Waterford House*. Foreword by Paul Henry. Waterford and Dublin, 1940: The Carthage Press. [pp 180] Reprinted from articles first printed in the *Waterford News*. [AE: pp 27–30, 52–7. Accounts also of meetings with James Joyce, Aristide Maillol, Paul Henry, Modigliani.]

CCCXVI Priestley, John Boynton. *Brief Diversions*. Cambridge, 1922:

Bowes & Bowes. [Parodies of AE's verse: pp 39 and 57. Another was printed in *Punch*.]

CCCXVII *Proposals for an Irish Settlement: being a draft Bill for the Government of Ireland, by Two Irishmen*. Dublin and London, 1917: Maunsel. [Brit. Museum pressmark: 8145. F. 21.]

CCCXVIII Pryse, James Morgan. In the *Canadian Theosophist* (Hamilton, Ont.) vol 16 No 6 pp 164–5 (August 15, 1935).

CCCXIX Ramachandran, G. "AE, Poet and Seer", in *Modern Review* (Calcutta) vol 42 pp 23–6 (July 1927).

CCCXX *Rathmines School Magazine*, later *Rathmines School News*, and subsequently *Blue, White and Blue* (Dublin) [1872–89]. Russell was enrolled on *Rathmines School Register* [item CLII] in 1882, number 1272. Headmaster Dr C. W. Benson. Russell was probably a day-pupil (not a boarder) until December 1884. The school *News* magazine contains no entries signed by AE (all were unsigned) and none which this compiler would care to attribute to Russell. There are innumerable sermons, and moral exhortations. References to Russell: June 1882 issue, p 8, details of Easter Exam 1882, form five-lower. In second rank, "Russell, George William. 235 marks" out of 450 possible marks. October 1882, p 35 *Intermediate* Exams, listed Russell, G. W., still in *Junior* grade. June 1882 issue, p 139, list of pupils attending the annual excursion to Holyhead, included *J.* Russell. The staff then included: Henry Cameron Lyster (Classics), F. C. Glanville (Greek and Latin composition), George Preston (mathematics), Meyrick Rainsford (Hebrew, Classics, History), J. C. M. Dawson (maths). The drawing master was Robert Walshe in 1883–4. Vol 2 No 1 (Nov. 1883) p 6: *Intermediate* exam lists incldg Russell, G. W. in the middle grade, with one ordinary pass and one with honors. For Christmas exams 1883: vol 2 p 31, *Lower Sixth* Russell, G. W. p 37 Russell won the *Mr S. Bewley Writing Prize* [donor said: "I consider the writings are, on the whole, better than the average of the last 2 or 3 years."] Russell also won prizes for Classics and English: he was "Dux in Lower Sixth" that term. Top marks, 2140 out of possible 3500. [Others in class: R. Dunlop, G. Braddell]. Pp 46–7 includes a/c of W. F. Russell in school football team. June 1884, vol 2 pp 62–4, a/c annual excursion to Holyhead: list included Russell, G. W. [Another Russell entered the school that term.] Vol 3 pp 6, 11–12 (March 1885) *Lower Sixth* Christmas exams 1884, prizes awarded to Russell, G. W., for General Proficiency, Mathematics, and French. The English prize was won by Joseph Symes. Russell's total marks gave him first rank, with 875 out of 1000. [A file of that school magazine is stocked in the British Museum Library at pressmark: Pp 6180. i.] In the "Report of the Headmaster of the Metropolitan School of Art, Dublin" [Robert Edwin Lyne] in the *32nd Report of the Science and Art Department for 1885*, Appendix H, mention was made of Russell, G.W., having obtained "full certificate of the second grade." Russell first studied at the art school in 1880. He attended evening art-classes at the Metropolitan School from Oct. 1883 until July 1885. The 1884 exam results for Russell included work in perspective, free-hand drawing and model-drawing: his geometry was "excellent." From Oct 1885 until Oct 1887 he attended Lessons at the school affiliated to the Royal Hibernian Academy, evening sessions. According to W. K. Magee he continued to attend some art lessons until 1900.

Rea, C. C. *See* Coates, C. C.

CCCXXI Reid, Forrest [1876–1947]. *Private Road.* [1940], Faber & Faber. [AE: pp 124–42]. See also: *Forrest Reid* by Russell Burlingham (1953, Faber).

CCCXXII Rhys, Ernest P. *Everyman Remembers.* 1931, Dent.

CCCXXIII —— *Letters from Limbo.* 1936, Dent.

CCCXXIV Roberts, George. "Reminiscences", in *Irish Times* (Dublin) July 13, 14, 19 and August 1 and 2, 1955. [Some factual mistakes.]

CCCXXV Robinson, Esmé Stuart Lennox. *Ireland's Abbey Theatre.* 1951, Sidgwick & Jackson.

CCCXXVI —— *Palette and Plough* [a Memoir of Dermod O'Brien, P.R.H.A.] Dublin, 1948: Browne & Nolan.

CCCXXVII Rolleston, C. H. [*See* Part 16, self-portraits.]

CCCXXVIII Rothenstein, Sir William. *Men and Memories, 1900–1921.* 1932, Faber & Faber.

CCCXXIX —— *Since Fifty. Men and Memories, 1922–1938.* 1939, Faber.

CCCXXX Russell, Diarmuid Conor [AE's younger son]. "Æ" in the *Atlantic Monthly* (Boston, Mass.) vol 171 pp 51–7 (February 1943). [Charles A. Weekes marked his copy "This is a lovely thing. Please return for others. 23.4.43."] Reptd [A] in *Modern Reading*, No 10 (London: edited for "Big Ben Books" by Reginald Moore), pp 23–34 (1944). Again reptd, [B] in *Irish Writing* (Tralee), No 15, pp 49–58 (June 1951). Quoted in *Irish Times* (Dublin) August 22, 1951.

CCCXXXI Sarr, Kenneth [*pseudonym of* Mr Justice K. Shiels Reddin]. *Somewhere to the Sea*. 1936, Nelson. [The book includes characterisations of AE and James Stephens, and others. Stephens disliked the characterisation of himself.]

CCCXXXII Sen, A. K. "Study of AE", *Calcutta Review* (Calcutta), vol 49 pp 143–75 (February 1932).

CCCXXXIII Shackleton, K. "Portrait of G. W. Russell (AE)", *Bookman* (London) vol 69 p 172 (December 1925).

CCCXXXIV Shahani, Ranjee G. "Some English Poets", *Asiatic Review*. (London), vol 31 (n.s.), pp [381–5] (April 1935).

CCCXXXV —— "AE: G. W. Russell", *Asiatic Review* (London) vol 44 pp 219–22 (April 1948).

CCCXXXVI Sharp, Elizabeth A. *A Memoir of Wm. Sharp* (*Fiona MacLeod*). 1910, Heinemann.

CCCXXXVII Shaw, George Bernard. "How Shaw and Russell Met", in *Pearson's Magazine* (New York) vol 47 p 5 (July 1921). To be reptd in [A] *The Matter with Ireland*, by Bernard Shaw: ed by Dan H. Laurence and D. H. Greene. London, 1961: Hart-Davis. [New York, 1961: Hill and Wang.] Vol 2 of the edition in 8 vols of Shaw's *Uncollected Writings*.

CCCXXXVIII Shiubhlaigh, Maire nic [died 1958]. *The Splendid Years* [told to Edward Kenny.] Dublin, 1955: Duffy.

CCCXXXIX Sinnett, Alfred Percy. *Esoteric Buddhism*. 1883, Trübner. [Other editions 1884–88.]

CCCXL —— *The Early Days of Theosophy in Europe*. 1922, Theosophical Publishing Co.

CCCXLI Sitwell, Constance. *Conversations with Six Friends*. 1959, privately printed. [AE: pp 55–9].

CCCXLII Solomons, Bethel A. H. *One Doctor in his Time*. 1956, Christopher Johnson. [Reptd, 1959.]

CCCXLIII Speakman, Harold. "Dublin Hours with AE," *Bookman* (New York) vol 57 No 3 pp 267–70 (November 1925).

CCCXLIV —— *Here's Ireland.* New York, 1925: Dodd, Mead. [AE: pp 276–88].

CCCXLV Srinivasan, P. R. "The Poet-Philosopher. His Mission in Life." In *Modern Review* (Calcutta) vol 58 pp 666–70 (December 1935).

CCCXLVI Stephens, James. "The Passing of AE", in *Observer* (London), July 21, 1935.

CCCXLVII —— "AE: the Wonderful Amateur", in *The Listener* (London) vol 27 pp 467–8 (April 9, 1942). [Mrs Charlotte Law, no flapper, wrote to Stephens from her home, Marble Hill, Co. Donegal: March 28, 1942. "We listened with deep interest and great appreciation to your broadcast on AE yesterday. Every word was just—most especially that the man AE was even greater than the sum of his great gifts. It was like a link with times we never cease to regret, as we never cease to miss his yearly Donegal holiday as June draws on. We shall not see his like again. So thank you." Mrs L. Mabel Purser wrote to Stephens, from Knockraheen, Roundwood, Co. Wicklow: April 30, 1942. ". . . Dear AE, it seemed to bring him back into the room again. I owe so much to him and to you for having advised me to go to his Hermetic talks. He was indeed a wonderful friend—he seemed to know how to speak to one's real self when that temperamental idiot, the personal self, was dumb! . . ."]

CCCXLVIII —— "The Purest Poet of them all", in *The Listener* (London) vol 34 pp 271–2 (September 6, 1945).

CCCXLIX —— "A.E.", in *The Listener* (London) vol 39 pp 144–5 (January 28, 1948).

CCCL "Stet". *Back Numbers by Stet of the Saturday Review.* New York, [1930]: Richard R. Smith Inc. [AE: pp 128–32].

CCCLI Strong, Leonard A. G. "A.E., a Practical Mystic", in *The Listener* (London) March 10, 1955: pp 427–8. A letter from Professor George O'Brien (issue March 17): from Francis Hackett and Strong (issue March 24): O'Brien (March 31) made a rejoinder to Hackett concerning the reason for discontinuance of the *Irish Statesman.* [The correspondence files concerning the *Irish Statesman* were used by this compiler before he wrote his introductory notes to item 59: but the notes were not printed. The correspondence is stored in the Plunkett Foundation for Co-operative Studies, London.]

CCCLII Synge, J. M. "Le Mouvement Intellectuel Irlandais", in *L'Européen: Courrier International* (Paris) May 31, 1902. [Synge compared the poetry written by Yeats and AE: and expressed unflattering judgments on AE's poems.]

CCCLIII Tagore, Rabindra Nath. "The Cult of the Charka", in *Modern Review* (Calcutta) vol 38 pp 263–70 (September 1925). [Reference to AE's *The National Being* on p 268.]

CCCLIV [——] *See* "The National Ideals of Tagore and AE" [compared] by Ajit Kumar Chakravarty [died 1918], in *Modern Review* (Calcutta) vol 54 pp 403–5 (October 1933).

CCCLV Tate, *Sir* Robert William. *Orationes et epistolae Dubliniensis 1914–40*. Dublin, 1941: Hodges Figgis.

CCCLVI Téry, Simone. *L'Îsle des Bardes*. Paris, 1925: E. Flammarion. [AE: chapter 4.]

CCCLVII Tierney, Michael. "AE: Prophet of Mystic Nationalism", in *Studies* (Dublin) vol 26 pp 568–80 (December 1937).

CCCLVIII In *The Times Literary Supplement* (London) an unsgd review of books by "Five Modern Poets" [T. S. Eliot, Herbert Read, AE, James Stephens and Wilfrid W. Gibson.] February 24, 1927. Reptd in *Living Age* (Boston, Mass.) vol 332 pp 695–701 (April 15, 1927).

CCCLIX Tomlinson, H. M. [1874–1958]. "Memories of AE" in the *Observer* (London) July 28, 1935.

CCCLX Tynan, Katharine [Mrs Henry A. Hinkson]. *Twenty-five Years*. 1913, Smith, Elder. [Reviewed by AE in item 98 vol 21 p 326 (April 25, 1914).] [AE: pp 248–52.]

CCCLXI —— *The Middle Years*. 1916, Constable.

CCCLXII —— *The Years of the Shadow*. 1919, Constable.

CCCLXIII —— *The Wandering Years*. 1922, Constable.

CCCLXIV —— *Memories*. 1924, Nash and Grayson.

CCCLXV Vachell, Horace Annesley. *Quests. The Adventures and Misadventures of a Collector*. 1954, Seeley Service & Co. [p 92 quotes with approval a remark by AE: "Throw your sharpest flints at the villain in the piece; be as kind as you can to hero and heroine."]

CCCLXVI Wadia, B. P. In *The Aryan Path* (Bombay) vol 6 No 12 pp 721–2 (December 1935).

CCCLXVII Wall, J. "AE and James Stephens", in *Poetry Review* (London: ed Stephen Phillips) vol 4 No 7 pp 29–36 (January 1914).

CCCLXVIII Wallace, Henry Agard, *The Hon.* In *Wallace's Farmer* (Des Moins, Iowa) August 15, 1913.

CCCLXIX —— "AE: a Prophet out of an Ancient Age", in *Colby Library Quarterly* (Waterville, Maine) Series 4 No 2 pp 28–31 (May 1955).

CCCLXX Webb, Beatrice [*Baroness Passfield*]. *The Diaries 1912–1924 of Beatrice Webb*, edited by Margaret I. [Postgate] Cole. 1952, Longmans. [AE: pp 131–3].

CCCLXXI Wells, Warre Bradley. *Irish Indiscretions*. Dublin, 1923: Maunsel. [AE: pp 140–54: 195–230].

CCCLXXII —— *and* Marlowe, Nicholas [*pseudonym of* J. M. Hone] *The Irish Rebellion of 1916*. Dublin, 1916: Maunsel.

CCCLXXIII —— *The Irish Convention and Sinn Fein*. Dublin, 1918: Maunsel. [Unsgd review by AE in item 98 vol 25 pp 704 and 707 (October 26, 1918).]

CCCLXXIV Weygandt, Cornelius. "AE: the Irish Emerson", in *Sewanee Review* (Sewanee, Tenn.) vol 15 pp 148–65 (April 1907).

CCCLXXV —— *Irish Plays and Playwrights*. 1913, Constable. [AE: pp 114–137.] [New York and Boston, 1913: Houghton Mifflin.]

CCCLXXVI —— *The Time of Yeats*. New York, 1937: D. Appleton Century.

CCCLXXVII —— *On the Edge of Evening*. New York, [1946]: G. P. Putnam's Sons.

CCCLXXVIII White, Jack R. *Misfit: an Autobiography*. 1930, Cape.

CCCLXXIX White, Terence de Vere. *The Road of Excess*. Dublin, 1946: Browne and Nolan.

CCCLXXX Williams, David John. *A.E., a Chymru*. [In Welsh]: pp 40. Gwasg Aberystwyth, [March] 1929: J. D. Lewis (Llandysul). [Qtns items: 19, 30, 35, and 44.] 18.2 × 12 cm.

CCCLXXXI Williams, Gertrude Marwin. *The Passionate Pilgrim. A Life of Annie Besant*. [1932], Hamish Hamilton.

CCCLXXXII —— *Priestess of the Occult. Madame Blavatsky*. New York, 1946: Knopf.

CCCLXXXIII Wilson, F. A. C. *Yeats and Tradition*. 1958, Gollancz.

CCCLXXXIV Wilson, Milburn Lincoln, *The Hon.* His correspondence with AE, and with administrative colleagues in America was printed in *Oriel Review* (New York) vol 1 No 1, at pp 66–7, 70–1, 86–103 (April 1943): collected and edited by Maurice Leahy.

CCCLXXXV Wolfe, Humbert. A review of item 46 in *Observer* (London) June 10, 1928.

CCCLXXXVI —— "New Books that ought to be known" in *Bookman* (London) vol 75 p 166 (December 1928).

CCCLXXXVII —— In *Observer* (London) March 8, 1931: p 5 col 4. A review of item 49.

CCCLXXXVIII —— In *Observer* (London) February 28, 1932: p 4. A long review of item 50, contrasting AE's ideas with Irving Babbitt's view that "poetry is the intellectualisation of sensation and not the sensualisation of reason".

CCCLXXXIX —— "The Mysticism of AE" in *The Aryan Path* (Bombay), January 1933.

CCCXC Wrench, Sir Evelyn. *Geoffrey Dawson and Our Times*. 1955, Hutchinson.

CCCXCI Yeats, John Butler [*the Elder*]. *Letters to his son W. B. Yeats and others*. Edited by J. M. Hone. 1944, Faber.

CCCXCII Yeats, William Butler. *Autobiographies*. 1955, Macmillan.

CCCXCIII —— *Mythologies*. 1959, Macmillan. [Reprints item LXXIV.]

CCCXCIV —— *Essays, 1931–1936*. 1937, Macmillan. [Includes a review of item 50, first printed in the *Spectator* (London) April 9, 1932.] See item 98, CC. issue, December 1897.

CCCXCV —— In the *Bookman* (London) vol 8 pp 48–9 (May 1895) Yeats reviewed the second edition of item 2 (and John Eglinton's *Two Essays on the Remnant*.)

CCCXCVI —— In the *Bookman* (London) vol 8 pp 167–70 (September 1895) Yeats' third article "Irish National Literature" includes on p 169 an extremely thoughtful summary of AE's work. See issue August 1894: review of item 2.

CCCXCVII —— "Some Passages from the Letters of W. B. Yeats to A.E." in item 100 vol 14 No 3 pp 9–21 (July 1939). [Including an interesting letter, not printed by Wade in item CCCXCIX, below.]

CCCXCVIII —— *Letters to Katharine Tynan*, edited by *Senator Dr* Roger McHugh. Dublin, 1953: Clonmore and Reynolds.

CCCXCIX —— *The Letters of W. B. Yeats*, edited by Allan Wade. 1954, Hart-Davis. [Especially interesting references to AE: pp 40, 76, 80, 91, 118, 175, 178, 231, 287, 289, 290–2, 296, 298–9, 302, 306, 312, 318–9, 344, 350, 364–5, 367–8, 372, 375–6, 381, 402, 415–6, 433–4, 461–3, 466, 477, 536, 623, 627, 666, 838.]

CD [——] See *A Bibliography of the Writings of W. B. Yeats* by Allan Wade. 1951: 2nd edition, 1958: Hart-Davis.

CDI [——] See *Scattering Branches: Tributes to the Memory of W. B. Yeats*, ed S. L. Gwynn. 1940, Macmillan.

CDII Young, Ella. *Flowering Dusk. Things remembered Accurately and Inaccurately.* London, 1945: Dennis Dobson. [New York and Toronto, 1945: Longmans Green.]

CDIII Zicarelli, Maria. *The Works of 'AE'—George Russell.* [Written in English: pp 2+111: and with an Italian summary, 3 pages, added.] Thesis presented to Università Commerciale Luigi Bocconi, Milan. Student No 5441: thesis No 1360: accepted January 20, 1958. Typescript only. [A hotch-potch lifted mainly from Eglinton's *Memoir*, but 'summarised'. The appended bibliography does not list accurately even those AE books which Miss Zicarelli had looked at in London. A scandalously inadequate performance. After several requests a copy was graciously sent to the National Central Library, London, by the University in Milan.]

PART 12C

POEMS ADDRESSED TO AE

Osborn Joseph Bergin (1873–1950) "If AE had written the *Iliad* and the *Odyssey*" [12 lines for each epic] first printed in the *Irish Tribune* (Cork) May 14, 1926 (signed: N.I.A.), impeccable parodies of certain stylistic features of AE's verse. Reptd by R. I. Best in item 100 vol 33 No 1, p 44 (January 1958).

Lord Dunsany (1878–1957). Three commemorative poems. The first printed in *The Times* (London), *Irish Times* (Dublin), and *New York Times*, July 19, 1935. Reptd in his book *Mirage Water* (1938. Putnam). The second poem "In Memory of AE" ("When the hills are cold in the sun") has been published. The third has not yet been published. Lord Dunsany also recited to this compiler an epigram championing AE, which expressed his conviction that his uncle Sir Horace Plunkett, by employing AE, deprived posterity of the great poetry which Lord Dunsany believed AE would have written in more profusion if not employed in such arduous work: "a camel tied to a steam-roller". That epigram was not written down and will not be printed.

Darrell Figgis. "To Æ" dedicatory sonnet in *The Mount of Transfiguration* (1915).

[William] Monk Gibbon. An eulogistic poem, "I have known one great man" printed in *Dublin Magazine* vol 5 No 4 p 1 (October 1930): reptd by Dr Gibbon in item 57 pp 6–7, and in his book *This Insubstantial Pageant* (1951, Phoenix House) another at p 103.

Oliver St John Gogarty (1878–1957). Two sonnets: item 99A, vol 9 pp 247, 456 (Nov 19, 1927: Jan 21, 1928), reptd in item 73, etc.

Katharine Tynan Hinkson, "A Song of May" in *Irish Poems* (London, 1913. Sidgwick).

John Irvine. "Valediction" in *Nocturne* (Dublin: 1941. Orwell Press) p 35.

James A. Joyce. AE was mentioned in *The Holy Office* (1905).

Alice L. Milligan. See *Part 12B*.

Susan L. Mitchell. See *Part 17*, item 13.

Mary Devenport O'Neill, in the *Irish Times* (Dublin) July 23, 1935.

Herbert Edward Palmer, in *The Vampire* (1936. Dent), pp 29–30.

Ruth Pitter, in *The Spirit Watches* (1939. Cresset Press), pp 43–4.

Keith Preston (1884–1927) [*pseudonym*: Pan] in *Pot Shots From Pegasus* (New York: 1929. Covici).

R. C. Reade. A poem printed in *Toronto Daily Star*, July 19, 1935.

James Stephens (187–?–1950), "The Mighty Mother" in *The Observer* (London) reptd in *Kings and the Moon* (1938. Macmillan) pp 82–3, and in his *Collected Poems*, 2nd ed (1954. Macmillan).

—— "The end of the road", and "Wind and tree" in *The Hill of Vision* (Dublin: 1912. Maunsel), pp 97–99.

John Millington Synge (1871–1909), in *Poems and Translations* (Dublin: 1909. Cuala Press) and later editions.

Charles Alexandre Weekes, "To an Artist" in *Reflections and Refractions* (1893. T. Fisher Unwin), at p 1.

Jack B. Yeats (1871–1957), an "Epitaph" among unpublished humorous verses kindly shown to this compiler by Dr Thomas Bodkin.

PART 12D

SOME BOOKS DEDICATED TO AE

Austin Clarke, *Collected Poems* (1936. Allen & Unwin).

Padraic Colum, *Wild Earth* (Dublin: 1907. Maunsel).

St John Greer Ervine, *Sir Edward Carson and the Ulster Movement* (Dublin: 1915. Maunsel).

Walter Yeeling Evans-Wentz, *The Fairy Faith in Celtic Countries* (1911. O.U.P. Dedicated to AE and W. B. Yeats).

Darrell Edmund Figgis (1882–1925), *The Mount of Transfiguration* (Dublin: 1915. Maunsel).

Paul Gregan (1876–1945), *Sunset Town, and other poems* (Kilkenny and Dublin: 1901. Standish O'Grady).

Isabella Augusta (Persse) *Lady* Gregory, *Dave*, Second in *Three Last Plays* (London & N.Y.: 1928. Putnam).

F. R. Higgins, *The Dark Breed* (June 1927. Macmillan).

Katharine Tynan Hinkson, *Late Songs* (September 1917. Sidgwick & Jackson).

Charles Johnston, *From the Upanishads* (Dublin: January 1896. Whaley).

Susan Langstaff Mitchell, *George Moore* (Dublin: 1916. Maunsel). Dedicated to Æ and John Eglinton.

Seumas O'Sullivan, *Common Adventures* (Dublin: September 1926. Orwell Press).

Herbert Edward Palmer, *Post-Victorian Poetry* (1938. Dent). Dedicated to AE and Robert Bridges.

James Morgan Pryse, *A New Presentation of Aeschylus' Prometheus Bound* (Los Angeles: February 1925. John M. Pryse).

Constance Sitwell, *Seek Paradise* (1948. Jonathan Cape).

James Stephens, *Insurrections* (Dublin: 1909. Maunsel), and *Collected Poems* (1926, 1954. Macmillan).

Simone Téry *L'Île des Bardes* (Paris: 1925. E. Flammarion).

Charles A. Weekes, *Reflections and Refractions* (May 1893. T. Fisher Unwin).

W. B. Yeats, *Fairy and Folk Tales of the Irish Peasantry* (1888. Walter Scott), and *The Secret Rose* (April 1897. Lawrence & Bullen).

PART 12E

FILM AND DISC RECORDINGS OF AE's VOICE

Russell arrived in New York (on the *Cedric*) on September 23, 1930. Next morning, whilst sitting on the walled perimeter of a fountain, in the forecourt of Barnard College, Columbia University, New York, he was recognised by Professor William Cabell Greet. Professor Greet invited AE to his rooms to recite some poems for private recording. AE complied gladly with that request, and immediately recited his own poems "An Idle Reverie" [*Biblio.* item 53, p 66], "Carrowmore" and "Promise" [item 21D, pp 106 and 320] in Professor Greet's apartment. His clear and rich voice closely resembled some recordings made later for Professor Greet by Dr Oliver St John Gogarty. Within three years, uninvited, an intruder broke open the locked private cabinet in which those records by AE had been stored, and attempted to play them on a gramophone fitted with a steel needle. The soft aluminum surface of the records was scraped and the sound of AE's voice was erased. Professor Greet had not any subsequent opportunity to ask AE to make more recordings.

Russell's voice has not been preserved among the old recordings in the store of Radio Éireann. Probably he was not invited to broadcast in Ireland, because the Director of the Irish Broadcasting station during his life-time was Mr Seumas Clandillon, the plaintiff in the 1928 libel action against the *Irish Statesman* and others. Russell did not broadcast for any other radio stations in the United Kingdom, nor in Ireland; nor was he invited to broadcast. An article signed A.Z. in *Irish Radio News* (Dublin) vol 33 No 1, p 1 (July 27, 1935) a conversation with AE was reported. [*Editor*, James Kitchen, A.M.I.R.E.]

During 1930 and subsequent years Russell's voice was broadcast over regional and national networks in America. He was also filmed for newsreels, with sound-track. Dr William Lichtenwanger (Director of the Music Division in the Library of Congress) wrote to this compiler "there are few guides to the many historical collections scattered around this country"; and to date no records of AE's voice have been located by this compiler.

In a poetry anthology recorded in England the Ulster poet Mr John Hewitt spoke AE's poems "Outcast", "Dust" and "Reconciliation" [*Biblio.*

item 21D, pp 303, 34, and 298] on a commercially issued disc: Beltona Record Company, number LBE 29 (12-inch disc, with several speakers). That recording was reviewed in *The Gramophone* (Kenton, Harrow, Middlesex) vol 37 p 477 (March 1960).

The libraries' directors and staff who have kindly searched their files for any form of recording of AE's voice, include:

The British Museum Library, London.

British Institute of Recorded Sound, 38 Russell Square, London, W.C.1. [*Secretary*, Patrick Saul.]

National Film Archive, 164 Shaftesbury Avenue, London, W.C.2. [*Curator*, Ernest Lindgren.]

The Permanent Record Library, British Broadcasting Corporation, Langham Place, London, W.1.

The Film Archive, National Library of Ireland, Kildare Street, Dublin. [*Honorary assistant*, George Morrison.]

The Library of Congress (all divisions), Washington, 25, D.C. [*Director of Reference Department*, Roy P. Basler.]

George Eastman House, 900, East Avenue, Rochester 7, New York. [*Director*, James Card.]

Hearst News of the Day Newsreels, New York City, N.Y.

20th Century-Fox, Movietone News, 460, West 54th Street, New York, 19. [*Producer*, Edmund Reek.]

The Houghton Library and the Widener Library, Harvard University, Cambridge, Mass.

[Mr Liam O'Leary instituted enquiries for newsreels including AE on sound-tracks, but failed to locate any.]

Radio Éireann broadcast Shelah Richards and Ian Aylmer, on July 12, 1937, reading "A Selection of Poetry by W. B. Yeats and A.E."

PAINTING

COMPILER'S NOTE

THE lists are intended to serve as a guide to future students, since the various problems posed by the attempt to compile exhaustive catalog details have proved insoluble.

Besides the pictures painted on canvas or board, listed in *Part* 14, AE decorated with mural paintings the Dublin houses in which he resided. All those murals have been erased, except only those at 3 Upper Ely Place, Dublin. He also painted murals, which have been erased, at Ghurteen Dhas, Dundrum (the late Miss Evelyn Gleeson's house); at Kilteragh, Foxrock, for Sir Horace Plunkett, and in the cottage at Ballaly, in the Wicklow Mountains, loaned to him (and to Arthur Griffith's other friends) by Constance Gore-Booth.

The houses at which AE and his wife resided are listed in the *Chronological Table*, pp 27–43—the premises were all progressively rated higher than the address preceding.

Notes concerning AE's attendance at art schools will be found in *Part* 12B under item CCCXX.

For about ten years, probably from 1902 AE frequently painted serpents into his pictures.

A NOTE ON AE AND PAINTING[1]
BY THOMAS BODKIN

WHAT follows is an account of a long talk I once had with AE in about the year 1914. It arose because I thought at the time of writing a little book on living Irish painters, to include Hone, Jack Yeats, Orpen, and AE. But the project fell through, as Orpen objected vehemently to be associated in a book with either Jack Yeats or AE. Jack Yeats, anyhow in my opinion, is a greater artist than Orpen was, though perhaps not so accomplished technically.

AE's earliest ambition was to become a painter; and when sixteen or seventeen he entered the Dublin Metropolitan School of Art and worked there at drawing from casts and the rest of the dull routine of the South Kensingtonian system. He was not promoted to drawing from the model and only remained in the school for six or seven months. W. B. Yeats, John Hughes, and Oliver Sheppard were all pupils at the time. Hughes modelled in clay a fine bust of AE as a dreamy, sensitive youth with full, mobile lips and a broad brow. A plaster cast from this, colored badly by AE himself, used to stand on the mantelpiece of the front sitting-room in 17 Rathgar Avenue.

From the Metropolitan School, AE progressed to the school of the Royal Hibernian Academy, securing admission on the test of a small drawing. It was here that he first began to work in oils. He won a prize of a pound or two in some student competition. The teaching, in his opinion, was sadly inadequate and ineffective. He described it many years later in the evidence which he gave before the Royal Commission appointed in 1906 to consider the quality of art training then available in Ireland: "When I was an art student there," said he, "I painted from life. There were four visitors who were Academicians. One visitor, Mr Duffy, was an excellent landscape painter and I have a great admiration for his work. Another was Mr Grey, who painted bulls and cows; the third was Mr William Osborne who painted cats

[1] Reprinted, with Professor Bodkin's generous permission, from *A Memoir of G. W. Russell*, by W. K. Magee ("John Eglinton"), 1937: pp 57–68.

and dogs, and the fourth was Sir Thomas Farrell who did not paint at all. These gentlemen, not one of whom painted figures, were put there to assist us in our work. They never put their fingers on the students' work, which was probably the best thing they could have done under the circumstances."

The Metropolitan School and the Royal Hibernian Academy began and ended AE's formal training in pictorial art. When he left the latter it was to abandon oil painting for some twenty years. W. B. Yeats described in *Reveries over Childhood and Youth* the beginning of AE's long divorce from the art: "One day he announced he was leaving the Art School because his will was so weak and the arts, or any other emotional pursuit, could but weaken it further." George Moore in *Salve* tells the story as he says he heard it from Mr Hughes: "He and AE were students together in the Art School in Dublin, and in a few weeks masters and students were alike amazed at AE's talent for drawing and composition: he sketched the naked model from sight with an ease that was unknown to them, and turning from the model he designed a great assembly of gods about the shores of the lake renowned in Celtic tradition. 'Compared with him we seemed at that time no more than miserable scratchers and soilers of paper.' Hughes' very words! Yet, in spite of extraordinary fluency of expression, abundant inspiration and the belief of the whole school that a great artist was in him, AE laid aside his brushes, determined not to pick them up again until he had mastered the besetting temptation that art presented at the moment. He feared it as a sort of self-indulgence which, if he allowed, would stilt his life."

AE himself told me positively that, though he had always desired to be a painter, he gave up painting because his lack of means forced him to enter into some more paying, if less congenial, business. Though he abandoned the idea of making painting his profession, he never ceased entirely to paint. During the decade or so which he spent in Pim's warehouse, he produced numbers of little water-colors, most of which must have long since disappeared. Katharine Tynan used to treasure a few. They were all mystic or symbolic in composition. He described to me one series of such drawings measuring about six inches by four inches. It was not less ambitious than a poetic illustration of the earth's history from its beginning in chaos to its dissolution. Early man, a winged demigod, fought with monstrous flying reptiles. The last man of all "dwindled to a tiny figure" crouched with his family in the shadow of a normal human skull, which served him for habitation in the twilight of time. When he recommenced, about the year 1900, to paint in oils, he made a version of this lost drawing for Lord Dunsany.

Another series of interest, done in what may be called the Pim period, were rough color prints of Irish gods and spirits. A brother mystic named Pryse who had some knowledge of printing, invented, in conjunction with AE, the manner of their production, from pewter plates etched in relief and colored by hand. Mrs George Coffey used to possess several of these, which are probably now in the ownership of her son, Diarmid Coffey.

When AE joined Plunkett and traveled for the Irish Agricultural Organisation Society all over the country, he began to sketch small landscapes at odd half-hours in hard, colored chalks. Someone found him so employed at the Rosses in Sligo and recommended him to try pastels as being more suitable for his purpose. He adopted that advice and drew constantly with pastels for several years.

In *Salve* George Moore describes a tour of three or four days' duration made with AE in the neighborhood of Drogheda, New Grange and Dundalk. AE drew several landscapes during their wanderings and a pastel of Moore, which the sitter described as "clearly the work of one who has been with the gods, for in it my hair is hyacinthine and my eyes are full of holy light." Moore did not retain his high opinion of AE as an artist; for many years before his death he was accustomed to refer to AE in tones of bitter contempt as "the Donegal Dauber."

Few of the pastels can now survive. They are perishable things and were done for the artist's purely personal pleasure, were never sold and never exhibited. Two or three used to hang in his own house. His work in the medium was not confined to landscape and occasional portraits. He delighted more to depict weird cosmogonies and hierarchies of ancient deities, plumed and crowned with light, ascending and descending in many-colored spirals of flame, or sitting in council along dim ridges of starlit clouds.

When, early in the present century, Count Casimir Markiewicz settled in Dublin, he made the acquaintance of AE and persuaded him to paint more in oils and to join with the Countess and himself in an exhibition of oil paintings. This was the first of AE's annual exhibitions, and took place in the Leinster Lecture Hall in Molesworth Street in

1904. It proved to be an artistic and financial success, and AE continued to exhibit regularly, in varied company, for ten or twelve years more. At each of these exhibitions he showed from forty to sixty small paintings and sold them all at prices which tended gradually to increase slightly, but ranged between three and eight guineas. Other exhibitors who joined AE from time to time in these ventures were Frances Baker; W. J. Leech, R.H.A.; Kathleen Fox; Dermod O' Brien, P.R.H.A.; William Crampton Gore, R.H.A.; Beatrice Elvery (now Lady Glenavy); Eli Delbert Maybee, and Grace and Paul Henry.

For the first few years these exhibitions were held in the Leinster Hall in Molesworth Street. After that they were transferred to the Mills Hall in Merrion Row. Only once did AE venture into the crowd of his fellow-artists: he showed three pictures at the Royal Hibernian Academy of 1905. They remained unsold during the exhibition: but shortly afterwards all three were disposed of for the prices asked at the Academy. One was bought by Lady Dudley, then Vice-reine of Ireland, the others by Lady Ardilaun. In the next year AE first came into contact with Hugh Lane, who greatly admired his work and bought several pictures for the Dublin Municipal Collection which he was then forming. AE told me that at one time every member of Mr Asquith's Cabinet possessed specimens of his work.

Among the masterpieces which Lane brought to Dublin in 1906 and 1907 were the first works by modern continental artists which AE had ever seen. He was enormously impressed by them, particularly by the Corots and Monticellis. In my opinion he did his best work as a painter at this period. "On the Rooftops" and "The Winged Horse," now to be seen in the Dublin Municipal Gallery, show not only the imagination which was always present in his work, but also a power of composition and a technical competence which he sometimes lacked. In later life AE said to me that he would like to replace some of the pictures which he sold to Lane by more recent examples of his art; but I think this would probably have been to the detriment of his reputation.

He regarded painting as a minor activity of his life and only worked at it, as a rule, on Sunday mornings and during his annual month's holiday in Donegal. From this holiday he was accustomed to bring back every year about thirty pictures. He was an amazingly rapid executant. In 1914 I spent a week-end with James Stephens and himself at Virginia, Co. Cavan, and was enabled to study his method of work. We went one morning together into the woods of Lord Headfort's demesne. AE selected a view-point, set up a little portable easel on which he placed his canvas, and opened one of the smallest and, certainly, the dirtiest paint-boxes which I have ever seen. His palette was clotted with old, dried pigment; his brushes were in a lamentable state. Without making any preliminary drawing he started to paint the scene before him. The result bore little resemblance to his model; but was yet an extraordinarily beautiful rendering of a sunlit glade. Before he had time to finish it we were expelled by one of his Lordship's keepers. That did not prevent AE from finishing the picture afterwards at his leisure in Rathgar.

His knowledge of the technique of his art was slight and, as a result, some of his pictures have deteriorated. He would occasionally start to paint a sunlit scene and his vision would alter as the work proceeded, till the final result was as likely as not to be a nocturne. Consequently, the layers of paint superimposed upon each other without having been given time to dry out, tended to go opaque and to crack. The only medium he used was turpentine, which, when used to excess, also induces cracks and fissures in the pigment. He never varnished his pictures, with one exception. This happened when, at the request of Sir Horace Plunkett, Mr Dermod O'Brien and myself were commissioned to buy a few pictures by modern Irish artists for the University of Wisconsin. Among our acquisitions was an unusually large painting by AE. As the paint surface was dull, I suggested that he should varnish it. He did so by smearing varnish on it in criss-cross strokes with a stiff, hog's hair brush. As a result the picture looked as if it was covered with a sheet of frosted glass: and we were compelled to bring it to a professional restorer to have AE's treatment remedied. Still, the majority of his pictures, painted as they were at one sitting, without niggling or much re-touching, will undoubtedly prove permanent. I have myself several, painted twenty or thirty years ago, which have not altered in the meantime in the slightest degree. The dark-toned ones are more liable, owing to his methods, to deteriorate than those painted with a considerable admixture of flake white.

Though he will probably always be far more famous as a poet than as a painter, I believe him to have had a streak of genius in the latter capacity. He had a fine sense of color, a great gift for composition. His draftsmanship, particularly in figures, left occasionally much to be desired. But, had he painted day in and day out, there can be no doubt that he would have taken rank as one of the most noteworthy painters of his age. The long landscape frieze which he did for Sir Horace Plunkett's house, Kilteragh, at Foxrock, was a composition, well realised, of extraordinary loveliness. It was certainly AE's masterpiece: and it is a pity of pities that it disappeared in the fire which consumed the house during the Irish Civil War of 1922–3.

He did a few, a very few, portraits, and was happy in catching a likeness. One of W. B. Yeats as a young man, in chalk, and another of James Stephens, in oils, hung in his own house. As he grew older he seemed to lose his taste for symbolic and mythological subjects and to confine himself mainly to pure landscape. For ten or twelve years before he died he painted little and exhibited not at all.

In conclusion, it may be interesting to add that in 1910 he told me that the six works of graphic or plastic art which he would most like to possess were these: a certain big landscape by Corot which, from his description, I judged to be the "Souvenir d'Italie"; "A Moorland Scene by Night" by Jean François Millet, which I cannot identify; "Mousehold Heath" by John Crome; "A Sunset" by Rousseau, now in the Lane Collection at the Tate; the statue of Theseus by Pheidias, and Rembrandt's "Jewish Merchant."

1937 THOMAS BODKIN

PART 13

PUBLIC EXHIBITIONS OF PAINTINGS BY A.E.

1884 Metropolitan School of Art, Dublin. Exhibition of Students' work, in the School, December 26 to January 5, 1885. The *List of Students' Work selected for the Annual Exhibition . . . Christmas 1884* was printed and published in Dublin by the Stationery Office. British Museum copy destroyed. See [*Science and Art Department*] "Report of the Headmaster [R. E. Lyne] for the Year ending July 31, 1885" Appendix H, p 372. Russell was probably an exhibitor. The Lord Lieutenant and Countess Spencer attended that exhibition, and 2,393 other persons. [See also Part 8, *Rathmines School Magazine.*]

1888 [Russell was characterised as "O'Reilly" in an unsigned article printed in the *Evening Telegraph* (Dublin) Saturday, January 14, 1888 (p 2 columns 6–8) "A Dublin Literary Côterie, Sketched by a Non-Pretentious Observer". The côterie was Katharine Tynan's: the author of this sarcastic sketch has feminine insight, adding accurate details of physical peculiarities, Russell's stutter for example (see also fn 2 to letter to C. C. Rea, conjecturally dated ?January 1888, in item 59). ". . . . 'Do you know that O'Reilly is an artist of splendid genius and promise?' this second Ruskin will say, introducing his new Turner to an unappreciative spectator. 'He excels Blake in weird and mystical fancies, and neither Puck nor Ariel is a more delicately inhuman and sprightly creation than one of his fairies. Look at this lovely little sketch of his. Is not it quite precious and spiritual? You mask the allegory. It was a dream, and you see that it is more exquisite far and more unseizable than anything Blake did.' . . ."]

1892 [In *The Path* (New York) vol 7 p 202 (September 1892): ". . . . Brother Russell has begun to illuminate the walls of the place with wonderful paintings symbolizing the journey of the pilgrim soul." Alluding to the murals in the ground-floor room of the Theosophical Society's Dublin lodge premises, 3 Upper Ely Place. The murals were covered for many years, and uncovered in 1936. One of the wall-paintings is signed "G.W.R., W.B.Y." Mr J. Kennedy asked W. B. Yeats whether he had any recollection of them: Yeats had none (unpublished letter written to Mr Kennedy in 1936 owned by Mr P. L. Pielou.) The murals are now preserved by Dr Colm McDonnell.]

1895 First exhibition by *The Arts and Crafts Society of Ireland*, held in the Royal University Buildings, Earlsfort Terrace, Dublin, from Tuesday, November 26 "for one month". Open daily 10.30 a.m. until 10 p.m.: admission 1/–, *Catalogue* price 6d. *Catalogue* [copy in the Victoria and Albert Museum, Art Library, London] p 25, item 295C, "Specimens of printing and colour reproduction for magazines [*Irish Theosophist*] by G. W. Russell and J. M. Pryse".

1902 [In a letter to Stephen L. Gwynn, April 29, 1902, Russell replied to Gwynn's mention of his "pictures of the Sidhe" by declaring "I intend to have an exhibition of them as the Invisible Inhabitants of Ireland, sometime during the autumn—and am preparing for the usual row which follows a new innovation here."]

1903 [In *The Celt* (Dublin: editor at Exbury, Southampton: 1–3, September–November 1903) vol 1 No 1 p 15 (September 1903), Miss Evelyn Gleeson (born at Knutsford, Cheshire, May 15, 1855: died at Dún Emer, Dundrum, February 20, 1944) wrote: ". . . only the privileged few have seen the delicate interpretations of nature given by AE. They are full of the beauty born of murmuring sound . . ." Russell also devised some designs for embroidery by Miss Gleeson and the Yeats' sisters in the Dún Emer Industries. See also *Part 1*, item 49D.]

1904 Tuesday, August 23, to Saturday, September 3. Paintings: by AE (Nos 158–220), with Casimir Dunin-Markiewicz (Nos 1–81E) and Constance Gore-Booth (82–157), in the Leinster Lecture Hall, Molesworth Street, Dublin. See comments on the exhibition in *A Dublin Playgoer's Impressions* by Joseph Holloway (died 1944) [National Library of Ireland, Ms 1802] 1904 vol, pp 382–3 (September 3). [C. D. Markiewicz, born in Poland 1874. He married Constance Gore-Booth, September 29, 1900: died December 2, 1932. See the *Golden Book of Russian Nobility*. Thieme & Becker refer to an article on him in *International Studio* (New York) vol 37 p 351 (1906): not checked by this compiler.] *Catalog*, 20.7 × 12.8 cm: pp 8.

1904 November onwards, in the Royal Hibernian Academy, Lower Abbey Street, Dublin. See *The Catalogue of Pictures Presented to the City of Dublin to form the nucleus of a Gallery of Modern Art . . . and Pictures lent by the Executors of the late J. Staats-Forbes and Others.* [*Catalog* in the Victoria & Albert Museum, Art Library.] Paintings by AE from the Hugh Lane Collection: Nos 76, 99, 239, and 241. "The Waders," (No 101) was presented by AE. This exhibition was reviewed by Forrest Reid in *Ulad* (Belfast) vol 1 No 2 p 21 (February 1905): mentions AE's pictures.

1905 The Spring exhibition in the Royal Hibernian Academy, Dublin, included three paintings by AE. [This compiler has not seen the *Catalog*. V. & A. Museum file lacks several R.H.A. *catalogs* including this: the National Library of Ireland, and Trinity College Dublin copies are missing.]

1905 Tuesday, August 22, to Saturday, September 2. With C. Gore-Booth (1868–1927), C. Dunin-Markiewicz and Percy Gethin, in the Leinster Lecture Hall. Noticed briefly in the *United Irishman* (Dublin) August 26, p 1 col 1.

[Percy Francis Gethin, second son of Captain George Gethin (1836–1913), born at Holywell, Sligo, on July 25, 1874. Second Lieutenant in the Devonshire Regiment, killed on the Somme, June 28, 1916. Some of his drawings are in the Dept of Prints and Drawings, the British Museum. A biographical notice of Gethin by his friend Campbell Dodgson was printed in *Burgundy and Morvan* by William M. Crowdy (born 1866), with illustrations by Percy Gethin (London: 1925. Christophers). Another brief note about him in *Irish Statesman* vol 6 p 354 (June 5, 1926).]

1906 Tuesday, August 28, to Saturday, September 8. With C. Dunin-Markiewicz, and C. Gore-Booth, in the Leinster Lecture Hall. Maurice Joy wrote "A Note on AE's Pictures" in *Sinn Fein* (Dublin) October 6, 1906, p 3. [Maurice Joy, born at Killorglin, County Kerry, in 1884. One of Horace Plunkett's secretaries for several years, until 1912; also a poet. He died in New York, April 27, 1944.] *Catalog*, 18.4 × 12.6 cm: pp 8. Russell, 50 paintings.

1907 Monday, August 26, to Saturday, September 7. With C. Dunin-Markiewicz, C. Gore-Booth, Percy Gethin, and W. J. Leech, A.R.H.A., in the Leinster Lecture Hall. See a notice in *Sinn Fein*, August 3, 1907; and an article "The Art of G. W. Russell" (sgd E.D.) in *Studio* (London) vol 42 pp 65–6 (November 1907). This article was also printed in *International Studio* (New York), at different volume and page numbers. There is a reference in *Letters from J. B. Yeats to his son W. B. Yeats* (ed J. M. Hone), English ed p 101 (to W. B. Yeats, August 30, 1907). [William John Leech, son of Professor H. B. Leech, born in Dublin, April 10, 1881. Associate of the R.H.A., April 18, 1907; full Academician, October 18, 1910. He studied at the Metropolitan School of Art, Dublin, at age 17, and the R.H.A. School at 18; later at the Académie Julian (in Paris, 1901) under W. Bougoureau and Gabriel Férrier, then Jean Paul Laurens and Henri Boyer. He lived and painted in Brittany from

1903–16. He has painted figures, landscape and still-life, in oils chiefly, throughout his life and has been a regular exhibitor at the Royal Hibernian Academy; recent one-man shows at the Dawson Gallery (Dublin) (Leo Smith), in June 1945, June 1947 and May 1951. Articles about him and his work: *Irish Statesman*, April 7, 1928, *The Leader* (Dublin) April 22, 1939, *The Leader* May 11, 1946. He has painted several self-portraits. He is still painting (1958) in his Surrey home.]

1908 Monday, August 24, to Saturday, September 5. G. W. Russell (55 pictures) with C. Dunin-Markiewicz (25), C. Gore-Booth (33), Mrs Frances Baker (23), W. J. Leech (63), and Dermod O'Brien, P.R.H.A. (16), in the Leinster Lecture Hall; admission charge sixpence. See notices in *Sinn Fein*, August 29, 1908; and in *Inisfail* (London) No 48 (1908), and in the *Irish Times* (Dublin), August 24, p 9, ending: "[AE] his subjects are always chosen with taste and invariably attract much attention." [Mrs Frances Baker (*née* Davies-Colley) born in London, May 3, 1873, eldest daughter of Surgeon J. N. C. Davies-Colley, of Guy's Hospital. Married Cecil Cautley Baker (died 1903 or 1904 in London); they settled at Rosses Point, Sligo, where Mr Baker owned an oyster farm. After Mr Baker died the family moved to Ballysodare, on the opposite side of Sligo Bay; Coilte Leyney remained their home until Mrs Baker's second marriage, in 1915, to Dr Frank Kennedy Cahill (a Dublin specialist); he died in 1930. Mrs Baker painted throughout her life, but did not exhibit after the association with AE in the Dublin exhibitions. Her portraits include several self-portraits. For several years Mrs Violet Russell and her two sons spent a summer holiday with Mrs Baker, before her second marriage. She was a close friend of Sarah Purser, the Yeats family, and Evelyn Gleeson (although she did not work in the Dún Emer Guild) and Sir Ronald Storrs. During 1930–1 she taught Arts and Crafts at the Aylesbury Borstal School (an English delinquents' Public School). She painted mainly landscapes adorned with figures, in oils and water-color. In later life (after she had moved from France to Cambridge, England) she painted on glass. She had established in 1919, in Dublin a hand-weaving industry, "The Crock of Gold". She died in Cambridge, November 14, 1944.]

1909 Monday, October 11, to Saturday, October 23. With C. Dunin-Markiewicz, C. Gore-Booth, Frances Baker, and W. J. Leech, in the Leinster Lecture Hall. Lengthy review (sgd S.A.W.) in *Sinn Fein*, October 16, p 1 cols 5–6. [S.A.W. may be Samuel Waddell (b. 1878), brother of Helen Waddell. As "Rutherford Mayne" author of plays.] *Catalog*, 18.4 × 12.8 cm: pp 8. Russell, 44 paintings.

1910 Monday, October 10, to Saturday, October 22. With Mrs F. Baker (20), W. J. Leech (35), Beatrice Elvery (21), Eli Delbert Maybee (1 portrait loaned), and P. F. Gethin (11) in the Leinster Lecture Hall. Lady Glenavy (*formerly* Beatrice Elvery) kindly notes: "AE exhibited 49 pictures. The expenses totalled £31 2s. 6d. The receipts at the door and from the sale of *Catalogues* was £16 16s. 3d. We all paid for our own share of the wall-space. AE paid £6 7s. 6d., the rest of us about £2 7s. 6d." [Beatrice Elvery, born in Dublin April 30, 1883. See a biographical notice in *Who's Who in Art, 1934*. Lady Glenavy wrote her reminiscences during 1957–59.] Unsgd review of exhib in *Daily Express* (Dublin) October 10, 1910. Rev by Ellice Pilkington in *New Ireland Review* (Dublin) vol 34 pp 173–6 (November 1910). *Catalogue*, 24.8 × 16.1 cm: pp 8.

1911 Monday, October 16, to Saturday, October 21. With C. Dunin-Markiewicz, Mrs F. Baker, Paul Henry, and Grace Henry, in the Leinster Lecture Hall. Unsgd review in *Irish Times*, October 16, 1911, p 7 col 2. [Paul Henry, the son of the Rev. R. M. Henry of Belfast, born April 11, 1880. Died August 24, 1958. A.R.H.A., 1926. His autobiography, *An Irish Portrait* (London, 1951. Batsford) includes reproductions of some of his best-known paintings of the western Irish landscape. His first wife Grace Henry (*née* Mitchell, of Aberdeen) died in 1953.] *Catalog*, 25 × 15.4 cm: pp 8. Russell, 46 paintings.

1912 Monday, November 4, to Saturday, November 16. With Mrs Gordon Campbell (*later* Lady Glenavy) and Mrs F. Baker, in the Hall, 8 Merrion Row. Review in *Sinn Fein*, November 16, 1912.

1913 May 21 to June 29. The summer exhibition "Irish Art" in the Whitechapel Art Gallery, London. Included 8 AE paintings, loaned by Hugh Law, Miss J. S. Cunningham, Sir John Simon, K.C.V.O., and the Hon Mary Massey. Russell loaned "The Tinker" by Jack B. Yeats. [Catalog in the Victoria and Albert Museum Art Library.]

1913 Monday, September 15, to Saturday, September 27. With C. Dunin-Markiewicz and Mrs F. Baker, in the Hall, 8 Merrion Row. Review (sgd X) in *Sinn Fein*, September 20, p 3 col 4. *Catalog* 25.5 × 16.5 cm: pp 4. Russell, 51 paintings.

1914 Saturday, October 31, to Saturday, November 7. With Mrs F. Baker, Dermod O'Brien, P.R.H.A. (1865–1945), and Kathleen Fox, in the Hall, 8 Merrion Row, Dublin. Unsigned review in *Irish Times*, November 2, 1914, p 6 col 9.

[K. Fox, *later* Mrs Pim, frequently exhibited at the Royal Hibernian Academy, from 1912; and occasionally at the Dawson Gallery,

Dublin. Resident and still exhibiting in Ireland, 1958.] *Catalog*, 20.2 × 13 cm: pp 8. Russell, 55 paintings.

1915 Monday, November 1, to Saturday, November 13. With Mrs F. Baker, D. O'Brien, and W. Crampton Gore, in the Hall, 8 Merrion Row. [William Crampton Gore, born at Enniskillen, October 24, 1871. He graduated Bachelor of Chemistry from T.C.D. and also qualified there in medicine. He worked as a ship's doctor from 1899, and practised subsequently in Sussex until 1901. His interest in painting was stimulated and trained at the Slade School (London), and in Paris after he left the Slade School (probably in 1903). He was elected Associate of the R.H.A. in 1917, and full Academician in 1919. His interest was life-long and he continued painting during the years of residence in France. He married Yvonne Farine in 1923 returning to England with their daughter probably in 1938. Among his other hobbies Dr Gore composed much music for songs. He died in Colchester, Essex, on January 10, 1946, mourned by his numerous friends: and survived by his widow and daughter.] *Catalog*, 24.7 × 15.8 cm: pp 4. Russell, 45 paintings.

SUBSEQUENT EXHIBITIONS IN IRELAND. During his annual holiday in Donegal, during June, Russell painted and sketched many scenes. His hostess was Miss Janie Stewart (died, aged 87, in 1940) at Breaghy, Ballymore: he was guest there first in 1913, and from 1917 annually for fifteen or more years he assembled his recent canvasses in a room and invited local residents among his friends Hugh and Charlotte Law, and others, to view them. These private shows were exclusively for friends, and their personal acquaintances. After 1915 his paintings were not publicly exhibited during his lifetime in Ireland.

1917 January 5–28. At the Art Institute, Chicago. The first representative exhibition in America of paintings by AE. 22 pictures were shown: 2 loaned by the University of Wisconsin: and one each loaned by Mrs John L. Fortune, John Quinn, Mrs William Vaughn Moody, Miss Elizabeth Brennan, Miss Mary Synon, Frank Keogh, and Mrs John Kinney. The paintings sent by AE for the exhibition were received by Miss Joanna Fortune. Those unsold after the exhibition were stored until 1919 by John Quinn. Eventually he sold all but three, which he returned to AE. From 1920 Mr Edmond Byrne Hackett (1879–1953) was agent in America for the sale of AE's pictures. [John Quinn wrote to Miss Joanna Fortune, December 18, 1916: ". . . Several times in the past few years I have suggested a small exhibition of his pictures here, but he was always so busy or so backward or 'had sold them all' and had 'none that he cared to send' that nothing came of it. I am sure you will make it a success . . ."].

1927 In American Art Galleries, Madison Avenue, 56th–57th Street, New York. Amongst John Quinn's paintings and sculpture, 47 pictures by AE were sold (after exhibition), February 5–12, 1927.

1928 Probably an exhibition of AE paintings in the Hackett Gallery (9 East 57th Street, New York City) to coincide with AE's first visit to America, January–February.

1929 Probably an exhibition during April, in the Hackett Gallery.

1929 October . Paintings exhibited in the Hackett Gallery, N.Y.

1930 March 1–8 in the Hackett Gallery, N.Y., 3 AE paintings exhibited with pictures by Jack B. Yeats, Paul Henry, Michael MacLiammoir (b 1899), Charles Lamb (b 1893), Frank McKelvey (b 1895), M. McGonigal, J. Keating, R.H.A. (b 1889), Patrick J. Tuohy (1894–1930), Humbert Craig (1878–1944), Hilda Roberts. See *New York Times* March 2: Section 10 p 12. "The Big Oak" and "The Glade" by AE. ["Humbert Craig, R.H.A." by Anthony Liddell, in *The Ulsterman* (Belfast) vol 1 No 4 p 19 (July 1933).]

1930 October 21 to November 2. Hackett Gallery: 24 AE paintings.

1931 January 11 onwards. 19 AE paintings exhibited at the Barbizon Plaza, New York City. Photograph in the *New York American*, January 12. [See also *Letters*, item 59A.]

1932 May–June. Exhibition of paintings by Paul Henry, AE, Jack B. Yeats, J. Keating, R.H.A., Michael McGonigal (b 1900), and Power O'Malley (d 1946), in the Museum of Irish Art, New York [owned by Mrs Mary H. Rumsey] which had superseded the Irish Theater Art Rooms in the Barbizon Plaza. The Patrons' Board, at the instigation of Mr Patric Farrell, appointed AE Honorary Director of the Museum. [See notice in *New York Times*, May 29, 1932: Section 8 p 7 col 6.]

1934 Late October to late November, "Wild Earth", the inaugural exhibition for the season in the Museum of Irish Art, Ritz Tower, New York City. Paintings by Power O'Malley (38), Robert Henri (1865–1929) (1), Jack B. Yeats (10), AE ("A small room"), Paul Henry, John Keating, R.H.A., Nathaniel Hone (1831–1917) and 2 drawings by Sir William Orpen. [Notice in *Art News* (New York) Vol 33 No 5 p 17 (November 3, 1934).]

1936 *Memorial Exhibition* of 74 paintings by AE, in Daniel Egan's Gallery, 38 St Stephen's Green, Dublin, from January 15 to February 1, 1936. Dermod O'Brien, P.R.H.A., opened the exhibition [speech reported in *Art News* (New York) vol 34 No 11 (February 15, 1936).] The *Catalogue* (copy in the National Library of Ireland) listed owners: Preface written by Mr C. P. Curran. The exhibition was arranged quickly, whilst an interest in AE was current in Dublin:

the exhibits being assembled from collections formed privately in or near to Dublin. Mr Curran expressed to this compiler his own view that, excellent as that collection was it should not be thought to have represented adequately the range of AE's expression as a painter.

1953 April to July in the Municipal Gallery of Modern Art, Dublin. See *Catalogue: An Tóstal Irish Paintings 1903–1953 . . . from the Municipal Gallery and from Private Collections . . . in Dublin.* No 38 "The Gulley" from Municipal Gallery; No 39 "The Dunes" lent by Mr William Murphy of Dublin.

1960 April and May, in the Crawford School of Art, Cork, "Some Paintings by Modern Irish Artists", organised by Professor Denis Gwynn (University College, Cork). *Catalogue* included a Foreword and notes on the artists by Professor Gwynn. Numbers 54–6 by AE. "On the Shore" lent by Mr and Mrs W. L. Murphy through Mr James White of the Friends of the [Irish] National Collections: "Silver Sand" lent by Mrs Dominic O'Connor (of Cork, a niece of the late T. M. Healy): "A Sunny Sea in Donegal", lent by Professor Gwynn.

PART 14

PRESENT OWNERS OF PICTURES BY AE: AND LOCATION

Institutions

The County Museum, The Mall, Armagh, Northern Ireland. (Several.)

The City Art Gallery and Museum, Stranmillis, Belfast. (3)

The Abbey Theatre, Dublin. (1)

Irish Agricultural Organisation Society, The Plunkett House, 84 Merrion Square, Dublin. (Murals painted in what was his office, by AE: "symbolic, visionary pictures" most aptly described by Professor E. R. Dodds. Probably painted *circa* 1909.) [The late Lady Fingall said AE several times re-painted these murals.]

Municipal Gallery of Modern Art, Parnell Square, Dublin. (Several.)

National Gallery of Ireland, Merrion Square, W., Dublin. (Several.)

Public Art Gallery, Limerick. (3)

American-Irish Historical Society, 991, Fifth Avenue, New York City. (2. Presented by Mrs W. Murray Crane on May 24, 1956. See the *New York Times*, May 23, p 34 col 8.)

The Library, Colby College, Waterville, Maine.

Department of Economics, University of Wisconsin, Madison 6, Wisc. (Several paintings.) [See *The Irish Collection of Books and Paintings at the University of Wisconsin*, by Alice Beatrice Cronin and Sydney Eleanor Horsley (Madison, June 1915).]

Private Owners

Dr and Mrs Francis P. Aumann, 112 East Como Avenue, Columbus 2, Ohio. (1) [Formerly owned by Mrs Aumann's father, the late Senator Charles McCarthy (died 1921).]

Lady Granville Bantock, Sherriff Cottage, 38 Bittell Road, Barnt Green Birmingham. (2)

Robert C. Barton, Glendalough House, Kilmacanogue, Annamoe, County Wicklow. (?)

Clifford Bax, F2, Albany, London, W.1. (1) [Formerly owned by his brother the late Sir Arnold Bax.]

The late Osborn Bergin owned several AE paintings. [*See*: Delargy, Farrington, Lavelle, and Mills.]

Mrs J. H. (Kathleen E.) Bewglass, The Manse, Ballindrait, County Donegal. (1) [*See*: Craig, Millen.]

The Hon Mrs Bickford-Smith, Younghouse, Liss, Hants. (1)

Dr Daniel A. Binchy, c/o Dublin Institute for Advanced Studies, School of Celtic Studies, 64–65 Merrion Square, Dublin. (2 early paintings, and one given to him by AE in 1929.)

Professor Thomas Bodkin's heirs, 259 Hagley Road, Birmingham 16. (2)

Mrs Madeleine Boyd, c/o La Grange, West Milford, New Jersey: *or* 159 East 56th Street, New York. [Widow of the late E. A. Boyd (1887–1946).]

Miss Kathleen Brabazon, 29 Nile Street, Kensington, Johannesberg, South Africa. [A niece of Susan L. Mitchell.] (2)

Mrs Nora F. Browne, 38 Braemar Park, Rathgar, Dublin. ("Some very early sketches on lined note-book paper, initialled by AE".)

Heirs of the late Mrs Charles Chambré [died *circa* 1958, in N. Ireland.] (?) [Mrs Chambré was a sister of Mrs H. A. Law.]

D. H. Charles, solicitor, 4 Clare Street, Dublin. [A picture formerly owned by the late F. R. Higgins.]

Mrs Sybil Childers, c/o Mrs Robert C. Barton [address as above].

Austin Clarke, Bridge House, Templeogue, County Dublin. (?)

Diarmid Coffey, Glendarragh, Newtownmountkennedy, County Wicklow. (2)

Marcus Coffey [son of Mr D. Coffey: address as for Mr D. Coffey. One oil painting of Horn Head, bought *circa* 1910 by his grandfather the late George Coffey.]

Padraic Colum, 415 Central Park West, New York City: *or* 11 Edenvale Road, Ranelagh, Dublin. (Several.)

Hugh Craig, 84 Rashee Road, Ballyclare, Belfast. (One oil painting of a child, with yellow hair and blue eyes.) [Sister Mrs Bewglass.]

Miss Janet Cunningham, Killymard House, Donegal. (About 12.)

Constantine P. Curran, *S.C.*, 42 Garville Avenue, Rathgar, Dublin. (About 30.) [AE gave Mr and Mrs Curran several pictures and *objêts d'art* when he moved to London; including a cast of the famous bust of Dante, a small figure of Cuchulain by Oliver Sheppard, a superb bronze cast of a figure of an athlete by his friend the American physician and sculptor Robert Tait Mackenzie, and a pencil drawing of Susan L.

Mitchell which had been given to AE in 1926 by Dr Thomas Bodkin, to try to console him in his grief over her death.]

Dr James Hamilton Delargy, 28 Kenilworth Square, Dublin. (1) [Presented to Dr Delargy as a wedding present, in 1934, by his friend the late Osborn Bergin. Exhibited, Dublin 1936. Dr Delargy described the painting: "Measurement, 31 by 20 inches. Not reproduced. It is in oils and shows a huge tree overhanging water with two typical amorphous AE females clinging to it in unconvincing fashion. But the tree is good—and the general effect pleasing."]

Alan Denson, c/o the publishers of this book. (One unfinished Donegal scene, badly faded. Oil on hardboard: 17 by 13 inches. Not reproduced. In addition 2 AE books with his own crayon illustrations.)

Mrs K. R. (Betty) Dickie, "Brackla", Warren Drive, Kingswood, Surrey. (1 oil painting: one self-portrait drawing.) [Formerly owned by her father, the late Charles Coates Riddal, to whom they had been presented by AE.]

Senator J. Harold Douglas, Moat Hill, Lucan, County Dublin. (Several.) [Formerly owned by his father, the late Senator James G. Douglas. The AE paintings were shared by Senator J. H. Douglas and his brother after their mother's death in 1959.]

Mrs Norah Douglas, 19 Taunton Avenue, Belfast. (1) [Reproduced in *Irish Life and Landscape* (1927).]

Mrs Wilhelmina Duggan, 3 Springfield Park, Blackrock, County Dublin. (2) [Formerly owned by the late Mr and Mrs Paul Gregan. One, a wedding present to the Gregans from the Russells.]

Mrs Aileen Dunlop-Sicré, "Ferncot", 27 Boase Street, Newlyn, Cornwall. (2) [Formerly owned by her parents, Mr and Mrs D. N. Dunlop.]

Lord Dunsany, Dunsany Castle, County Meath, Ireland. (14?)

Mr St John Greer Ervine, "Honey Ditches", Seaton, Devon. (?)

Mrs F. C. Farrell, "The Crock of Gold Ltd", Newtownpark Avenue, Blackrock, County Dublin. (3)

Dr Anthony Farrington, c/o The Royal Irish Academy, 19 Dawson Street, Dublin. (Several.) [Formerly owned by his uncle, the late Osborn Bergin.]

Mrs Stephen Farrington, Coolgarten Park, Cork. (1)

Heirs of the late Professor William Robert Fearon (1892–December 27, 1959), lately resident at 24 Trinity College, Dublin. (Several.)

Heirs of the late Dr James Joseph Flood, *M.D.* (died at 31 N. Frederick Street, Dublin, November 20, 1937). (Several.) [Memorial Exhibition, 1936.]

Mrs Victoria D. Franklin (lately at 16 William Street, now resident in) Wolfe Tone Street, Sligo Town. (10)

Baron Geddes, "Malleny", Balerno, Midlothian. (Several, formerly owned by the late Sir Patrick Geddes.)

Dr William Monk Gibbon, "Tara Hall", 24 Sandycove Road, Sandycove, County Dublin. (Several.)

Lady Glenavy, Rockall, Sandycove, County Dublin.

Mr Oliver D. Gogarty, S.C., 22 Earlsfort Terrace, Dublin. (?)

Mr H. G. Goodwillie, "Ennismore", King Edward Road, Bray, County Wicklow. ("A few of his earlier paintings". Formerly owned by his father, the late Henry Goodwillie: died December 31, 1944.)

Mr David Gould, "The Corner", 104 Station Road, Barnes, London, S.W. 13. (1)

Heirs of Isabella Augusta *Lady* Gregory. (Several.)

B. J. Gwynn, "Temple Hill", Terenure, Dublin. (2)

Professor Denis Gwynn, 4 Lower Montenotte, Cork. (1)

Heirs of the late *Provost* Edward J. Gwynn (1868–February 10, 1941). [Memorial Exhibition, 1936.]

J. D. Gwynn, 49A Lytton Grove, Putney, London, S.W. 15. (1)

Mrs O. M. Gwynn, 3 Winton Road, Leeson Park, Dublin. (1)

Mrs George Hall, Campstoun House, Drem, via Athelstaneford, East Lothian, Scotland. [Some, formerly owned by the late Hugh Law.]

Sir Patrick Hannon, 9 Campbell Court, Queens Gate Gardens, London, S.W. 7. [Sir Patrick generously gave away to younger people the paintings by AE which he treasured, trusting such pleasant wedding presents would induce idealism "from the lofty spiritual exaltation" out of which AE had lived and worked.]

Lady Constance Geraldine (Deena) Hanson, 79 Upper Leeson Street, Dublin. (A bright landscape, painted at Marble Hill, County Donegal, and a dark faded landscape.) [Lady Hanson, widow of Sir Philip Hanson (died October 23, 1955), private secretary to George Wyndham, 1898–1903, and Commissioner of Public Works (Ireland) 1903–14 and 1919–34. The bright landscape was given to Sir Philip by Sir Horace Plunkett.]

Rev. Canon Anthony Hanson, *D.D.* (Canon Theologian of St Anne's Cathedral, Belfast), 53 Malone Avenue, Belfast. (1) [Formerly owned by his mother Lady Deena Hanson.]

Rt Rev T. Arnold Harvey, 1 Dartry Road, Dublin. (2)

Mrs Irving H. Hare, 167 Dolphin Road, Palm Beach, Florida. (Several sketches.)

Mrs Kate M. Hasler, East Mount, Brunswick Road, Douglas, Isle of Man. (1)

Miss Irene Haugh, B.A., 31 Northumberland Road, Dublin. (Several.)

Mrs Beatrice M. Higgins, Brabazon House, 2 Gilford Road, Sandymount, Dublin. (1)

Miss Pamela Hinkson, 3 Clifton Terrace, Monkstown, County Dublin. (3)

[*The Rt Hon* Jonathan Hogg died in Dublin during July 1930, aged 80. His small, choice collection of AE paintings was sold at auction in Dublin, during September or October 1930.]

Mrs Joseph M. Hone, 4 Winton Road, Leeson Park, Dublin. (?)

Dr Andrew J. Horne, 10 Merrion Square, Dublin. [One landscape given to his father by Dr Thomas Bodkin. Dr Bodkin esteemed this as possibly the finest surviving AE picture. Bought before 1914. Size: 32 by 21 inches.]

Mrs Robert H. Hutchinson (*née* Hesper Le Gallienne), The Barlow House, West Redding, Connecticut. [Bequeathed to her by her aunt the late Mrs E. J. Weekes.] (2)

John Irvine, 88 Ulsterville Avenue, Lisburn Road, Belfast. (One water-color: page from a sketch-book, given to Mr Irvine by the late Dr J. S. Starkey. 2 brown crayon drawings.)

Heirs of the late Mrs Clara Annabel Caroline Huth Jackson [author of *A Victorian Childhood* (London, 1932. Methuen).] (?)

Emeritus Professor T. Campbell James, "Valsolda", Caradoc Road, Aberystwyth, North Wales. (2). [Photographs held by the National Museum of Wales, Cardiff.]

Mrs Sage Jennings, c/o Edwin O. Holter, 150, East 73rd Street, New York City. (2 crayon sketches, one oil.) [Mrs Jennings was a friend of Mrs Jessie Orage, and of Mr D. C. Russell.]

Mrs Holford Knight, c/o 146 Carlton Avenue West, North Wembley, Middx. (1)

Miss E. K. Lavelle, Dugort, Achill, County Mayo. (1: formerly owned by Osborn Bergin. After his death this was given by his heirs to Bergin's housekeeper. She passed it on to her friend Miss Lavelle.)

Lt Col Francis Law, Barony House, Lasswade, Midlothian, Scotland. (2) [One given to him as a wedding present, by AE: the other purchased by Colonel Law, from AE. See also further particulars concerning pictures owned by his sisters, Mrs Hall, Mrs Mackenzie-Kennedy, Mrs Tidswell: and by his aunts Mrs Chambré and Mrs Perry.]

Sir J. A. Shane Leslie, *Bt.*, Glaslough, County Monaghan. (?)

Mrs Florence C. Lewis, Currabawn, Putland Road, Bray, County Wicklow. (1)

Henry McEllivray, Glenveagh Castle, County Donegal. (?)

Mrs A. G. Mackenzie-Kennedy, Beltony Lodge, Mountjoy, via Newtown-stewart, County Tyrone, N. Ireland. (?)

Mr Séan MacBride, Roebuck House, Clonskea, Dublin. (?)

Miss Grace and Miss Katherine MacCormack, 12 Kenilworth Road, Rathgar, Dublin. (1)

Mrs Deirdre MacDonagh, "Carmencita", Airfield Road, Rathgar, Dublin. (?)

Dr Thomas McGreevy, c/o The National Gallery of Ireland, Dublin. (?)

Mrs Maureen McGuire, 37 FitzWilliam Square, Dublin. (2)

Dr Edward E. MacLysaght, Raheen, Tuamgraney, County Clare. (Several.)

The late *Hon* Ethel MacNaghten (died *circa* 1949–50: daughter of late Baron MacNaghten of Runkerry) left her AE ptgs to Belfast Gallery.

Mr B. Y. McPeake, c/o The National Magazine Co, 28–30 Grosvenor Gardens, London, S.W.1. (1)

Mrs W. K. Magee, 21 Carbery Avenue, West Southbourne, Bournemouth. (2)

Mr Arnold Marsh, Woodtown Park, Woodtown, Rathfarnham, County Dublin. (5)

Heirs of the late Miss Mary Massey. [Whitechapel Exhibition, 1913.]

Lady Dorothy (Robert) Mayer, 2 Mansfield Street, London, W.1. (2)

Heirs of late *Mr Justice* James Creed Meredith (died Aug 14, 1942). [Memorial exhibition, 1936.] (?)

Heirs of the late Miss Millen, of Belfast (died *circa* 1957). [*See also* Bewglass, and Craig.]

Dr Rosemary M. Mills, The Manse, Castletroy, County Limerick. (1—formerly owned by Osborn Bergin.)

Miss Susan M. Mitchell, 1 Iona Crescent, Glasnevin, County Dublin. (1)

Mr Niall Montgomery (architect), 27 Merrion Square, Dublin.

Heirs of the late Mrs Wm. Vaughn Moody, Boston, Mass.

Mrs T. G. Moorhead, 23 Upper FitzWilliam Street, Dublin. (1). [Daughter of the late S. L. Gwynn.]

Mr and Mrs Wm. L. Murphy, 413 Griffith Avenue, Dublin. [Or c/o James White, The Friends of the National Collections, Dublin.] (1)

Mrs Frances Nuttall, Tittour, Newtownmountkennedy, County Wicklow. (5)

Dr Brendan Edward O'Brien, M.B., B.Ch., F.R.C.P.I., 65 FitzWilliam Square, Dublin. (?) [Pictures formerly owned by his father, the late Dermod O'Brien, P.R.H.A.]

Professor George O'Brien, 3 Burlington Road, Dublin. (?)

Mrs Dominic O'Connor [a niece of the late T. M. Healy, and wife of the distinguished Irish architect, Dominic O'Connor], Arundel, Ballintemple, County Cork. (1)

Mrs Jessie Orage, 15 Oakley Street, London, S.W.3. (1)

Dr and Mrs Donal O'Sullivan, 40 Anglesea Road, Ballsbridge, Dublin. (2 sepia sketches: one in black and white.)

Heirs of Herbert Edward Palmer, 22 Batchwood View, St Albans, Herts. (1)

Miss Margaret C. Patten, 2120 16th Street N.W., Washington 9, D.C. (several crayon sketches).

Mrs Louise Perry [sister of Mrs Chambré and Mrs Law], Banlin Lodge, Milford, County Donegal. (3: 2 seascapes, and one landscape. One, "The Bathing Pool", purchased about 1913 or 1912, includes Mrs Charlotte Law with her daughter, now Mrs Hall.)

Heirs of the late Mrs Catherine Mary Phillimore (Mrs Wm. Lyon Phillimore) [author of *The King's Namesake* (London, 1928: new ed, Sheldon Press)].

Mr Pierce Leslie Pielou, "Annandale", 17 Sandford Road, Dublin (1: given to Mr Pielou, his wife's sister's husband, by the late James H. Cousins.)

Miss Ruth Pitter, "The Hawthorns", Chilton Road, Long Crendon, Bucks. (4)

Heirs of the *Hon and Most Rev Dr* Benjamin J. Plunket, Bishop of Tuam, Killala and Achonry (1870–January 26, 1947) [Memorial Exhibition, 1936.]

Benjamin W. A. Plunket, *M.V.O.*, "Dromin", Delgany, County Wicklow. (3?)

[The frieze painted by AE for Sir Horace Plunkett at his home, Kilteragh, Foxrock, was destroyed by fire in the Irish Civil War. This compiler has not located any photographs of that frieze. Probably Plunkett specified in his will disposition of any other AE paintings in his custody.]

Heirs of the late Sarah H. Purser, R.H.A. (?)

District Judge Kenneth Shiels Reddin, "Ashleaf", Templeogue, County Dublin. (?)

Heirs of Miss Barbara Robertson [Memorial Exhibition, 1936].

Mrs E. S. Lennox Robinson, 20 Longford Terrace, Monkstown, County Dublin. (?)

Sir John Rothenstein, *C.B.E.*, Beauforest House, Newington, Warborough, Oxford. (2?: one given to his father the late Sir William Rothenstein, by Miss Ruth Pitter.)

Mr Charles Cary Rumsey, 130 East 79th Street, New York City. (Some portrait sketches, and almost certainly some paintings. The late Oliver St J. Gogarty advised Mr Rumsey and his family to present some of their AE relics, including letters, to Colby College, Waterville, Maine.)

Mr Brian Hartley Russell, Furzy Cottage, South Weirs, Brockenhurst, Hants. (?)

Mr Diarmuid Conor Russell, Hook Road, Katonah, New York. (?)

Miss Cathleen Sheppard, 38 Dawson Street, Dublin. (2: Memorial Exhibition, 1936: then owned by her father the late Oliver Sheppard, R.H.A. In addition a pencil drawing of Oliver Sheppard.)

Viscount Simon, "Pollard", Whiteleaf, Princes Risborough, Bucks. (9) [Four of his AE pictures were exhibited at Whitechapel, 1913: loaned by his father John, first Viscount Simon.]

Mrs Constance Sitwell, 1 Victoria Square, London, S.W.1. (2 oil: one crayon woodland scene in Northumberland.)

Mrs A. Kathleen Smith, 74 Woodlawn Park, Churchtown, County Dublin. (2) [Mrs Smith is the widow of the late Herbert Smith, sometime Private Secretary to Sir Horace Plunkett, in the Dept of Agriculture.]

Dr Bethel A. H. Solomons, "Laughton Beg", Rochestown Avenue, Dun Laoghaire, Dublin. (2)

Mrs Estella Starkey [widow of the late Dr J. S. Starkey. He advised this compiler that he owned "about thirty paintings and many sketches and notebooks by AE".] 2 Morehampton Road, Dublin.

Mr and Mrs Charles Stewart, "Hillcrest", Breaghy, Portnablagh, County Donegal. (1: given to the late Miss Janie Stewart, by AE.)

Miss Mary Synon, c/o The Catholic University of America, Washington, D.C. (1)

Mr Gilbert Thomas, "Hesper", Yannon Drive, Teignmouth, Devon. (A copy of AE's *Collected Poems* decorated with drawings by AE.)

Mrs Edward S. W. Tidswell, "Summers", Mill Street, St Osyth, Essex. (?)

Dr Michael Tierney, University Lodge, Stillorgan Road, Dublin. (2?)

Mrs Louise Tottenham, "Struan", 42 Links Lane, Rowlands Castle, Hants. (1)

Mrs Pamela Travers, 50 Smith Street, Chelsea, London, S.W.3. (?)

Miss Caroline P. Trenain (2). [Miss Trenain had worked on the staff of Alexandra College, Dublin, until 1914. Probably there she met AE's friends Harry and Edith Norman. She owned several AE paintings when she moved to Aberystwyth, where she was for many years senior warden of the Hostel for Women Students in the University. She died in 1935, and bequeathed 2 of her AE paintings to Professor T. Campbell James.]

[Miss Helen Waddell owned about 10–11 AE paintings. Miss M. M. Martin (her niece) advised this compiler that those paintings have been disposed of at the direction of the Official Solicitor, since 1959.]

Samuel J. Waddell ("Rutherford Mayne"), "Fuzefield", Westminster Road, Foxrock, County Dublin. (?)

Mr Victor Waddington, c/o Waddington Galleries, 2 Cork Street, London, W.1. (?)

The Hon Henry A. Wallace, Farvue Farm, South Salem, New York. (2)

Mr Karl Walter, c/o Dr William Grey Walter, M.A., 35 Mariners Drive, Bristol 9. (?) [Perhaps some from Sir Horace Plunkett?]

Mrs Bernard Werthan (*née* Leah Rose Bernstein), 4440, Tyne Lane, Nashville 5, Tennessee. (Several sketches.)

Augustus W. West (born 1871), M.R.A.C., formerly one of the Assistant Land Commissioners for Ireland, resident at Leixlip House, County Kildare. Presumably now deceased. [Mem. Exhib. 1936.]

Mr Walter Muir Whitehill, Director and Librarian, The Boston Athenaeum, Ten-and-a-half Beacon Street, Boston 8, Mass. (?)

Mr and Mrs N. Wise, "Eversleigh", 28 Queen's Walk, London, N.W.9. (3)

Heirs of the late Miss Elizabeth Corbet Yeats, and the late Miss Lily Yeats. (?)

Mrs W. B. Yeats, 46 Palmerston Road, Dublin. (?)

[The murals in the front ground-floor room at 3 Upper Ely Place, Dublin, have been preserved: they were painted by AE, probably in collaboration with W. B. Yeats. See above, *Part 13*, under date 1892. The present tenant of the 3 Upper Ely Place property is Dr Colm McDonnell.]

PART 15

PRINTED REPRODUCTIONS OF DRAWINGS AND PAINTINGS BY AE

Irish Theosophist (Dublin): vol 3 No 11 (August 15, 1895) frtspce: vol 3 No 12 (Sept 15, 1895) p 222: vol 4 No 1 (Oct 15, 1895) p 4: vol 4 No 2 (Nov 15, 1895) p 28 [illus to *Collected Poems*, p 90]: vol 4 No 7 (April 15, 1896) p 126: vol 4 No 9 (June 15, 1896) p 174: vol 4 No 10 (July 15, 1896) p 190 [illus to *Collected Poems*, p 108]: vol 4 No 12 (Sept 15, 1896) p 230: vol 5 No 1 (October 15, 1896) p 6. Repros sgd AE and "Aretas" (James M. Pryse) in several colors (AE's, blues only): vol 3 Nos 11, 12 (Aug, Sept 15, 1895) pp 197, 224–5; vol 4 Nos 2, 3, (Nov, Dec 15, 1895) pp [29], 49.

The Artist (London) vol 17 p 139 (March 1896) with review of exhibition (*Part* 13, 1895) repro of one sketch by Russell & Pryse from *Part* 5, item 96, from the "Songs of Olden Magic". In item 96 the sketch was printed in reds and yellows. "There was a refreshing daringness and quaint originality in the specimens of color reproductions for magazines (No. 295) . . . that for the 'Songs of Olden Magic' being most remarkable." [Item 96 vol 4 No 1 (Oct 15, 1895) p [4].]

Irish Homestead (Dublin) One of the December issues annually from 1897 until 1910 inclusive was called the *Celtic Christmas* issue. Most had separate pagination from the annual volume. In them AE illustrated poems and stories written by Padraic Colum, Lord Dunsany, Susan L. Mitchell, Kate F. Purdon, J. S. Starkey (Seumas O'Sullivan), George Roberts, Ella Young and others. vol 21 p 107 (February 7, 1914), "Giant Middleman".

Tatler (London) No 42 (April 16, 1902). A review of the Dublin performance of AE's *Deirdre*, with photographs [by *Chancellor*, Dublin] including the scenery designed and painted by AE. [See also *Letters of W. B. Yeats* (ed. Wade) p 368 for his verbal description.]

The Passionate Hearts. Love Stories by Ethna Carberry. (London: June 1903. Isbister). The cover-design, printed in three colors, was designed by AE.

The Green Sheaf (London) No 2 (1903): an AE illustration between pp 10–11, of a huge skull and a man. Identical subject in a small painting now in the County Museum, Armagh. Another owned by Mrs W. B. Yeats.

Myths by Ethel Longworth Dames (Dublin: 1903. Hodges, Figgis). The cover was designed by AE.

Studio (London) vol 37 pp 351–2 (1906).

Studio (London) vol 42 pp 65–6 (November 1907).

Orpheus (London) No 14 (April 1911): No 15 (July 1911) facing p 295: No 16 (October 1911) facing p 327.

Irish Review (Dublin) vol 1, between pp 312–3 (September 1911): vol 2, opposite p 281 (August 1912): vol 3, frtspce (March 1913). [Also reproduced in that journal were monochrome photographs of paintings by Jack B. Yeats "In the possession of Mr G. W. Russell": vol 1, opp. p 365 (October 1911) "The Tinker's Curse" (a water-color, now owned by Mr C. P. Curran's daughter) a picture praised by Padraic Colum in a contemporary review in *Sinn Fein*, when it was first exhibited in the Leinster Lecture Hall, Dublin, early October 1906: vol 2, opp p 337 (September 1912) "Romance".]

Bulletin of the Art Institute of Chicago (Chicago) vol 11 No 1 p 251 (January 1917), "On the Sand Hills".

Vanity Fair (New York). Reproductions from paintings by AE, to accompany an article on general Irish topics, written by Padraic Colum. Probably in the issue dated January or February 1917.

Art News (New York) vol 24 No 13 p 3 (1925–6).

John Quinn 1870–1925. Collection of Paintings, etc., with a Foreword by Forbes Watson (Huntingdon, New York: 1926. Pidgeon Hill Press) includes repro in monochrome of paintings by AE: "Nocturne—The Well", p 154: "Bedtime", p 155: and on p 156 "John B. Yeats" from the pencil drawing by Russell—but the caption is surely a mistake for W. B. Yeats.

The Quinn Collection. Paintings and Sculptures of the Moderns. [Exhibition and sale catalog] (New York: 1927. American Art Association). [Free public exhibition from Saturday, February 5, 1927: unrestricted public sale Wed–Sat February 9–12, 1927.] Sale conducted by Mr O. Bernet and Mr H. Parke.] "The Shining Shallows", item 330: "In the Forest", item 343: "The Cockle Gatherers", item 487, by AE reptd in monochrome. Other AE paintings exhib and sold were items numbered: 70, 79, 81, 82, 84, 85, 86, 87, 89, 99, 101, 105, 177, 180, 198, 206, 207, 209, 213–216, 223, 232, 235, 237, 315, 320, 326–328, 336, 345, 452–3, 459–463, 471–2, 475, 484.

Irish Life and Landscape (Dublin: [1927] Talbot Press) by J. Crampton Walker. P [107] color repro of AE's oil painting "River and Sands at

Dunfanaghy, County Donegal". [The book date-stamped at Brit. Mus. 10 Aug 27.]

International Studio (New York) vol 92 p 76 (April 1929). Some AE pictures were sold in New York during October 1929.

New York [*City*] *American* (New York) January 12, 1931. [Reference to Barbazon Plaza exhibition.]

New York Times (New York) May 29, 1932: section 8 p 7 col 6: AE's "Lost in the Woods" repro in monochrome. [Review of exhib in the Museum of Irish Art.]

Art Digest (New York) vol 7 p 20 (September 1933). [Article.]

AE—G. W. Russell. Sein Leben und Werk im Lichte seiner theosophischen Weltanschauung, by Friedrich Biens (Greifswald: 1934. Verlag Hans Dallmayer). Monochrome reproduction of some AE sketches etc, probably from originals supplied by D. N. Dunlop, from the *Irish Theosophist*. [pp 95]

Art Digest (New York) vol 9 p 16 (August 1935) [Article.]

Listener (London) vol 39 pp 144–5 (January 28, 1948) with article by James Stephens.

NOTE

AE designed the woodcut winged sword, within circles, printed in red, in *Words for Music Perhaps and other poems* by W. B. Yeats (Dublin: November 14, 1932. Cuala Press), on p [xi].

PART 16

PORTRAITS BY AE

1 *Cesca Chenevix-Trench* (1918). Crayon drawing: size 30 × 22 inches. Owned by her husband, Dr Diarmid Coffey. Exhibited, Dublin 1936. [Francesca G. Chenevix-Trench (February 3, 1891–October 29, 1918) was a painter, using professionally the name Sadb Táinseac (Sadhbh Trínseach).]

2 *Cesca Chenevix-Trench* (1918). Oil portrait, slightly larger than No 1, above. Owned by Dr D. Coffey. He has presented it on long loan to the Friends of the Irish National Collections. Exhib., Dublin, 1936.

3 *Mary Catherine Maguire Colum* (1922). Oil on canvas. Owned by Mr Padraic Colum. [Mary Colum, the critic and poet (1887–1957).] Described by Mrs Colum (to AE's amusement), "Portrait of a deaf woman, by a blind man." [Presented by Padraic Colum to Sligo Library, 1961.]

4 *Padraic Colum* (1905?). Drawing, reproduced in the *Irish Homestead* vol 11 p 737 (October 7, 1905). Not located. This may have been one among several drawings of Mr Colum which were once owned by the the late Dr J. S. Starkey ("Seumas O'Sullivan"), sold during 1960. See the list of *Sales*, in this book, p. 174.

5 *Miss Janet Cunningham* (*circa* 1910). Oil on canvas: approx. 30 × 22 inches. In Miss Cunningham's opinion an improbable likeness to herself. Owned by Miss Cunningham.

6 *Elizabeth Curran*, aged 10 (1923–4). Oil. Owned by her father Mr C. P. Curran, S.C.

7 *Helen (Laird) Mrs C. P. Curran* (1903). Colored chalk drawing, sketched by AE during rehearsals of W. B. Yeats' play *The King's Threshold* (produced by the Irish National Theatre Society, in the Molesworth Street, Hall, Dublin, on October 8, 1903).

8 *Helen (Laird) Mrs C. P. Curran* (1903?). A pen drawing which is considered by her husband (owner of both portraits) to be half caricature. ["AE made no claims at all for his portraits. He constantly sketched likenesses in his notebooks. They were what he regarded as a light relaxation. He was always playful over his sketches. He devised a book-plate for my wife, using the legend 'Helen Laird, not her book'." —Mr C. P. Curran's comment.]

9 *Mike Elkins* [the photographer] (1930). Drawing reproduced in the *New York Journal*, September 29, 1930.

10 *Kathleen Celia Franklin* ('Kitsy') (1923?). Oil on canvas. Owned by her mother Mrs Victoria D. Franklin. Miss Franklin was a niece of Susan L. Mitchell. [K. C. Franklin, born April 28 (or 29), 1906: died February 1, 1958.]

11 *Oliver St John Gogarty* (1930?). Pencil drawing in a copy of his book *Wild Apples* (1930). Sold among AE's books, at Sotheby's, November 11, 1935. Not located.

12 *Lady Isabella Augusta Gregory* (1904). Oil portrait: sitter's name painted in upper right corner. Owned by the Abbey Theatre Collection, Dublin. Repro in *Ireland's Abbey Theatre*, by Lennox Robinson (London: 1952. Sidgwick & Jackson), facing page 13. Memorial exhibition, 1936.

13 *Robert Gregory* (1899?). [Drawing?] Not located.

14 *Christopher Murray Grieve* ('Hugh MacDiarmid') (1928). Crayon drawing profile, left, signed and dated 17.8.28. Repro in Mr MacDiarmid's fine book *First Hymn to Lenin* (London: 1931. Unicorn Press). Owned by the subject.

15 *Sir Patrick Hannon* (1902, etc). Many portrait sketches made during the years in which Sir Patrick and AE were happy associates in the I.A.O.S. Several ink sketches of Sir Patrick adorn a letter written to him by AE, January 24, 1902.

16 *Mrs Jeannette Hare* (early July 1931). Crayon pastel drawing sketched by AE one Sunday whilst he was Col and Mrs Hare's guest in their home at Forest Hills Gardens, Long Island, N.Y. Owned by Col and Mrs Hare.

17 *Miss Irene Haugh* (1929–30). Several crayon sketches. One full-face, sgd, repro to her book *The Valley of the Bells* (Oxford: 1933. B. H. Blackwell). Owned by Miss Haugh.

18 Fr John Hegarty (1897?). Drawing repro in the *Irish Homestead* vol 4 p 54 (January 15, 1898), with AE's first co-operative article, "Co-operative Banks". Not located: the drawing may have been inherited by his brother Mr Edward Hegarty of Rathduff, Ballina. [At the time this drawing was made Father Hegarty was priest at Kilmore Erris although the drawing was captioned "Fr. Hegarty of Belmullet". Later he was for many years parish priest at Belmullet, County Mayo. He was born in Moygownagh. First apprenticed to a Ballina merchant, and then trained for the church: he was ordained at Maynooth, 1891. He was later appointed Canon in the diocese of Killala, and was promoted Archdeacon in 1934. He died at Belmullet, aged 85,

November 10, 1942. Obituary, with a photograph, in *Western People* (Ballina, County Mayo) November 14, 1942: p 6 col 4.]

19 *Mrs Beatrice May Higgins* (1929). Crayon drawing, owned by the subject—widow of F. R. Higgins, the poet.

20 *Mrs Charlotte (Hugh) Law and her children* were often portrayed by AE in his landscape scenes painted at Marble Hill, Donegal. Mrs Law's surviving sister, Mrs Perry, owns one. In many such landscapes the children are playing tig, or swinging from a tree: often, again, they are merely suggested, rather than portrayed in detail, in woodland scenes.

21 *Miss Katherine MacCormack* (aged 10?) (*circa* 1903–4). Oil on canvas, painted at Dún Emer, Dundrum, home of Miss MacCormack's aunt, the late Miss Evelyn Gleeson. Owned by the subject.

22 *Miss Jeannie Mitchell* (1905?). A drawing to illustrate one of her own stories. [Miss Jeannie Mitchell, younger sister of Susan L. Mitchell: died December 1, 1941.] Owned by Mrs V. D. Franklin.

23 *Miss Elinor Mitchell* (aged 8) (1903). Oil on canvas: owned by her sister Miss Susan M. Mitchell. [Elinor Mitchell (March 2, 1895–December 13, 1943) a niece of Susan L. Mitchell.]

24 *Susan Langstaff Mitchell* (1905). Pen and ink drawing, lightly colored by hand with mauve and green. Full length. Repro in the Celtic Christmas issue of the *Irish Homestead* (December 1905). Unsigned, not dated. Also printed onto a postcard: one copy inscribed to 'Seumas O'Sullivan' "With best wishes from the original", is now owned by this compiler.

25 *Susan L. Mitchell* (190–?). Pencil sketch, now owned by the National Gallery of Ireland.

26 *Susan L. Mitchell* (191–?). Oil portrait, on canvas, half-length: owned by Mrs V. D. Franklin. [This may portray their sister Jeannie.]

27 *George A. Moore* (the novelist) (1903?). Pastel drawing. Not located.

28 *Jessica Nelson North* (1928). Drawing, repro in her book *The Long Leash* (Boston and New York: 1928. Houghton Mifflin) [Reviewed by AE in the *Irish Statesman* vol 11 pp 341–2 (sgd Y.O.) (December 29, 1928).] [Mrs MacDonald, [*née* North) born 1894. She wrote about AE in *Poetry* (Chicago) vol 48 pp 290–2 (September 1935).]

29 *Self-portrait* (1893). Pencil sketch: now owned by the County Museum, Armagh. From the late Charles Weekes' papers.

30 *Self-portrait* (1900?). In 1937 the late Dr J. S. Starkey ('Seumas O'Sullivan') owned "an early self-portrait". In 1954 he refused to divulge to this compiler whether or not he had retained possession of it.

31 *Self-portrait* (1914). Pastel: once owned by Miss Jane Mitchell. Not located. Dublin, Memorial exhibition, 1936.

32 *Self-portrait* (*circa* 1914?). Oil on canvas: once owned by the late

Susan L. Mitchell. By her bequeathed to her youngest sister Mrs V. D. Franklin. Mrs Franklin generously presented that portrait to the County Museum, Armagh, in 1954. [In *Portrait of an Irishman* by C. H. Rolleston (London: 1939. Methuen) there is a photograph of AE painting a self-portrait.]

33 *Self-portrait* (191–?). Pencil drawing, signed, on white paper. This is full-face. "Looking straight at you!" is the present owner's description. Presented to the late Charles Coates Riddall, by AE (*circa* 1930): now owned by his daughter, Mrs Betty (R. K.) Dickie. [This may be the same drawing as number 31 above.]

34 *Oliver Sheppard, R.H.A.* (?1885). Pencil drawing reproduced in this book. Owned by the subject's daughter Miss Cathleen Sheppard. [Oliver Sheppard, 1865–1941.]

35 *James Stephens* (?1910). Oil portrait, on canvas (?), owned by the late Mrs Cynthia Stephens. Approx 10 × 16 in.

36 *James Stephens* (1930). A pencil sketch, three-quarters facing right inscribed in lower right corner: "James Stephens 13/4/30. AE to W. H. T. Howe". Repro in *New York Times*, June 22, 1930: section 5 p 13 (with an article by F. L. Minnigerode, quoting Stephens' comments on AE. [Wm. Thomas Hildrup Howe, died August 19, 1930, aged 65. He was President of the American Book Co., and had been Stephen's host in America.] Not located.

37 *James Stephens* (?1930). Another pencil drawing, reproduced elsewhere. Not located.

38 *J. M. Synge* (190–?). An oil portrait was listed as "lost" by Maurice Bourgeois in *J. M. Synge and the Irish Theatre* (London: 1913. Constable). Not yet located?

39 *J. M. Synge* (1904. "A full-face pencil sketch, in the possession of Seumas O'Sullivan" (Bourgeois). Dr Starkey in 1954 would not divulge to this compiler whether that drawing was still his property.

40 *Simone Téry* (*Mme Chabas*) (August 1928). Two drawings, not located. Mme Chabas assumes they were destroyed, or irretrievably dispersed with all her personal possessions, during the German occupation of Paris in the second world war. [Mr C. P. Curran, S.C. recalls many occasions in 1920–3 when AE sketched Simone Téry.]

41 *Jean Wallace* (aged 10) (1930). Two crayon sketches owned by the subject's father the Hon Henry Agard Wallace. [Mr Wallace generously gave this compiler a colored photograph of one of these sketches (the second having been mislaid). Loaned to AE's old friend (—.—.—) the photograph has not been returned.]

42 *Charles Alexandre Weekes* (March 1891). Pen and ink drawing, on white paper. Mrs E. J. Weekes presented this drawing to the County

Museum, Armagh, a few weeks before her death in 1957. Repro in this book.

43 *Mrs (Bernard) Leah Rose Werthan (née Bernstein)* (1928) several crayon sketches, owned by Mr and Mrs Werthan.

44 *Mrs Leoline Leonard Wright* (?June 1896). "An amusing sketch caricature" made in Killarney. Abandoned and lost with all her personal possessions, when Mrs Wright left Germany in 1914. [Mrs Wright, widow of Claude Falls Wright (1867–1923).]

45 *W. B. Yeats* (189–?). A pastel sketch twice reproduced in the *Irish Homestead*: vol 3 p 765 (November 13, 1898), and again in the Celtic Christmas issue of the *Irish Homestead*, vol 3 (December 1898: separate pagination from the volume: page 3). Not located.

46 *W. B. Yeats* (190–?). A pencil drawing, signed in the lower right corner "AE", not dated. 7×10 inches. Repro in *Quinn, 1870–1925. Collection of Paintings, etc*, with a Foreword by Forbes Watson (Huntingdon, New York: 1926. Pidgeon Hill Press), p 156 captioned erroneously "John B. Yeats". This drawing was not listed in the Quinn sale *Catalogue* (1927). Not located.

47 *W. B. Yeats* (1903). Black chalk drawing: signed and dated in lower left corner, "Æ Aug 1903". This drawing was framed and hung above the mantel-shelf in AE's home, until 1933. AE gave it to F. R. Higgins when he left Dublin. This drawing is now owned by the National Gallery of Ireland. Memorial exhibition, Dublin, 1936.

48 Robert Andrew Anderson (1861–1942), pencil drawing on white paper, *circa* 1904: signed lower right, GWR. Size: 13.6 × 9.5 inches. This shows Anderson profile, facing left, with a cigarette protruding from his mouth. Owned by Sir Patrick Hannon.

[Several sketches made in America by AE were owned by Mary Harriman Rumsey. Her son Mr Charles Cary Rumsey advised this compiler that they were dispersed several years ago: either to the subjects, if portraits, or else to the Library at Colby College. Details concerning Colby College holdings were not divulged to this compiler.]

PART 17

PORTRAITS OF AE

1 Bust modelled in plaster, at the Metropolitan School of Art, Kildare Street, Dublin, by John Hughes. Colored by AE. Hughes presented the bust to Russell. He gave it to Mr C. P. Curran in 1933. Mr Curran gave it to the Municipal Gallery of Modern Art, Dublin, after AE's death. Exhibited: AE Memorial Exhibition, Dublin 1936. Repro in *Part 1*, item 59, and in this book. 1885–6

1A See *Part 16*, No. 29 p 241. 1893

2 Pencil drawing by John Butler Yeats [J. B. Yeats the Elder]. Now in the National Gallery of Ireland. Exhibited: Work by J. B. Yeats and Nathaniel Hone, in 6 St Stephen's Green, Dublin, October 19 to November 2, 1901. [Review, sgd AE in *Freeman's Journal* (Dublin) Oct 21, 1901, p 5 col 3. Reptd in *Part 8*, item 177 and in item 28, etc.] Signed and dated. January 1898

3 "An early self-portrait" once owned by the late Dr J. S. Starkey. *Part 16*, No 30 p 241. *Circa* 1900?

4 Oil portrait on canvas by Sarah H. Purser (1848–1943). Now in the National Gallery, Dublin. Exhibited: Memorial Exhibition, 1936. 27 × 20⅛ inches. *Circa* 1902.

5 Oil portrait on canvas, by J. B. Yeats the Elder. Owned by Mrs W. B. Yeats. Painted in Dublin: 4 sittings, Sundays during August 1902. [See reference in *Freeman's Journal*, September 5, 1902, p 4 col 8. And in a contemporary letter, AE to W. B. Yeats.] Repro in *Part 9*, item 198: vol 8, facing p 2986. August 1902

6 Oil portrait on canvas, by Count Casimir Dunin Markiewicz. Now in the Municipal Gallery, Dublin. Exhibited: *Part 13* (1904); Whitechapel Gallery (1913); Memorial Exhib, 1936. [AE wrote to Messrs Macmillan & Co., January 16, 1919, alluding to this as the best "likeness".] Repro: *Catalogue of the Municipal Gallery* (Dublin: 1908. Dollard Printing House), from a photograph by Combridge & Co, Grafton Street, Dublin. Again in the new (select) *Catalogue* of the Municipal Gallery (Dublin: 1958. Sealy, Bryers): in the *Irish Review* (Dublin) vol 2 No 1 (June 1912); in *Part 1*, item 54 (vignette on title-page); in the *Irish Times* (Dublin), July 29, 1959, April 2, 1960, etc. 1903

7 Pencil drawing by J. B. Yeats the Elder. Once owned by John Quinn. Repro in *Quinn . . . Sale Catalogue* (1927) [see *Part 15*], p 65. *Early* 1903?

8 Pencil sketch by J. B. Yeats the Elder. Once owned by John Quinn. [See letter AE to Quinn, May 17, 1903: in *Part 1*, item 59.] May 1903

9 Oil portrait by J. B. Yeats the Elder. Signed, and dated 1903 (upper right. Repro in *John Quinn 1810–1925* (Huntingdon, N.Y.: 1926. Pidgeon Hill Press), p 158. By Quinn's executors presented to the National Gallery, Dublin. 44¼ × 34¼ inches. 1903

9A A fine photograph of AE, by Baker Brothers (Belfast): repro in *The Bookman* (London) vol 27 p 163 (January 1905). *Late* 1904?

10 Full-face pencil drawing by J. B. Yeats the Elder: sgd, and dated upper right side. Repro in *The New Orient* (New York: quarterly), June 1925. [Miss Ruth Brown of New York kindly mentioned that repro to this compiler.] The drawing was then owned by Julia Ellsworth Ford (*née* Shaw) (1852–August 15, 1950). J. E. Ford wrote: "AE the neo-Celtic mystic" in *Poet Lore* (Boston), December 1905, vol 16 No 4 pp 82–6: that was reprinted, bound into a booklet as *AE: A Note of Appreciation* (New York: 1906). September 1905

11 Oil portrait by J. B. Yeats the Elder. Now in the Abbey Theatre Collection, Dublin. Repro in *The Lady of the House* (Dublin) Christmas issue, 1912; p 40. Exhibited, Whitechapel Gallery, 1913. [A portrait of AE by J. B. Yeats was repro in *Connoisseur* (New York) vol 130 p 8 (September 1952).] Signed and dated. 1905

12 Full-face pencil drawing by J. B. Yeats the Elder. Signed in lower left corner, not dated. Once owned by John Quinn. Repro opp p 822, *Complete Catalog of the John Quinn Library Sale* (Nov 12, 1923–March 20, 1924) (New York: 1924. Anderson Galleries). 1907

13 A cartoon by Beatrice Elvery, decorating the front cover of Susan L. Mitchell's *Aids to the Immortality of Certain Persons in Ireland* (1st ed only: Dublin: 1908. New Nation Press). [From l. to r. the caricatures portray: Edward Martyn, W. B. Yeats, George Moore, Anthony MacDonnell (*later* Lord MacDonnell of Swinford), Douglas Hyde, AE, Horace Plunkett, Hugh Lane, William Orpen, Capt Shawe Taylor.] Also repro in *Theosophical College Magazine* (Madanapalle, Madras) October 1935, p 1; with report of an address delivered to commemorate AE in the College on July 23, 1935, by J. H. Cousins. *Circa* 1908

14 Pastel. Signed: Mathilde de C[...... ?]. Once owned by the late F. R. Higgins. Memorial Exhibition, 1936. 1911

15 Lithograph by Miss Mary Duncan. Hitherto dated 1915–6. Miss Duncan kindly searched her records for this compiler, advising him

by letter (September 3, 1957) that the portrait was executed in her studio, 7 North Gt. George's Street, Dublin, either in 1912 or 1913. Given by the artist to the National Portrait Gallery, London, April 1956 (Regstn No 3980). Black ink on white paper; three-quarters lkg left. Sgd lower rt. Repro in the *Dublin Magazine* (Dublin) Series 1, vol 1 No 4, p 262 (November 1923). [Miss Duncan kindly notes she was born February 27, 1885, in Bromley, Kent, daughter of John Kinmont Duncan. She was trained in the Slade School. See *Who's Who in Art, 1934*. She has practised mainly as an oil painter and etcher. Whilst resident in Dublin she was a member of *Craobh na gCuig gCuigi*; Miss Evelyn Gleeson and Miss Una Duncan exhibited in that group, in 7 St Stephen's Green, on October 6, 1913. The group was a branch of the Gaelic League. Miss Duncan and Estella Solomons, A.R.H.A. were "inseparable partners" then.] 1912 *or* 1913

16 "A pen sketch by Beatrix Duncan" [not dated?] and "A reproduction of a pencil sketch" [no specifications printed] are now in the library of Colby College, Waterville, Maine. See *Colby Library Quarterly*, May 1955, p 54. [Beatrix Duncan, the daughter of Mrs Ellen Duncan (d. 1939), (secretary, and practically the originator of the United Arts Club, Dublin; Curator, Municipal Gallery, Dublin, 1914–22) and James Duncan (a Civil Servant in the Teachers' Pension Office). Miss Duncan and Miss U. and Miss B. Duncan were not related. Miss B. Duncan was successively the wife: of Douglas Goldring (1887–April 1960), Brian Lunn (see his reminiscences *Switchback* London: 1948. Eyre & Spottiswoode) and finally of a Yugoslav.] *Circa* 1913?

17 Self-portrait in oils. See *Part 16*, No 32 p 241. *Circa* 1914

18 Self-portrait in pastels. Once owned by Miss Jane Mitchell. See *Part 16*, No 31 p 241. *Circa* 1914

19 Portrait in oils on canvas by Dermod O'Brien, P.R.H.A. In the Abbey Theatre Collection, Dublin. Exhibited Dublin 1914; priced 15 guineas. 1914

19A Self-portrait See *Part 16*, No 33 p 242. 191–?

20 Portrait in oils on canvas by Dermod O'Brien, P.R.H.A. Now in the Horace Plunkett Foundation, London. Memorial exhibition, 1936 (repro on front of *Catalogue*). Repro in *With Horace Plunkett in Ireland* by R. A. Anderson (London: 1935. Macmillan). *Probably* 1914

21 Black pencil drawing, head in profile, to left, by Sir William Rothenstein. [Sir John Rothenstein's *Iconography* (1926. Chapman & Hall) No 296.] Twice inscribed: "W.R., Dublin, Nov. 1914." Height, $5\frac{1}{2}$; width, $5\frac{3}{8}$ inches. Repro in *Twenty-Four Drawings* [first series]

(London: 1920. Allen & Unwin) with unsgd prose note by James Stephens. November 1914

22 Marble bust carved by Oliver Sheppard, R.H.A. (1865–1941). Exhibited Royal Hibernian Academy 87th annual exhibition, 1916 (No 507). Destroyed in the R.H.A. fire, 1916. [Noticed in *Studio* (London) vol 68 p 58 (June 1916): "In the sculpture section the most important exhibit was (——), a fine and dignified work intensely modern in feeling."] Two photographs given by the sculptor to the County Museum, Armagh. 1915

23 Marble bust carved by Oliver Sheppard, R.H.A. Now in the National Gallery of Ireland. Repro as a vignette on title-page of *Part 1* item 57; and in *Some I Knew Well* by Clifford Bax (London: 1951. Phoenix House), and in the *Colby Library Quarterly* (Waterville, Maine), May 1955, p 58. Memorial Exhibition, Dublin, 1936. 1916

24 Black Crayon drawing by "Sidney Davies" [Philip Naviasky (born Leeds, 1894)]. Profile, turned slightly left. Now in the National Gallery, Dublin. 1917

25 Two photographs taken by Messrs Lafayette Ltd, Dublin. AE wrote to Macmillan & Co (London) admitting the faithful resemblance he
25A bore to one of these photographs (January 16, 1919). Probably he sent a print of one to E. A. Boyd; if so this might prove to be the photograph which was printed as frontispiece to the *Colby Library*
25B *Quarterly*, May 1955. One repro in *The Christian Commonwealth* (London) vol 38 p 49 (October 31, 1917). *Circa* 1917

26 "Homage to Hugh Lane" painted by John Keating, P.R.H.A., to Dr Thomas Bodkin's commission. The figures represented in it from left to right are: (back row) Thomas Bodkin, Dermod O'Brien, P.R.H.A., the portrait by J. S. Sargent, R.A. (1856–1925) of Sir Hugh Lane, and Alderman Thomas Kelly; in the front row, seated: W. B. Yeats, A.E., Sir William Hutcheson Poë (1848–Nov 30, 1934), and Richard Caulfield Orpen, R.H.A. (1863–March 27, 1938). The drawing represented in the upper right-hand corner was by William Walcot (1874–June 1943) of Sir Edwin Lutyens' design for the Bridge Gallery over the Liffey, to contain the Lane Bequest pictures. Mr Keating kindly wrote to this compiler, April 24, 1959: "I never did any other portrait or drawing of AE—nor indeed of any of my, by this time, innumerable sitters. Having had a thorough academic training in the old-fashioned way, *viz* study of the antique, drawing and painting from the life, and anatomy, I had no hesitations but began on the fresh canvas and if I didn't like what I got I rubbed it out and began again. Orpen was my master and I had the good fortune to work in his studio in London for a time. Orpen, Tonks, Legros, Ingres, and so on

right back to the renaissance; such is my line, or so I would like to think." The late Dr Bodkin, the owner, expressed his conviction that this is the finest portrait of AE in his prime. It was exhibited at the Royal Hibernian Academy, 1920. In the *Aonal Tailteann* (*Tailteann Games*) in Dublin, 1924, this painting won the *Tailteann Trophy* and the silver medal for portraiture in the *Arts and Crafts Exhibition.* [In 1924 and 1928 AE served as one of the "Literary Board of Adjudicators."]

26A The painting was reproduced in *The Sphere* (London) April 17, 1920 (with a note by C. K. Shorter), vol 81 p 80. 1919

27 Two cartoons including AE, by Sir William Orpen (1878–1931). "A
27A talented picnic" and [A] "I meet Æ in the street." Repro in *Stories of*
27B *Old Ireland and Myself*, by W. Orpen, at pp 58 and 60, (London: 1924. Williams & Norgate). *Before* 1924

28 Drawing, sanguine and black, head three quarters to left, by William Rothenstein. Height, 9⅛: width, 5⅜ inches. J. Rothenstein's *Iconography*
28A No 581. [A drawing of AE by Rothenstein was repro in [A] *Arts and Decoration* (New York) vol 16 p 276 (February 1922).] 1921

28B Drawing, head three-quarters to left, by Sir William Rothenstein: sgd and dated "W.R., 1921." Height, 9⅝: width, 5¾ inches. Presented by the artist to the National Gallery, Dublin, in 1936. J. Rothenstein's *Iconography*, No 582. 1921

29 Wax portrait medallion by Theodore Spicer-Simson [born in Le Havre, June 25, 1871: died in Florida, February 1, 1959.] Owned by Mr Diarmuid C. Russell. Repro in *Men of Letters of the British Isles* by T. Spicer-Simson (with essays by Stuart Sherman) (New York: 1924. William E. Rudge), pp 111–13. Signed and dated 1922. 1922

30 Drawing by Beatrice Elvery (Lady Glenavy), repro in the *Irish Times*
30A (Dublin) October 20, 1923, accompanying an article on AE, signed "Bruyere". *Circa* 1923?

31 "Chin-angles, or How the Poets Passed," a cartoon by "Mac" (sgd lower rt corner). The original is in the United Arts Club, Dublin. A
31A colored print is in the County Museum, Armagh. Later repro in
31B miniature in the *Irish Times* [B] December 19, 1946: then off-printed
31C [C] announcing a talk "Reminiscences of an Irish Caricaturist" to be given on *Radio Éireann* by the artist "Mac" (" on Friday at 7.40 p.m.").

31D Another cartoon of AE by "Mac" repro in *The "Celebrity Zoo" (First Visit) Some Desultory Rhymes and Caricatures by "Mac"* ([Dublin] 1925. Browne & Nolan. 200 copies: sgd and colored by hand.) No 3 "The Russell Bear" of AE, at pp [11–12]. Item 31 was reptd in *The Masterpiece and the Man* by Monk Gibbon (London: 1959. Hart-Davis). Dr Gibbon described another "Mac" cartoon of A.E., in

31E *Bibliography* item 57 p 19. [Miss Isabelle M. MacNie died, aged about 94, early 1958.] *Circa* 1925?

32 Lithograph by Marion E. Broadhead [biographical notice in *Who's Who in Art, 1934*.] *Perhaps circa* 1925

33 Sketch-portrait by Dermod O'Brien, P.R.H.A. Item No 66 in an *Exhibition of Paintings and Sketches by D. O'Brien*, held in Dublin, October 1926. Not priced or marked. *Catalogue* in the Victoria and Albert Museum *Art Library* (not dated: sponsoring gallery's name omitted). *Circa* 1926?

34 Bust by Jerome Connor, cast in bronze. One cast is now in the Public
34A Art Gallery, Limerick. The plaster original was repro in *Irish Life and Landscape* by J. Crampton Walker (Dublin: [1927]. Talbot Press) p [95]. Bronze repro in *A Memoir of . . . AE* (1937) and in *Irish Press* (Dublin) December 24, 1951. [J. Connor: 1876–August 21, 1943. As child, to U.S.A. To Dublin, 1925.] *Circa* 1926?

35 An unsigned and undated pencil sketch, three-quarters facing left, is owned by Mrs William Sitwell. She believes it to be a sketch by Estella Solomons, A.R.H.A. That artist had no recollection in 1954 of having made any sketches of AE, nor preliminary drawings before painting the oil portrait listed below (1930). [This drawing closely resembles portrait number 15 above.] *Perhaps circa* 1928

36 One of Mr Pirie MacDonald's magnificent photographs of AE, taken in New York, was reproduced in *Photograms of the Year 1928* (London: December 1928. Iliffe). Also repro elsewhere. *Early* 1928

37 Photographs taken in New York by Mrs Zlata Llamas Coomaraswamy [Mrs Ananda K. Coomaraswamy]. One repro in *AE's Letters to*
37A *Mínanlábáin* (1937): another in *A Memoir of AE* by "John Eglinton"
37B (1937). A third repro in *N.Y. Herald Tribune*, Feb 6, 1938: section 9 p 4 cols 2–3. *Early* 1928

38 Portrait in oils by Hilda Roberts [Mrs Arnold Marsh, of Rathfarnham]. Now in the City Art Gallery and Museum, Stranmillis, Belfast. Repro in its publication No 116, the *Quarterly Notes* of the Museum, No 53, p 8 (June 1937). Exhibited in the Hackett Gallery, New York, March 1–8, 1930. Dr Thomas Bodkin judged this to be the most attractive
38A likeness of AE in later life. [A pencil(?) drawing, presumably a sketch for No 38, owned by artist.] 38: 39 × 36 inches. 1929

39 Portrait in oils by Estella Solomons, A.R.H.A. [Mrs J. S. Starkey]. Owned by the artist: not yet exhibited. 1930

40 Portrait [in oils?] by George Luks: probably commissioned by the late Mrs Mary H. Rumsey. Made in America. Detail not yet discovered by this compiler. [G. Benjamin Luks: born at Williamsport, Pa., Aug 13, 1867. Died, New York, Oct 29, 1933.] *Probably* 1930–1

41 Bust by Jeannette Hare, cast in bronze. Commissioned by the late Mrs Mary H. Rumsey. Ten sittings, approximately 2 hours each, in New York. Two casts: one presented by the artist and her husband Col Irving H. Hare, to the National Portrait Gallery, London: the other owned by Col and Mrs Hare. [Mrs Hare, daughter of Peter Francis De Souter and Maria J. A. (Neels) De Souter: born in Antwerp, August 24, 1896. To U.S.A., 1908. Studied at the Art Students' League, N.Y., under George Bridgeman and Sterling Calder: sculpture under C. C. Rumsey and Harriette Frishmuth. Married Col Hare in 1923. Mrs Hare has made portrait busts of Dale Carnegie, Lowell Thomas, and others. Among recent heads, Mrs Polly Wayne Kiltelle.] Photo in *New York American*, June 5, 1931. May–June 1931

42 A brochure circulated privately by Mr Colm McLoughlin, and others. A single sheet of off-white paper lettered in black. The sheet was twice folded: the front of the brochure reads, *United Arts Club* | *Dublin* | [*Gaelic inscription*] | *From* | *The Artist and The Gunman* | *To* | [wide space] [at foot of page] | *Nodlaɣ 1931.* | Opened out the brochure comprises on the left flap (i.e. the *verso* of the front page) a full-page illustration "To Dance": the middle page, verses in English: and the right-hand flap a second illustration captioned "—And Dine", and signed "B.Q.R. [?]". In this second illustration, a sketch-caricature, AE and Bernard Shaw were among those characterised. On the *verso* of the flap carrying the second illustration there are verse "Interpretations". The verses were written by C. F. Mc.L[oughlin] [Mr McLoughlin is the founder of the Dublin printers *At the Sign of the Three Candles.*] On the verso of the middle flap is the printer's mark *At the Sign of the Three Candles*. The two flaps fold inwards.

20.1 × 12 cm. 1931

43 Bust by Donald Gilbert, F.R.B.S., R.B.S.A., modeled in plaster: height, 24.5 inches. One bronze cast purchased by the City Museum and Art Gallery, Stranmillis, Belfast, in 1957. The plaster original, and copyright, are owned by the sculptor. Mr Gilbert kindly wrote to this compiler (July 4, 1960): "The late Sir Granville Bantock, a very old friend whose portrait bust I made also, introduced me to AE, and suggested I should make the bust. AE sat to me in what was then my London studio, 9 Pembroke Studios, Kensington, W.8. At this distance of time I cannot tell you how many sittings he gave me, but it was probably 10 or 12 of 2 to 3 hours duration. He was an excellent sitter and we got on very friendly terms very quickly . . . He was most interesting to listen to as he ranged from agricultural economics to oriental philosophy and mythology, interspersed with factual accounts of his encounters with 'the little people', anecdotes of incidents such

as the time when both sides held their fire during the 'troubles' while he crossed the street; and every now and then breaking into a recitation of one of his own poems in a rich voice that made them live in a way cold print never can. It was a great experience to listen to him. I think the essence of what was so wonderful about him was that he was at one and the same time profoundly sensitive as poet, practical as a man of the world, and deeply versed in knowledge and scholarship . . ." [Concerning AE's later years Mr Padraic Colum wrote to this compiler (August 1, 1950): "O'Casey is very wrong about AE. He was disinterestedly helpful to the young poets—I know he spent hours discussing anything I wrote with me; not only did I get encouragement from him, but practical, technical help. If the young poets dedicated their volumes to him it was because there was no one in Dublin so worthy of receiving such homage. I will say this: I think O'Casey came to know AE at a time when the disease he died of was beginning to make inroads on him. He had lost a certain control; he talked far more than he listened."] AE admired the bust by Mr Gilbert. This compiler has seen a letter which AE wrote to James Stephens in autumn 1933 eagerly urging Stephens to visit the artist's studio to see the bust. Unaware of that letter Mr Gilbert recalled Stephens' visit with AE (1960). The bronze cast was exhibited at the Royal Hibernian Academy summer exhibition, 1934. (Notice in the *Irish Press*, April 9, 1934.) Since that Dublin exhibition the bust has been displayed elsewhere, including the Bournemouth Art Gallery, in September 1948. [Hubert D. McGeoch Gilbert, born 1900 at Burcot, Worcs. Died June 17, 1961. Biographical notice in *Who's Who in Art, 1958*.] Repro in this book. October–November 1933

44 Dry-point etching by Walter Tittle. Reproduced in *Fine Prints of the Year, 1933* (New York: 1934. Minton, Balch & Co). Also repro in *New York Times*, November 25, 1934: section 5 p 5 cols 2–3. [W. Tittle, born Springfield, Ohio, 1883. Painter and etcher. Author of *Portraits in Pencil and Pen* (New York: 19—?. ———— ?).] The print was published separately in New York, by Messrs Kennedy. It was also reptd in *The Sunday Times* (London) July 28, 1935: p 6 cols 3–4. 1933?

45 Drawing by Alfred Hugh Fisher, A.R.E. Signed. Once owned by the artist. [A. H. Fisher, born 1867: died in London, July 2, 1945.] 1934

46 Etching by Alfred Hugh Fisher, A.R.E. Signed. Once owned by the artist. Repro in *London Mercury* (London) vol 31 p 452 (March 1935), and in *Art Digest* (New York) vol 9 p 16 (August 1935). 1934

47 Two photographs taken for the U.S. Department of Agriculture, by one of their staff photographers, Mr E. C. Purdy, in Washington D.C.,

47B on February 21, 1935. One reproduced in item 59, and the other [B] in this book. February 21, 1935

48 Three pencil drawings by Séan O'Sullivan, R.H.A., depicting AE's face after death, as he lay in his deathbed. Drawn in the Stagsden Nursing Home, Canford Cliffs, Bournemouth, the morning after AE died. [Mr O'Sullivan's extremely sensitive drawings were commissioned by Mr C. P. Curran, S.C. He knew Mr O'Sullivan's address, *en route* through London to Paris, and invited him to interrupt his journey with a diversion to Bournemouth. This compiler told Mr O'Sullivan of the sharp impact and sense of horror which one of these drawings had made on him. Mr O'Sullivan described the circumstances. As he set to work the atmosphere in the room seemed quite unlike similar scenes he had known, he was quickly penetrated by some consciousness of a type of vitality. That room was not warm, nor receiving direct sunlight, but Mr O'Sullivan sweated profusely. A man otherwise inexperienced in such phenomena his sense of some intangible vitality there persisted, and vanished only when he emerged from that room. Mr O'Sullivan offered no comment, and does not know why he had that experience.] The first of the drawings is owned by Mr C. P. Curran, S.C. The
48A second [A] once owned by the late Albert Wood, K.C., is now in
48B the Public Art Gallery, Limerick. The third [B] is in the Municipal Gallery of Modern Art, Dublin. One displayed in the AE Memorial Exhibition, Dublin, 1936. July 18, 1935

49 Violet Russell. An oil portrait on canvas, by Mrs Frances Baker (*later* Mrs Cahill). Owned by her younger daughter, Mrs Frances C. Farrell of Blackrock. 1909 *or* 1910

INDEX

[ITEM not PAGE numbers are given]

Titles of items in Parts 1–7 only. Personal names are listed for Parts 1–7. In parentheses their life dates are recorded only if a note is not appended in the text. Full biographical notes on those people should be sought in item 59.